Pride & Poise

The Oakland Raiders of the American Football League

by

Jim McCullough

Bloomington, IN   authorHouse™   Milton Keynes, UK

AuthorHouse™
1663 Liberty Drive, Suite 200
Bloomington, IN 47403
www.authorhouse.com
Phone: 1-800-839-8640

AuthorHouse™ UK Ltd.
500 Avebury Boulevard
Central Milton Keynes, MK9 2BE
www.authorhouse.co.uk
Phone: 08001974150

First published by AuthorHouse   4/25/2006

ISBN: 1-4208-5979-X (sc)
ISBN: 1-4208-5980-3 (dj)

Printed in the United States of America
Bloomington, Indiana

This book is printed on acid-free paper.

To coach Erdelatz and his "Guys Named Joe" whose great spirit will live forever within the following pages

CHAPTER ONE
LIMPING INTO EXISTENCE
1960

With all systems seemingly go for the new American Football League, the unthinkable had happened. The National Football League, forty years established and fearing costly competition from this upstart, had found success in offering an NFL franchise to an AFL owner, Max Winter, and he and his Minneapolis franchise were bought away. Sensing he couldn't compete with an NFL expansion team in the twin cities, Winter accepted an offer to join the NFL with his new club beginning play in 1961. The remaining seven AFL franchises needed a new home for number eight and by early January 1960, the new home had been narrowed to four possibilities: Atlanta Georgia, Oakland California, Miami and Jacksonville Florida. Having only three cities that enjoyed good weather in late fall, this new league was eager to add a fourth to compliment their four cold weather cities: Denver, New York, Boston and Buffalo.

Out west, the Oakland city council wasted no time in endorsing efforts to bring professional football to their city and empowered mayor Clifford Rishell to appoint a committee to propose ideas on building an Oakland stadium and investigate the availability of San Francisco's new Candlestick Park while the Oakland facility was being built. City councilman Dan Marovich reported the Port of Oakland had already made an offer of land for a new facility, which could be financed by revenue bonds to eliminate the financial burden from local taxpayers. This was seen as a major boom for the city as not only would it bring professional football to Oakland but make the area more attractive for other professional sports.

Time, however, was of the essence. There were concerns of other cities getting a head start on them by building a new stadium first, as was the case in Miami. Oakland had an advantage. Some AFL owners wanted a Northern California team to create a natural rivalry with its Los Angeles franchise, the Chargers. Another city councilman, Robert Osborne stated that he was interested in joining a syndicate backing a club and pledged $200,000 of his own money in the venture and gave assurances to his fellow councilmen that he would be able to handle any financial requirements set forth by the new league.

Hopes for a temporary stadium were initially placed on the University of California's Memorial Stadium. City leaders were optimistic they could persuade UC regents to allow them use of the facility on a temporary basis, in spite of a longstanding policy that disallowed professional events. Though conditional upon the team having its beginnings in the East Bay, Oakland industrialist Ted Hareer expressed his interest in obtaining the club.

Barron Hilton, owner of the Los Angeles Chargers and catalyst for the addition of a Bay Area team, suggested that if Oakland officials were only interested in playing at Memorial Stadium then perhaps another group should come forward, possibly putting the team into Candlestick Park, which was available to rent by a professional football team. In the coming days, Hareer softened his "East Bay only" stance, conceding it would be better to have an Oakland team in San Francisco than no team at all. A second syndicate was formed by Oakland auto dealers Bill Jackson and Ed Goldie. A $25,000 "faith payment" was submitted to the league accompanied by a formal application for the final franchise. Unless Berkeley's Memorial Stadium was made available to them, this new group was intent on playing in San Francisco until a permanent home was built in Oakland. Arrangements were made to bring these two groups together, but the talks broke down over the issue of control.

San Francisco mayor George Christopher did Oakland no favors by publicly questioning the wisdom of placing a second professional football team in San Francisco, which would be in direct competition with the 49ers. Oakland city councilman Frank Youell reminded Christopher of how Oakland had opened its heart to San Franciscans during the aftermath of the 1906 earthquake and appealed to Oakland's neighbor to do the city a good turn by granting the use of either Kezar Stadium or Candlestick Park until a home was erected in the East Bay. Having no control over the rental of these two stadiums, mayor Christopher relented slightly, urging serious study regarding the effects of a second football team in San Francisco.

Y. C. "Chet" Soda, councilman Robert Osborne and San Francisco contractor Charles Harney formed a third and final syndicate. All three factions were confident a stadium would be built in Oakland and accepted the team would have to play in San Francisco for its first season as UC regents refused to allow use of its stadium for professional, Sunday games. This third group had also made the necessary $25,000 "faith payment" to the AFL and submitted a formal application of their own. Ted Hareer refused to involve his camp in a battle over the team and withdrew.

To decide where the eighth and final franchise would be located, league owners held meetings at their headquarters in Dallas. With the elimination of Miami and Jacksonville, only Oakland and Atlanta interests remained and had their syndicates present. Support for the Atlanta franchise was remarkably strong. Houston Oilers owner Bud Adams was a strong supporter of the Atlanta franchise, wanting create a natural Eastern Division with Boston, New York and Buffalo, with his Houston team joining Dallas, Denver and Los Angeles in forming the Western Division. Adams argued that the southeastern United States was a top producer of football talent and Atlanta was a natural home base for the area. The possibility of an AFL club in the Bay Area appeared remote as the owners voted 6-1 in favor of the Georgia capital.

As Bill Jackson withdrew his and Ed Goldie's bid for the team, Chet Soda and Robert Osborne gave presentations to the league. Telegrams were introduced from the San Francisco Park and Recreation District, affirming the availability of both Kezar Stadium and Candlestick Park. This, along with intense lobbying from Barron Hilton, who threatened to pull his Los Angeles team out of the loop should Oakland not be awarded the franchise and league commissioner Joe Foss proved to be successful. The league's owners ultimately ignored a bylaw requiring a unanimous vote and voted 5-2 to grant the eighth and final original franchise to Oakland. Eight men, councilman Robert Osborne, Chet Soda, Charles Harney, Wayne Valley, Harvey Binns, Art Beckett, Ed McGah and Don Blessing, who ten days earlier hadn't made any notification or application for the team, won out and brought professional football to Oakland.

(2)

Now the real battle began. Sleeves were rolled up as work on an unprecedented task commenced with training camp only six months away, followed by a five-game preseason and a fourteen-game regular season. Oakland's football franchise needed to assemble an office staff, coaches and at least sixty players for training camp that would be reduced to thirty three for the regular season. While they had rights to the players drafted by Minneapolis, none were under contract and were free to seek employment elsewhere. Many had, while other teams around the league only returned the players they saw fit, as draft choice Abner Haynes remained a Dallas Texan. These issues, along with the need for uniforms and equipment, needed to be resolved. The clock was running and the other seven teams were enjoying a seven-month head start.

The owners announced their intentions of bringing in the best possible football minds to guide the new franchise. Former University of San Francisco Athletic Director Jimmy Needles was retained for a two-week period to oversee the hiring process of the club's first general manager and head coach. As co-owner, Chet Soda was first appointed spokesman for the team and within a matter of days was named chairman of the board before inheriting the role of general manager.

The day after his appointment, Soda announced the team had reached a "gentleman's agreement" with former Navy head coach Eddie Erdelatz. Still a week to ten days away from actually signing a contract (a process delayed because the club was still to obtain office space) Erdelatz was considered one of the best college coaches of his time, leading the Midshipmen to victories in the 1954 Sugar Bowl over Mississippi and in the Cotton Bowl over Rice in 1957, after taking over a sagging program at Navy in 1950. An imaginative coach known for tough defense and getting the most out of his players, Berkeley native Erdelatz was thrilled to have found a coaching position in the Bay Area and was a leading candidate for the head coaching position at Cal until the surprise appointment of Marv Levy. Erdelatz was the obvious and unanimous choice to guide this new franchise.

The AFL came to Oakland on the 3-4 of March for its next series of meetings. The main topics of discussion were how to stock the Oakland franchise with talent and to establish a schedule for the upcoming season. It was agreed that to have a competitive balance the Oakland team needed its share of top players. Coach Erdelatz had reservations about what kind of talent could be pooled. Oakland was given jurisdiction over the Minneapolis clubs' fifty-two-man draft list aside from Abner Haynes, however many had signed with the NFL, the Canadian Football League or decided against playing pro ball altogether. In all, 13 players remained from the original bunch, including Iowa All American receiver Don Norton, Boston University tight end Gene Prebola, defensive end Carmen Cavelli from Richmond, North Texas State quarterback Sam McCord and University of Miami center James Otto who had distinguished himself as well on defense performing as a linebacker but was considered too small for professional football.

The plan to fill the remainder of the Oakland roster was known as the twelfth man draft. The seven other teams would present Oakland with a list of eleven untouchables for five rounds. Oakland was allowed to select from each team in every round giving the team thirty-five more names to fill its roster. This was thought to give Oakland its best chance to field a competitive ball club. Much scouting was to be done by coach Erdelatz and his two recently hired assistants, Ernie Jorge, his top assistant at Navy, and former Stanford assistant Marty Feldman. The drafts' first two rounds were two and a half weeks away with the remaining rounds set to follow on weekly intervals. It was time for a cram-study session of all available talent as training camp was only four months off.

League commissioner Joe Foss announced the United States Justice Department was compiling testimony, for a possible anti-trust action against the National Football League. It was first thought the two leagues could co-exist peacefully, until the passing of NFL commissioner Bert Bell and the appointment of Los Angeles Rams general manager Pete Rozelle to his post. Almost immediately the NFL, which had previously been unwilling to expand, moved the Cardinals franchise from Chicago to St. Louis and began making offers of new NFL teams to AFL owners. Along with the successful conversion of Max Winter, the NFL placed a new franchise in Dallas, home of league founder Lamar Hunt's club and the new league's offices. During his deposition to the Justice Department, Foss testified that it was obvious that through their actions the NFL was attempting to injure or deal a deathblow to the American Football League in its infancy.

Enthusiasm in Oakland from civic leaders and football fans for their new team and the upstart new league was unmatched by any other AFL city. While most football fans in the East Bay were supporters of the cross-bay San Francisco 49ers, they were elated to have a team of their own. Many promised to buy season tickets and many more offered suggestions as to what to name the team. To capitalize on this, the Oakland Junior Chamber of Commerce, along with the Oakland Boosters and *The Oakland Tribune* held the "Name Your Football Team" contest in which fans could submit their ideas along with an explanation in twenty-five words or less, their reasoning for the suggested moniker. The grand prize was a weeklong, all-expenses-paid vacation in Acapulco, Mexico. Thousands of entries were received, reviewed and judged by a five-man panel consisting of George Jacopetti, chairman of the Oakland Chamber of Commerce Stadium Committee, Oakland city councilman and president of the Oakland Boosters Dan Marovich, Oakland Junior Chamber of Commerce chairman Harold Price, Francis Dunn, chairman of the Alameda County Board of Supervisors and Chet Soda. Most entries drew ideas from three sources, the old West with suggestions such as the Wranglers or the Mavericks, California's Spanish heritage with submissions such as the Diablos and Gauchos or the original with such entries as the Oakland Bay Jets, the Knights or the Dolphins. Of the thousands of entries received good, bad and awful, the grand prize entry, attempting to originate from the state's Spanish forefathers was clearly chosen from the latter and the Oakland team was christened "the Senors." Stating in her entry letter "Senors symbolizes the history, strength and solidarity of old world California," the twenty-year-old Oakland policewoman was surprised her entry was chosen. Most fans and citizens alike were simply amazed it was ever conceived, reaction to the Senors was outrage.

Though unlikely, it may have gone over better had it been spelled correctly. Unfortunately, it was misspelled in Spanish and ridiculous in English. Many fans openly questioned whether the team's mascot would be a bull or a Chihuahua and wondered if tamales, chili and tequila would be served at concession stands as opposed to the traditional hot dogs, pop corn and beer. Within a week, the entire Senors fiasco was laid to rest when a new moniker was chosen and the Oakland franchise was given arguably the strongest and most recognizable name in all of sports, "the Raiders."

In his grand-prize-winning submission statement, nearby Hayward resident Kendrick Martin chose the name "Because our team and its supporters must be fired and inspired by a fighting name. 'Raiders' implies early sustained offense, carrying the fight to their opponents." All of the previously awarded prizes were also awarded to the Raiders submissions, including the Acapulco trip, the second-prize Los Angeles trip to see the

Oakland team play the Chargers in November and season tickets for the inaugural 1960 campaign was awarded to the third place entry. Twenty-three other "Raiders" submissions were awarded single-game tickets in the upcoming inaugural season.

(3)

Thomas Kalmanir and Edward Cody were brought in to complete the Raiders coaching staff and Wes Fry was appointed director of player personnel and chief scout. These three, along with coach Erdelatz and assistant coaches Feldman and Jorge, had a long road ahead of them and a shorter time to travel as the team was still almost fifty players short of the sixty it needed to begin drills, now just three months away. Vanderbilt center Ben Donnell was the first new player announced to be coming to Oakland from the twelfth man draft. Joining him were Ohio State defensive halfback Joe Cannavino, fullback Billy Lott selected from Houston along with Jerry Epps, a New York Titans draft choice from West Texas State and former Wisconsin star Robert Nelson, a center who was selected first by the Boston Patriots. Along with the draft, coach Erdelatz and his staff were busy signing free agents, such as former University of California and Chicago Cardinals quarterback Paul Larson and University of California star halfback Wayne Crow, who originally decided to return to Cal for his senior season before changing his mind and turning pro in Oakland. Raiders coaches were beginning to feel more comfortable with their talent prospects as training camp neared.

The club's owners were buried in work as well. This included ironing out the details of where they would train in the coming summer and which San Francisco facility would be called home. The second question was answered first. It was decided that Kezar Stadium would hold their first games. Easier to access from Oakland than Candlestick Park, Kezar was constructed for football and they would be able to print and sell tickets, allowing those fans that wished to purchase them the luxury of seeing where they would be located in the stadium, unlike Candlestick, which had never held football games. Candlestick's baseball scoreboard was unsuitable for football and would cost thousands of dollars to modify or install one suitable for the Raiders. The cash-conscious owners also struggled to keep themselves intact with two defections and additions. Art Beckett withdrew from the General Partnership (which the eight Oakland owners had come to be known) and was "replaced" by Roger Lapham Jr. the son of a former San Francisco mayor and Harvey Binns, the Oakland restaurant owner resigned from the group because of the team's direction with Soda serving as general manager, being succeeded by Wallace Marsh, a Bay Area industrialist.

Three East Bay cities were viewed as possible homes for the Raiders summer training camp: Richmond, north of Oakland in Contra Costa County at the Salesian Seminary, which featured two turf practice fields, a new cafeteria and dormitory facilities, the Alameda County Fairgrounds in Pleasanton to the east of Oakland, again offered up by the Alameda County Board of Supervisors as it had been when the team was looking into a temporary home in the East Bay; and tiny Moraga, at coach Eddie Erdelatz's alma mater St. Mary's College, which was already equipped with everything a team could want for its training. Even with three suitable facilities in the East Bay, the Raiders training camp would be held in Santa Cruz, approximately seventy miles to the south along California's central coast, with the team headquartered at the Hotel Palomar. Training would take place at the local high school. They would open their first training camp with a total of seventy-five players on July 10, where they would remain for six weeks.

After being returned to Oakland from Los Angeles after Minneapolis bowed out, All American end Don Norton was dealt back to the Chargers for former 49ers defensive end Charlie Powell, who had retired from football four times to pursue a boxing career. Agreeing to return to pro football just a few days before being traded, Powell was a proven player on a team full of question marks. Also signed was College of the Pacific quarterback Tommy Flores. At age twenty-five, the 6' 1" 195-lb. Flores had been in camp with both the Washington Redskins of the NFL and the Calgary Stampeders of the CFL. Cut from both squads due to an injury in his throwing shoulder, Flores had worked diligently in rehabilitating the injury and was in top shape when observed by coach Erdelatz, who was scouting Flores in an alumni game at the urging of Ernie Jorge.

While the Raiders were gearing up for training camp, the AFL was fighting for its very existence. The league was moving forward with a $10,000,000 anti trust lawsuit against the NFL and its thirteen teams for seeking to induce members of the AFL to refuse or abandon their teams by promising them National Football League franchises. The suit also charged that the NFL was seeking to prevent teams in the new league from obtaining necessary commitments for playing facilities by various harassing tactics, including making announcements that the NFL would be playing in AFL markets and sharing their facilities. The NFL was also granting franchises to cities where AFL clubs were already in place, knowing these markets could only support one professional football team and threatening players and coaches involved with AFL teams with NFL blacklisting as well as attempting to induce AFL players to break contracts with their AFL clubs and seeking to prevent teams from obtaining reasonable compensation for the sale of television rights. The complaint also asked for a court order preventing the NFL from granting or transferring any new teams into markets where the AFL was already established. Commissioner Rozelle publicly denied there was a war between the two leagues and gave assurances that one wouldn't ensue but admitted there was little harmony. Stating it takes two to make war and claiming there was only one league as the AFL was yet to play a single game, the NFL head also made claims of AFL player tampering, specifically with Rufus Grunderson of the Detroit Lions. Rozelle's allegations accused AFL teams of contacting Grunderson via telephone, making claims the Lions didn't want him and encouraging him to sign with the American League. Grunderson confirmed that he was in contact with the Dallas Texans until his signing with Detroit. From then on, he would have no contact with the club and claimed to have received no calls or offers from any AFL franchise.

Just two days before the start of training camp, commissioner Foss brightened the hopes of the seventy-five Raiders hopefuls by increasing the roster allotment from thirty-three, to thirty-five for the fast-approaching 1960 season. Coach Erdelatz and his staff were finally able to get a look at many of these players, after only being able to speak with most of them over the telephone. Every position was truly up for grabs and with only thirty-five roster spots, many players would be required to play multiple positions.

The first day of training camp was fun for these hopefuls, with each player looking like All-Americans, hamming it up for reporters and their cameramen. The fun would end on July 11 as coach Erdelatz began two-a-day work out drills, whipping these aspiring Raiders into shape. Although roster cuts weren't mandated until August 8, when all teams rosters were to be reduced to forty-three, Erdelatz had designs on making the first cuts by the end of the first week to weed out those he felt were unwilling to make the necessary sacrifices and to concentrate on the players who had the best chance at being Oakland Raiders on opening day.

Doing away with some traditional practices such as bed check and other forms of policing, coach Erdelatz made it clear to each of his players what was expected of them, both in practice and in public. The idea was to treat his players as men and expect them to conduct themselves as such. The morning drills lasted no more than one hour, while the afternoon drills went no longer than two. Standing around was not tolerated and players were required to run from place to place. Also they were given no instruction that would serve little purpose to them once the season began. Erdelatz's running camps were considered unorthodox at the professional level but these players soon found themselves in great shape. Even the veterans who were used to being in game shape prior to the start of the regular season were thrilled to admit they would now be physically game ready at the commencement of the exhibition schedule.

The first week concluded with an hour and a half high-speed dummy drill, work on their first plays, followed by a well-deserved day of rest. The roster had slimmed with fourteen players being cut and six more quitting voluntarily. Coach Erdelatz was pleased with the players remaining on the squad, noting good backfield speed, improving line speed as his linemen worked themselves into better shape and his defensive backs were performing well.

Additional talent was brought in and up to speed with their teammates, while the coaching staff continued to evaluate these players and mold their roster with practices and scrimmages continuing until July 26 when the team was taken by bus to Oakland (a first for many of the players, as some had no idea where the city was located until signing with the club) to participate in the "Welcome Raiders" parade, beginning in Jack London Square. Upon completion of the parade, which was seen mostly by unimpressed shoppers, the players were herded back onto buses and returned to Santa Cruz for a late-afternoon workout as their first preseason game was just five days away. In a benefit game for Children's Hospital of the East Bay, the Raiders played host to a Dallas team that featured eleven All-Americans and jumped the gun by starting their training camp a week early. Although Dallas was fined $2000 for the violation by commissioner Foss, the Raiders coaches and officials (while conceding that after starting several months behind the rest of the league an extra week of preparation would have been well worth the penalty) were appalled by the poor sportsmanship exhibited by league founder Lamar Hunt's club. Despite being three-touchdown underdogs, Raiders players and coaches alike expressed confidence in their chances for a win.

Quarterbacks Tom Flores and Paul Larson were named team captains for the first game. Flores, listed as questionable for the contest earlier in the week due to a leg injury, had shown the same resilience that had brought him back from his shoulder ailment, would start. In spite of an announced 20,000 advance tickets sold for this inaugural contest, only an estimated 12,000 spectators made their way through the turnstiles at Kezar Stadium to watch the Raiders battle for the first time. Handicapped by a lack of a potent running game to keep the Texan defenders off balance and an offensive playbook that featured just eleven plays; Flores completed 9 of 12 passes in the first half and a 1-yard Buddy Allen touchdown run put the Raiders up, 7-0.

Former Baltimore Colt Cotton Davidson managed just 9 completions in 31 tries on the afternoon but his running game carried the Texans offense, picking up 211 yards. Two of Davidson's completions put the Raiders in a hole midway through the second quarter. A diving goal-line grab by Stanford grad Chris Burford put six Dallas points on the scoreboard and a reception by LSU rookie Johnny Robinson doubling as a halfback on offense and defense gave the Texans an 8-7 halftime advantage. Able to make adjustments at the intermission, the Raiders used just one defense that was being run without its leader, middle linebacker Tom Louderback (out of action due to injury) that was exploited midway through the third period. Burford made a spectacular reception on third down and 11 from the Dallas 34 in front of defensive back L.C. Joyner at the Raiders 47. Gaining 22 more with a Davidson toss to Max Boydston, Running back Jim Swink powered for 9 yards and Jack Spikes picked up 12 more on the ground before scoring from 2 yards out. The ensuing 2-point conversion failed when Joe Cannavino halted Robinson short of the goal line. Using 17 plays to move 73 yards, a pass interference call gave the Raiders first and goal on the 1. Buddy Allen then added his second touchdown. Former New York Giant Billy Lott's failure to reach the end zone on a 2-point try left the Raiders down a point at 14-13. The next Dallas drive resulted in a field goal attempt that fell short but Oakland's opportunity to regain the lead resulted in disaster as linebacker Mel Branch intercepted Flores on the Raiders 27 and brought the ball back 14 yards. With four minutes to go, Jack Spikes scored his second 2-yard touchdown. Eddie Macon deflected Davidson's 2-point conversion attempt to hold Dallas to a 20-13 advantage that they would enjoy as time expired, winning their first exhibition.

Being competitive against a team that had more highly regarded personnel with more preparation time gave the Oakland club plenty of reason for optimism. Dallas coach Hank Stram expressed confidence in coach Erdelatz's abilities while star receiver Chris Burford gave assurances that the Raiders would be a much tougher opponent the second time around. Tom Flores looked poised to be a major star in the new league; with a 14 for 25 performance for 151 yards, the young passer drew praise from all around, including San Francisco 49ers quarterback Y.A. Tittle. In what amounted to only their third scrimmage, they performed valiantly in front of a partisan home crowd that hadn't given them much of a chance prior to kickoff.

It was two weeks away from their next exhibition game and a meeting with the New York Titans in Sacramento's Hughes Stadium. Until then it was back to their Santa Cruz training ground to resume two-a-day practices and a surprise scrimmage. The roster was trimmed to forty-three players by the August 8 deadline and those remaining were ready for the August 13 contest against New York. Again they were expected to fail miserably, with fears that Titans end Don Maynard would run wild over them. In Hughes Stadium, he would be required to do so from behind. Opening the contest with a near-perfect 10-play, 80-yard march, Flores, commanding the offense for the entire outing, found Tony Teresa in the corner of the end zone for a 7-0 lead. Maynard's receiving mastery accounted for 9 catches and 135 yards as he made catches for 10 and 28 yards in the opening quarter and an interference call as the secondary tried to coral him netted 10 more. Dick Jamison, sharing quarterbacking duties with veteran Al Dorow, tied the contest late in the opening period with an 8-yard toss to halfback Bill Shockley who knotted the game with a conversion. The New York defense halted the Raiders three straight times and were rewarded by their offense which tacked on 10 more points. Down 17-7 with time waning in the opening half, the offense clicked. A screen pass to Billy Lott picked up 51 yards and Larry Barnes brought his squad to within a touchdown with a 35-yard field goal as time expired.

Scoreless through the third quarter, Flores and the offense began to operate on their own 26. Spreading short passes to Charley Hardy to pick up 16 yards and to tight end Gene Prebola for 12 more, Jack Larschied raced over his fallen left guard for a 28-yard, game-tying score. Before the

9,551 on hand in Hughes Stadium could come down from their collective joy of Larschied's run, their jubilation was sustained when Bob Dougherty intercepted an Al Dorow pass on the New York 21. A quick toss to Prebola picked up 13. Flores handed off to fullback Dean Philpott who found the end zone after running over right guard. Ex-Cleveland Brown Thurlow Cooper blocked Barnes' conversion try but the 23-17 advantage was enough for the Oakland club to earn its first exhibition victory.

The Raiders returned to Kezar Stadium to face the formidable Los Angeles Chargers, who, like the Texans, received a $2,000 fine from the league for starting training camp a week early. In other familiar news, these Raiders found themselves three-touchdown underdogs to the more prepared, highly talented and undefeated Los Angeles team. A sparse crowd of 6,521 witnessed this contest, the first of three for Oakland over the next nine days. Tied at 3, the Raiders capitalized on a Chargers' fumble on their 20. An 18-yard Flores pass to Lott gave them a first and goal from point blank range and another toss to Brad Meyers put them ahead 10-3. The lead was fleeting. Coming back to tie the game in 10 plays, Jack Kemp, struggling to find success on the ground went airborne to Paul Lowe, first for 18 yards to enter Oakland territory then for 43 more and a touchdown as the Chargers runner took Kemp's throw in stride to tie the game. Taking over on his 20 after a punt. Flores began to pick the Los Angeles defense apart. Aided by receptions of 20 and 16 yards by Billy Lott and another from Gene Prebola for 16 more, the offense drove to the 7-yard line with 90 seconds remaining in the half. Running a sweep to the left, Lott was escorted to the end zone by the superb blocking of his offensive line. Larry Barnes converted and the Raiders enjoyed a 17-10 halftime lead.

Looking to pad their lead and run the clock in the fourth quarter, Flores made an ill-advised throw that defensive back Dick Harris intercepted on the Raiders 39 and returned to the 1. Howard Ferguson leapt over the line and Ben Donnell, the first player selected by the Raiders in the twelfth man draft tied the game with the conversion. Scoring again on their next drive, Los Angeles captured a 24-17 lead as Ferguson swept around the left for 10 yards and a touchdown. From their 19, the Oakland offense began carving away big chunks of yardage. Moving in deep, Flores fired complete to Alan Goldstein on the 3. Dick Harris quickly wrestled with Goldstein for possession. An unfathomable ruling that the pass was intercepted ended the final Raiders threat. Though coach Gilman conceded immediately post game that they had won a contest in which they had no business doing so. The Chargers held onto the ball, ran out the clock and escaped Kezar Stadium undefeated in the preseason. A bright spot emerged from the loss as defensive back Wayne Crow established himself as the punter, kicking 5 times for a 52.8-yard average including one bomb that traveled 77 yards beyond the line of scrimmage in place of Larry Barnes.

Breaking camp the day before they were to fly into Buffalo to face the Bills in War Memorial Stadium, the Raiders were experiencing their first quarterback controversy. With Flores the clear starter, coach Erdelatz needed to decide which of his two remaining back-ups would be cut by September 6 when all teams were required to scale back to their final thirty-five players. Both Paul Larson and newly acquired Vito "Babe" Parilli were former All-Americans, having each logged time on NFL squads. They would both see action in the Buffalo game due to the reoccurring injury in Flores' throwing shoulder. Giving an obvious sign as to which was the coaching staff was leaning "Babe" Parilli, part of the squad for a little more than a week, was given the starting nod. Jack Larschied, who was unable to beat the last man en route to the end zone on the Buffalo 48 with the opening kickoff, got open for a Parilli pass on the 35 and outraced the Bills defense to the goal line. A Larry Barnes field goal added to the cushion created by touchdowns by former Chicago Bear Ron Drzewieki and Parilli to give Oakland a 23-0 lead. Holding a 23-7 advantage at the break, Barnes added his second field goal after a fumble recovery by Bob Dougherty. With the Oakland starters resting, the Bills made things interesting. Adding a pair of touchdowns to pull within 5 points, Paul Larson came on late in the fourth period, kept the ball away from Buffalo and ran out the clock, preserving a 26-21 win.

One final preseason contest remained in Amherst, Massachusetts against the Boston Patriots. The perennial underdog from Oakland arrived amid controversy stemming from alleged "hiding" practices. A member of the Boston media had accused coach Erdelatz of denying game films to the Patriots, when in fact the opposite was true. Films of each team were exchanged, unfortunately for Oakland the films of the Boston club didn't arrive until the morning before the game; too late to do the coaching staff much good as a great deal of their time was devoted to finding adequate practice space. Despite these factors and the fatigue of a third game in nine days, Oakland's Raiders soldiered on. In front of a miniscule crowd of 3,500 spectators sweltering in 90 degrees of humidity, Billy Lott took a hand off from Parilli (who would command the offense through the entire contest) on a draw play and eluded several Boston defenders on his way to a 42-yard touchdown and a 7-7 tie. Down by a touchdown in the second quarter, Larschied knotted the contest again, picking up 21 of his 124 rushing yards. In the third quarter, the exhaustion finally took its toll. Driving to the Boston 14, Larschied's second fumble (of three) began an 86-yard journey for the Patriots that resulted in a 25-yard Butch Songin to Mike Long touchdown. Having already halted Boston with an interception, L.C. Joyner's next gem proved disastrous. Batting a Songin pass down in the end zone, a fallen Jim Colclough, lying flat on his back, had the good fortune to be underneath the pass as it fell. Securing it, Colclough wrapped up a 28-14 Boston win. At 2-3 in their first exhibition season, these Raiders had proved to be the most exciting team in the new AFL as all three losses came against teams that either had more preparation time or had withheld vital scouting information until the last possible moment. Seemingly, the first installment of the Oakland Raiders could compete with anyone in the new American Football League.

(4)

Immediately this was put to a test. Still the underdog, the Oakland club opened their inaugural season on Sunday, September 11, 1960 at home in Kezar Stadium against the Houston Oilers. Featuring top talent such as quarterback George Blanda and the current Heisman Trophy winner, halfback Billy Cannon, the highest paid player in professional football with $100,000 in salary guaranteed to him over the next four seasons.

Tied at seven at halftime as each team exchanged 29-yard touchdown passes, the lead swung in Oakland's favor as a deflected Blanda throw was picked off by Eddie Macon. Redeeming himself for his miscue on the Houston touchdown, Macon raced 28 yards to score. The Houston club countered quickly and often. Aided by fullback Dave Smith's 104 yards on 19 carries, the Oilers practiced ball control while their hosts' squandered opportunities. A first and goal from the 3 netted zero Oakland points as a trio of running attempts were quashed by Houston's defensive front that held the Raiders ground attack to just 27 yards of offense and a Teresa fumble on a kickoff return helped the Oilers to compile 23 unanswered points. Setting up the first Raiders score with a 38-yard pass on a halfback option, Jack Larschied found himself on the receiving end of a short throw from Flores that paid a huge dividend as the 160-lb. halfback turned and raced 46 yards for a touchdown. A Flores pass to former Compton City College standout Jim "Jetstream" Smith brought the Raiders to within eight points midway through the final period. To avoid an upset Houston worked the clock. Running precious time away, the Oilers mounted a final scoring drive and put their first regular season game out of reach with Blanda's fourth touchdown pass of the afternoon to win 37-22.

Granted Monday off, the players and coaches returned Tuesday to prepare for a Friday night contest against another tough opponent, the Dallas Texans. For his struggles, Flores was benched in favor of Babe Parilli, after a 6 of 13 outing, punctuated by two interceptions that ended promising early drives. Down 10-0 Parilli got Oakland on the board early in the second quarter with a picture-perfect 36-yard pass to Tony Teresa. Dallas maintained their 10-point edge after an exchange of field goals and a 15-yard touchdown run through the heart of the Oakland defense. Given a drive start on the Oakland 42 after a pair of obvious clipping penalties went uncalled on a punt return, Johnny Robinson hauled in a 25-yard pass from Cotton Davidson for a score and captured another on a sweep following a Parilli interception for a 34-10 Texans' lead. Mounting one final scoring drive "Jetstream" Smith grabbed an 11-yard touchdown reception with 1:47 remaining. The 2-point attempt failed holding Oakland to 16 points to the Texans 34 as the Raiders stumbled to an 0-2 start.

The schedule makers had done the Oakland squad no favors by having them open up against two teams considered the best in the new league, and their first road trip looked to be a double whammy as they were booked to play those same high-powered squads over the next three weeks. They would be starting in Houston to face the Oilers before a swing to Colorado for their first meeting with the Denver Broncos, then a return to Texas for a rematch with Dallas. Before they could leave, the coaching staff experienced true adversity. Coach Erdelatz came down with a nasty case of laryngitis after the second game then broke a toe while demonstrating an option play in practice the day before the third. These ailments, debilitating for an emotional, sideline walking coach, paled in comparison to the heart attack suffered by Ernie Jorge before the team boarded the plane for the Lone Star State. Forced into bed for the next six to seven weeks, coach Jorge would not return to the Oakland sidelines.

For the first time in his coaching career, Eddie Erdelatz asked his team to win. Asked to win this one for Ernie, his players responded. Eddie Macon grabbed his second interception of the young season off George Blanda on the Oakland 44 and a 35-yard return gave his squad a first down in Oilers territory at the 21. A screen pass from Parilli to Billy Lott gained 17 yards and a hand off to "Jetstream" Smith on second and goal resulted in an early 7-0 lead. Pinned on their 15-yard line by some outstanding work by the visiting coverage team, a 36-yard Dave Smith run brought Houston to the Oakland side of the field. Having a pair of passes batted down by former Michigan defensive tackle Don Deskins, Blanda was forced to throw outside and found John Carson for a game tying score

Ahead 10-7 at the break, Houston added another Blanda field goal to extend its lead to 6 points. Forced to punt from their 19, the ball rolled dead on the Raiders 42 and Tom Flores took over. Performing well throughout the afternoon, the Oilers defense were no match for Flores, who picked them apart with passes to Alan Goldstein and Charley Hardy for 16 yards each before firing a perfect strike to Gene Prebola for a touchdown and a 14-13 lead. Forced to endure a pair of field goal attempts that sailed wide to the right under the intense pressure from the defenders, the Raiders held on to capture their first victory 14-13.

The elation of this historic win was shared by the fans back home. San Francisco mayor George Christopher, reversing his earlier opposition to the Oakland club, announced "Raiders Week" would be held in his city upon their return from the road. The players would be given a heroes' welcome at a rally in Union Square, where both mayor Christopher and Raiders owner and general manager Chet Soda would speak and each of the players would be introduced to the crowd by coach Erdelatz.

AFL Player of the Week Tom Flores led his Raiders teammates into Denver to face the unseen Broncos, unseen because the teams had never met before and because league mandated film sharing again had failed to produce any game films of the Raiders opposition. At 2-1, the Broncos opened their home schedule with a top-rated defense that Oakland exploited in the fourth week of league play on the ground for 180 yards of offense. Wayne Crow's punting clinic rivaled his preseason exploits against the Chargers, as he boomed 5 punts through the thin Denver air that averaged 53 yards and one that changed field position 72 yards beyond the line of scrimmage. The 18,372 on hand, the largest crowd assembled to date to see the Raiders including mayor Rishell, saw these successes trumped by mistakes. Taking a 7-3 lead into the second quarter, the advantage slipped away first with a spectacular Lionel Taylor touchdown reception followed by interceptions that contributed to scores as Taylor reached the end zone for a second time and an ill-advised throw found its way into the hands of defensive end Bill Yelverton. Out of position on the play, Yelverton was in the perfect place to return the pass 20 yards for points. Climbing back into the contest with a Billy Lott touchdown in the third quarter, a pair of fumbles forced them to slide off the mountain. One led to a 57-yard Bob McNamara touchdown that saw the Bronco receiver bust through six tackles on the way to the end zone, sending the visiting club to a resounding 31-14 defeat.

The 1-3 Raiders returned to Texas to finish out the season series with Dallas. They were trailing 7-0 at intermission after Dave Webster nabbed a tipped Flores pass on the Dallas 20 and hauled his good fortune 80 yards up field for a score. At halftime, coach Erdelatz tore into his offensive unit in the locker room for their poor execution and for their lack of physical play. Promising to find players willing to play the game properly should the current squad continue in their current practices proved to be perfect motivation as his players responded beginning with the second half kickoff as "Jetstream" Smith tied the score with a 96-yard return. With the momentum on their side they began to dismantle the Texans. Driving on the strength of Billy Lott's running and an 11-yard Prebola reception, the Raiders resorted to trickery, handing off to an aching Tony Teresa, who was suffering from severe back pain. The former San Jose State Spartan lobbed a pass to a wide-open Alan Goldstein for a 14-7 lead.

The defense performing superbly the entire afternoon, created another opportunity as Abner Haynes fumbled and Joe Cannavino recovered on the Dallas 16. Calling a reverse, Goldstein was able to showcase his running ability. A devastating Ron Sabal block cleared a path and Goldstein scored the Raiders third touchdown of the half. With six minutes to go on the game clock Dallas reeled off eight plays in less than three minutes. Bo Dickinson found the end zone on a 1-yard run to cut the Oakland lead to 20-13. Jack Spikes' extra point attempt was blocked but an opportunity arose as his kick off was fumbled on the Oakland 33-yard line. In five plays, Dallas returned to the end zone when Max Boydston grabbed Cotton Davidson's 6-yard pass. Playing for the win, coach Stram called for a 2-point conversion. Sending Bo Dickinson through the left side of Oakland's defensive line proved fruitless as the Dallas running back was buried a yard shy of the goal line. Regaining possession, the Raiders ran out the clock and won for the second time.

Returning home to their heroes' welcome, they were just one win shy of a .500-mark and respectability. Standing in their way was a Boston team, coming off a 35-0 shutout of the Los Angeles Chargers. For the first time in their brief history, the Oakland club wouldn't go into a contest playing the role of underdog as they were given even odds. Like the Raiders, the Patriots were proving to be road warriors after starting their season 0-2 at home before evening their record on the first two games of their current road trip. Unfortunately for the Boston club, they met an Oakland team that was beginning to gel. From the game's second play, the visiting Patriots were on their heels. The Raiders grabbed a 7-0 lead as Jack Larschied tore through a gaping hole in the line provided guard Don Manokian and Sabal and a block downfield by Charley Hardy enabled an 87-yard touchdown jaunt. Despite giving up a big play, the Boston defense was a meddlesome bunch, intercepting five passes (three by Gino Cappaletti). The first, by Bob Soltis on the Oakland 42, was returned 33 yards to the 9. Diving over from the 2, fullback Alan Miller got the Patriots on the board but former Chargers' linebacker Riley Morris, performing well since his acquisition prior to the previous road swing overcame the severe back pain that hospitalized him following the Dallas contest, batted down Cappaletti's conversion try to preserve a 7-6 lead. Forcing Oakland to punt, Boston's opportunity to take the lead slipped away as Crow's kick was fumbled by Dick Christy who was attempting to make a fair catch. With a first down on the 40 after Charley Hardy's recovery, Flores found Gene Prebola open on the 20. Eluding a defender, the Oakland tight end raced to the end zone and the Raiders went ahead 14-6. Taking over on the 24 after a failed field goal attempt, Flores had the offense on the march. A pair of completions to Doug Asad gained 35 yards and helped to bring Oakland to the Boston 10-yard line in 7 plays. On the eighth play, Flores found Al Hoisington alone in the end zone and the home team began to pull away 21-6. After losing a scoring opportunity when a fumble rolled into the end zone and was recovered for a touchback, Boston found second half success on its first possession when Butch Songin snuck over from the one, pulling to within a touchdown as Gino Cappaletti took the ball he was supposed to kick in for a 2-point conversion. The Patriots were countered by a 40-yard Billy Lott run for a touchdown. A failed extra point was meaningless as Oakland won easily 27-14.

Embarking on a three-week road trip, the Oakland club traveled to the northeastern United States with games in Buffalo, New York and Boston. In Buffalo they took a giant step backward against the 1-4 Bills. Favored to win by a single point, the Raiders ran into a Bills squad that ended the competitive phase of the game within its first 30 seconds as the newly acquired Johnny Green found fullback Wray Carlton with a 38-yard touchdown pass. The unfortunate circumstance of the remaining

59:30 of game time proved to be an endurance test as coach Erdelatz said post game "the longer it went, the worse we got." Down 21-0, Parilli engineered a scoring drive that nearly ended in disaster. Unable to find an open receiver, Parilli ran into an eligible one, "Jetstream" Smith, who took the ball, dove into the pile and was credited for a touchdown despite his fumbling and the ball being recovered by receiver Doug Asad. Later a center snap to the Bills punter sailed high through the back of the end zone, the final Oakland tally in a 38-9 whitewashing in rain and mud of War Memorial Stadium.

Another mud bog awaited Oakland at New York's Polo Grounds in their game against the Titans. This was also the first time Raiders defensive end Charley Powell had a chance to see his little brother Art, a flashy 215-lb. offensive end and a rising star in the new league in action. Clinging to hopes his little brother wouldn't demonstrate his full potential. Baby brother Art happily disappointed his older sibling in what proved to be a week-eight war. Along with Don Maynard, Powell ran wild over the Oakland secondary in the first half. Maynard opened the scoring, hauling in a 47-yard Al Dorow pass for a touchdown. The Raiders responded; moving 80 yards in 6 plays and tying the score with a 25-yard Flores pass to Billy Lott. The lead swung quickly back to New York on the ensuing kickoff as Leon Burton sprinted 101 yards untouched, putting the Titans up 14-7. With five minutes remaining in the half, Oakland took over on their own 22. After picking up 17 yards on two running plays, Flores fired deep to split end Al Hoisington on the Titan 25-yard line. Hauling in the picture-perfect pass full two full strides beyond the nearest defender, Hoisington waltzed in for the score unmolested for a 61-yard touchdown and a 14-point tie.

Dorow would not relinquish the momentum, answering with a strike to Powell who fought off Alex Bravo for possession then broke a tackle at the Raiders 20. Powell completed a 76-yard journey by crossing the goal line and claiming a 21-14 halftime lead. In the second half, Oakland's defense bent but did not break. After allowing a field goal in the third quarter, the Raiders halted a touchdown march when Eddie Macon picked off a Dorow pass on the 9-yard line. A pair of penalties helped while a slant pass to Tony Teresa and the running of "Jetstream" Smith gained big chunks of yardage. The 12-play march came to fruition and the Raiders were within a field goal at 24-21 when Smith crashed over from the 3. An exchange of fourth quarter interceptions preceded Bill Shockley's second field goal. From the 29, it took nine plays for "Jetstream" Smith to run around the left side of the Raiders' line for a 9-yard score and a 28-27 advantage with

3:34 to go. Afforded one final shot to get into field goal range and pull out a victory, Titans quarterback Al Dorow was met hard by defensive tackles Ramon Armstrong and George Fields, whose savage handling of the New York passer on fourth down was reminiscent of hungry animals ripping apart their prey in the wild. After taking over on downs, the Oakland offense ran out the clock and pulled their record even at 4-4 with their third 1-point victory of the season.

Trailing the Chargers by a game in the Western Division, they arrived in Boston for their second regular season meeting with the Patriots and again encountered a rumor mill in full production. Reports in the Boston media had coach Erdelatz leaving Oakland for a head coaching position with the New York Giants in the NFL. Also, that the Raiders organization was considering a mid season jump to the East Bay, having the team use a high school field in nearby San Leandro, while speculation arose in regard to Chet Soda's interest in either selling or moving the team out of the Bay Area altogether. These rumors all proved false, misguided and prophetic. Coach Erdelatz immediately denied any intent on leaving, citing his two-year agreement with the Raiders and his wanting to stay in his native East Bay Area. The team's home status was very much in question. None of the Raiders home games had been televised locally due to an AFL blackout rule, which states that no home games can be televised within a 75-mile radius of a home stadium holding the game in question that was not sold out. With an average attendance of just more than 10,700 for its first three regular-season home games, Kezar Stadium was far from capacity and would hurt the Raiders in building its local fan base while cutting deep into the AFL profit sharing plan from its broadcast deal with ABC. All eight teams shared equal monies from the broadcast of AFL games. This agreement brought much needed financial relief to the clubs, none of which were turning a profit.

Despite the club's financial and stadium uncertainties, the Oakland squad took the field on the following Friday night to face the Patriots. With a win, the Raiders would move into a tie with Los Angeles for first place in the western division. Instead, Oakland returned the favor the Patriots had done them in week six. After spotting Boston a 20-7 halftime lead, they began to climb back in the second half with an 8-yard Flores scamper to bring them within six. A 1-yard touchdown plunge by Dick Christy and a 38-yard scoring connection between Butch Songin and Jim Colclough with a little more than 10 minutes to go left Oakland needing a miracle. A pitch to Tony Teresa who ran around the left side of his protective wall, proved the perfect call as he raced 8 yards for Oakland's second score of the half. George Fields' recovery of halfback Billy Wells' fumble of the kickoff return on the Patriots 32 gave the Raiders added life. A 12-yard Parilli pass was complete to Alan Goldstein and with 5:06 to go the Raiders had climbed back into the contest with the momentum clearly on their side, trailing 34-28. Burning only 1:37 before being forced to punt, Boston faced defeat when the Raiders took possession just 57 yards from a winning score. Alas the prayers from Oakland went unanswered. On first down, Parilli's pass was intercepted by Chuck Shonta and returned to the Oakland 14. Regaining possession on downs, time remained for just two offensive plays. Time ran out, with the Oakland team on the short end of the score.

Returning home with a record of 4 wins and 5 losses, the Raiders were focused on winning their remaining five games to maintain their hopes of a division title. The first pitted them in a rematch with a Bills team that they crumbled against three weeks prior. Since that time, Buffalo had sported the league's top defense and quarterback Johnny Green was emerging as the league's newest star. This time the Raiders wouldn't falter. Led by a ferocious defense that kept Buffalo trapped between the 30's. The outcome of the contest was never in doubt. Oakland was enjoying a 13-0 lead as Larry Barnes connected on a pair of field goals complemented by a 1-yard scoring blast by Billy Lott. The margin widened to 20-0 as the third period ended when Tony Teresa, already averaging 5.5 yards per carry added seven points and gave the Raiders their first 100-yard rusher by picking up 83 of his 141 rushing yards on a beautiful touchdown run. Buffalo, referred to post game as "quitters" by head coach Buster Ramsey, received a break when a questionable pass interference call was made against Eddie Macon. Macon's harsh protest sent the home crowd into a fit of jubilation but ultimately fell on the deaf ears of the officials, whose opinions mattered most. With Johnny Green sitting after 18 of his 32 passes fell incomplete, quarterback Tom O'Connell went over from the 1 on a quarterback sneak for Buffalo's lone score, a meaningless feat as Oakland evened their record at 5-5 with a 20-7 victory.

As the Raiders enjoyed a bye week, the AFL got a leg up on the NFL by holding their draft in mid-November. Selections were to be made in reverse order of the eight teams won-loss record. Buffalo, with the leagues' worst record, would be picking first followed by New York, Boston and Denver, who with records of 4-5 would alternate the third and fourth picks in each round, followed by Oakland, Dallas then Los Angeles and Houston alternating the final pick of each round due to their 6-3 records.

The Oakland Chamber of Commerce held meetings to establish a non-profit stadium organization (to be called Coliseum Inc) charged with building an East Bay home for the Raiders then leasing the facility back to the city and county. The Raiders themselves scrapped the San Leandro High School idea and signed a lease with the San Francisco Parks and Recreation Department for the new Candlestick Park facility for the remainder of the 1960 campaign, providing they return Candlestick to its baseball setting upon their season's conclusion. Kezar had become problematic due to scheduling and contractual conflicts with the 49ers, forcing the Raiders out. Despite rumors of his impending sale and his reported desire to move the club away from Oakland, the Raiders ownership had given a vote of confidence to Chet Soda with their recent success, but any hopes the Raiders had for a division title came to an abrupt halt with a home and home series against the Los Angeles Chargers.

Just a game behind Los Angeles going in, they would fall to three back with two games remaining when the dust had settled. Linebacker Tom Louderback's interception of Jack Kemp on the Los Angeles 13-yard line gave his squad an excellent scoring opportunity, which they used to erase a 7-0 deficit, with a 1-yard blast from "Jetstream" Smith. Kemp's 13 completions on the afternoon accounted for 307 yards and a pair of touchdowns, the last of which ended the competitive phase of the ball game just four plays after it had been tied. It was the beginning of an uninterrupted parade to the end zone that began as running back Paul Lowe took a short pass 63 yards for a score before breaking Tony Teresa's single game league rushing record by carrying the ball for 157 yards and adding another score. Sustaining scoring drives of 77 and 55 yards did little to help a shell-shocked Oakland club that already trailed 38-7. The Chargers answered nearly every Oakland score, establishing a new league scoring record at 52 points. Combined with the Raiders 28, a new combined league scoring mark was also set at an astounding 80 points.

A locally biased home crowd numbering 12,061 filed into the Raiders new digs at Candlestick Park for the first of a three-game home stand that would conclude the 1960 campaign. Aside from the controversy surrounding Soda's protest over Sid Gillman's activation of Al Bansavage, a draft pick the Oakland club held the rights to, they were treated to the best 45 minutes of football their Raiders had strung together in their inaugural season. Trailing 17-14 after three quarters, the visitors from Los Angeles began to resemble one of professional football's elite, while the home squad reminded their boosters of the Keystone cops. Lowe took a Jack Kemp pass on the Oakland 30 between a pair of defenders. Slipping away, the elusive Charger made a would-be tackler miss in the open field on the way to the end zone for a 49-yard score and a 21-17 lead. A Flores fumble on the Oakland 44 gave Kemp and the Chargers excellent field position and before the quarter was half over, Los Angeles led by 11 as Kemp scored on a 6-yard roll out. Stopping the Chargers' attack also proved futile when both Jack Larchied and Billy Reynolds signaled for a fair catch of a Bob Laraba punt. With neither man yielding to the other, they collided. Touched by Reynolds, the live ball was recovered by the Chargers on the Raiders 17 and quickly Oakland trailed by 18 at 35-17 as Kemp found Dave Kocourek for a touchdown on first down. The avalanche came to a conclusion three plays later when Babe Parilli lost control of the ball on the 49 and linebacker Rommie Loud scooped it up and rumbled untouched for a score. The 41-17 victory gave the Chargers the Western Division title and dropped Oakland to 5-7 and into third place as the Dallas Texans scored a 24-0 win at home over the Eastern Division leading Houston Oilers.

A .500 finish for a team that had limped into existence seven months later than the rest of the league and lost the rights to one of the league's best running back's Abner Haynes to a division rival would be a remarkable feat. With the Denver Broncos coming to town to finish their schedule after going 1-7-1 since their 31-14 win over the Raiders in week four and the New York Titans, who blew a 21-14 halftime lead against the same Oakland team at home in the Polo Fields it was a feat that now appeared feasible. Much like the contest in New York, the rematch for the California team would be an uphill battle. From the games second play, a 72-yard Al Dorow pass to Art Powell that the former San Jose State Spartan took the final 40 yards untouched for a lightning quick 7-0 Titans lead. Another Powell touchdown left the host squad trailing 14-7 at the break but a Flores pass to Charley Hardy on the goal line following a 78-yard kickoff return by Larschied opened the second half. Powell's third score came nine plays later. Capping a 56-yard march, the Titans went ahead 21-14 with a 5-yard Dorow pass.

A fumbled punt gave New York another opportunity from midfield that they cashed in with a 27-yard Bill Shockley field goal. Down by 10, Tony Teresa went to work against the New York defenders. Running stride for stride with Titans' defensive back Corky Tharp, Teresa made an amazing fingertip grab. The play covered 46 yards and resulted in a first and goal from the 9. Picking up eight yards on first down, Teresa followed up by plowing through the line for a score. His efforts inspired his defense. Allowing only 96 yards of offense on the ground, Ramon Armstrong and company stopped New York and following a punt, Teresa was back at it. After completing a 17-yard pass to Alan Goldstein on the halfback option to move into Titans' territory, a blatant pass interference call put the Raiders on the New York 5 with another first and goal. Sending Teresa into the defensive backfield, Flores fired his third touchdown pass of the afternoon as his hot-handed halfback made another spectacular grab and the Raiders took the lead for the first time 28-24 with 12 minutes to go. With the Titans ground to a halt, the Raiders offense took over looking to bury their guests. Firing to Doug Asad, Flores' pass was batted around like a volleyball before landing in the arms of Larry Grantham on the New York 31. Aided by a pair of pass interference penalties as the Oakland defensive backs showed their intent on beating the Titans physically as well as on the scoreboard. New York moved into Oakland territory. The inspired defenders finally brought up a fourth down and five situation from their 20. Looking to end the rematch in the same way that the first contest concluded, the defensive line hounded and harassed Dorow. Ducking under the intense pressure, Dorow fired a prayer to Dewey Bohling. Perfectly covered by Bob Dougherty, Bohling had no chance of making a reception until Dougherty tripped and fell. Dorow's pass fell into Bohling's hands and with it, New York's seventh win of the season 31-28.

As is the case with all things, Oakland's first season as a professional football town would come to a close. As a treat to the miniscule crowd of 5,159 that made the ascent into Candlestick Park to witness the Raiders-Broncos rematch, the home squad, on both sides of the ball saved their best performance for last. Tied at three at the conclusion of the opening period, the Raiders took advantage of an excellent drive start on the Broncos 45-yard line and a 37-yard Billy Lott run that brought them a first and goal from the 8. Three Teresa runs resulted in positive yardage but he failed to score as he was held just 2 inches from the goal line. Following Jim Otto, Flores plunged over for a touchdown and a 10-3 lead. Having already established a professional football record for most receptions in a season with 88, Lionel Taylor added four more to his record pace and tied the game with a 6-yard reception with 1:22 remaining in the half. The Broncos' offense, managing to lose 5 yards on the ground on the day, wouldn't be heard from again until 1961. Rattling off seven plays, Flores displayed his prowess for the big play by launching a perfect 47-yard strike to Charley Hardy to the 5. On fourth down and goal, Teresa blasted over for a 17-10 halftime lead.

An interception in the end zone by Goose Gonsoulin ended Oakland's lone scoring opportunity in the third quarter, but, late in the period, circumstances for the visiting Broncos went horribly awry. Eddie Macon's interception of Frank Tripuka ended a promising Bronco drive on the Oakland 20. Another long Flores pass, this one finding Alan Goldstein for 44 yards, moved the Raiders to the 6 and extended their lead to 10 with Larry Barnes second field goal. Forced to punt, George Herring was buried trying to find the handle on a bad snap at his 21. Rolling to his right after taking over on downs, Flores found the end zone for the second time with a 7-yard run. Accustomed to having his way with opposing pass defenders, Lionel Taylor took exception to Joe Cannavino's interception on the 33. An 11-yard personal foul penalty (half the distance to the goal line) was added to a 10-yard return and the Raiders had a first down on the Broncos 12. A Babe Parilli sneak added to the lead and a Denver failure on a fourth down and 4 situation gave the Raiders possession on the Broncos' side of the field at the 49. Firing deep, Parilli found flanker Nyle Mcfarlane behind a beaten Bob McNamera and for the second time in as many games, the Salt Lake City sheriff's deputy had a touchdown. Taking a page from the Oakland playbook Denver showed their incompetence with the halfback option as Alex Bravo snagged George Herring's pass intended for Pat Epperson. Charley Hardy's second score of the day accounted for the Raiders sixth touchdown as the Raiders amassed 48 points to the Broncos' 10 and only the time running out on the game clock stopped them from establishing a new league scoring mark. Evaluating his squad post game, a beaming coach Erdelatz couldn't help but exude praise for his players. "These 'Guys named Joe' are ok, and they've made this season one of my best in football."

CHAPTER TWO
TURMOIL 1961

With the ownership defections of Harvey Binns and Art Beckett prior to the 1960 preseason, Raiders management appeared to be on shaky ground. By the end of the inaugural 1960 season, team management proved as stable as an East Bay fault line. A running feud had developed between the eight owners over stadium and management issues, causing at least half of them to look for prospective buyers for their stakes in the franchise. While no owners were willing to comment publicly, many reports had Chet Soda himself selling out, while others had Wayne Valley leading a group of current owners, including Soda in buying out the unhappy parties and reorganizing the team's front office.

With this constant bickering and an unnamed owner leaking the club's dirty laundry to the local media, Chet Soda badly wanted to step down as the team's president and general manager. While claiming to have no plans to sell his share in the team, Soda would resign from both posts on his third attempt. His wish to be "just another owner" had twice been thwarted by the Raiders' board of directors. Soda's embarrassment, stemming from management squabbles taking public precedent over the team's efforts and accomplishments on the field, was seemingly unshared by many in the Raiders hierarchy.

When Eddie Erdelatz was hired as head coach, he was expected to take over the GM reins as well. In removing himself from consideration a second time, Erdelatz opened the door for acting general manager Bud Hastings to take the position over on a permanent basis. Newly appointed, acting team president Ed McGah wasted no time in elevating Hastings, leaving only one question mark in team management, his own. With a term originally slated to last as briefly as three days, McGah found himself Oakland's top man officially when the AFL owners dispatched commissioner Foss and two league attorneys to settle the Oakland discord once and for all.

Other AFL franchises were owned and operated by ownership groups, yet Oakland stood alone in the league with its management disharmony. Many owners saw Oakland's potential to be one of the league's great cities. However if commissioner Foss were unsuccessful in squashing the team's strife, he would then be required to revoke the Oakland franchise and the Raiders would be lost forever.

Though proving they could not get along in managing the team, each of the eight owners agreed it was in the Raiders' best interest to remain in Oakland. Through a seven-hour negotiation session, commissioner Foss and the attorneys constructed a buy-out arrangement, in which the team's directorship would now be reduced to three, McGah, Wayne Valley, the teams vice president, and treasurer Robert Osborne, each retaining their executive positions in the new regime.

The figurative wrestling matches put on by Raiders' management were not the only item of interest apparent to the AFL. The efforts of two "guys named Joe" received recognition from the league. Center Jim Otto, bulking up to 235 lbs. prior to the 1960 season (from less than 200 lbs.) and approaching 250 lbs. nearing its conclusion without losing any of his quickness or agility, quickly proved himself as the best center in professional football with only a few disbelievers holding out for Jim Ringo of the Green Bay Packers. Otto was named All-AFL first team in his rookie season with identical honors coming from the Associated Press (AP). A fellow lineman was named to the All-AFL second string. Guard Don Manokian was considered by some to be the best at his position in the new league, though Bob Mischak from the New York Titans and the Dallas Texans' Bill Krisher would be awarded the top honor. Otto also found himself honored by United Press International (UPI) by being named to their second-string AFL team. Nine-year veteran defensive back Eddie Macon was named to the UPI's first team in recognition of his 9 interceptions and 105 return yards in 1960.

Players such as these, along with teams such as the league champion Houston Oilers, the (now) San Diego Chargers and the Dallas Texans who were stocked with them, gave commissioner Foss an extreme sense of confidence. Early in 1961, the commissioner targeted the NFL, making challenges of a championship game between the two leagues. Many in the AFL felt the smothering defense of a Houston Oilers team along with its offensive backfield featuring Dave Smith, Heisman Trophy winner Billy Cannon and quarterback George Blanda, could compete with the best squads the NFL could produce. Jack Kemp, on the other hand, led a Chargers offense as potent as anyone had seen at any level. NFL commissioner Rozelle scoffed at these challenges, citing the impending $10,000,000 anti-trust suit in his reasoning.

Despite getting off to a slow start with fans, the AFL's popularity had grown over its first season. With only a half-million fewer viewers for its championship game than the NFL enjoyed for its game pitting the Philadelphia Eagles against the Packers, it was thought the AFL would only have to be competitive with their well-established adversary to score a major victory with fans.

The general feeling was that all AFL franchises would be greatly improved for the 1961 season. The Raiders, generally happy with the squad they fielded the prior season, began to upgrade. In signing their fifteenth pick, they added the nation's fourth-ranked receiver in Bob Coolbaugh. A University of Richmond standout, reputed as tough to cover after being named to the All Southern Conference first team, Coolbaugh displayed a good set of hands, establishing a conference record by snagging eight passes one afternoon against the Citadel. Georgia Tech captain Gerald Burch, Oakland's thirteenth pick, chose the Raiders of the AFL despite being drafted #6 by the NFL's new Minnesota club. The sure-handed Burch, capable of showing good speed and moves, was expected to be a potent weapon in the Raiders' arsenal and reduce the number of passes falling incomplete, a malfunction that plagued the offense throughout 1960.

The most notable draft pick signing with Oakland in 1961 was that of their number-two selection George Fleming. With a lucrative off-season job at a Los Angeles brewery, Fleming chose Oakland over the Bears in the NFL and the Toronto Argonauts of the CFL. The lack of a breakaway threat hampered the Oakland offense in 1960. His ability to score from anywhere on the field provided the team with this badly needed element. The 44-yard blast from his foot in the Rose Bowl was the catalyst for Washington's 17-7 victory over Minnesota. With Larry Barnes at times missing both wide and short in his field goal attempts from within 40 yards, Fleming was valued highly for his kicking abilities.

Defensive backfield coach Ed Cody departed for an assistant's position at Washington State University and offensive line coach Ernie Jorge returned to the Naval Academy in 1961. Former University of San Francisco assistant Bob Maddock, coming off a three-year stint in Canada with the Saskatchewan Roughriders, took over the offensive line for coach Feldman, who reverted to his original position of mentoring the defensive line. An unusual choice was made to fill the vacancy made by the departure of coach Cody. Notre Dame grad and University of the Pacific assistant George Dickson assumed the defensive backfield chores. A high school tailback, who switched to quarterback in college, where he would serve as a back up to the Broncos' quarterback Frank Tripuka. Dickson, until his new appointment had only coached and played on the offensive side of the ball his entire career, would receive a trial by fire in Oakland.

(2)

The AFL's dramatic rise in popularity over its first season was not lost on ABC TV, which rewarded the new league by renewing its broadcast contract with a raise of $200,000 to be shared equally among the clubs. The Raiders needed this money for their new players salaries and to calm some irate veterans. Defensive back and punter Wayne Crow held out over a withholding clause and linebacker and defensive captain Tom Louderback was being asked to take a pay cut large enough for him to first mistake it as a misprint. The AFL's third-ranked kick returner Jack Larschied, along with end Charley Hardy, guard Wayne Hawkins and top halfback Tony Teresa would all return contracts unsigned, holding out for larger pay increases.

All six players would re-sign as training camp was set to begin. With some of their teammates pursuing off-season interests such as acting or even professional wrestling, new ticket manager Al Salisbury would come up with a clever way to keep three of the disgruntled six employed during the off-season. Louderback, Crow and Larschied along with tackle and Oakland native Ron Sabal began knocking on doors of local businesses selling season tickets. Called the "Four Men In Motion" and armed with a $3.50 discount over seven regular season games, the four also offered an installment plan with an $8 down payment with the remainder to be paid in $5 monthly increments. These players also got an off-season taste of the passion local fans had for their Raiders. Unfortunately for these zealous fans, they were required to travel cross-bay to watch their team in 1961 as home for the Oakland franchise remained at Candlestick Park. With a heavy evening fog and winds that blew Giants' relief pitcher Stu Miller off the mound during the 1961 All-Star game, the AFL granted Oakland no night games for the impending season, opting instead for 1:30 p.m. kickoff times, just in time for the bay tide to come in and saturate the Candlestick field from below.

In Oakland, the perfect spot was located for the new coliseum. The East Bay Municipal Utilities District (EBMUD) sold the city 104 acres of land it used as a pipe yard along the city's Nimitz Freeway. Along with another 36 acres to be donated by the Port of Oakland, the site was able to easily support both the proposed 54,000-seat outdoor coliseum, as well as an adjacent 13,000-seat sports arena, with plenty of room remaining for huge parking lots on both the north and south ends of the facility, to easily handle traffic that would pour in from the surrounding freeway exits. A proposed mass transit station just to the east would make the facilities accessible from San Francisco and the entire East Bay after a short walk. With the nation's top architects spending between fifty and one hundred thousand dollars of their own money drawing the plans for the new coliseum, a weather survey was also done on the site as well. The cold, wind and fog players and fans endured at Candlestick Park would be a thing of the past, as the Oakland site enjoyed the best weather conditions of any locale in the entire Bay Area.

With eight patrons reportedly suffering fatal heart attacks at Candlestick Park, from climbing the stairs into the stadium in the facilities first year and a half, the Oakland Coliseum and Arena would both feature gradual slopes upon entry and feature stairs only in the seating aisles. Baseball's American League had already shown interest in the East Bay with a brief flirtation with relocating the Boston Red Sox in 1960, a move halted by the lack of a suitable home. Now with both the Cleveland Indians and the Kansas City Athletics faltering at the ticket gate, the AL was primed for a move. With both football and baseball in the outdoor coliseum and the arena suitable for pro basketball, ice hockey, expositions and cultural events, Oakland could attract millions of yearly visitors willing to spend money. Hundreds of jobs would also be created to maintain and operate both buildings, such as maintenance, ushers, stagehands, groundskeepers, concessions, security, box office, parking and management to ensure smooth operation. These facilities would provide an economic boom not only to Oakland, but to the entire East Bay for decades to come.

(3)

As the breeze blew softly in Oakland, the winds of trade began whipping through the Raiders' franchise early on in 1961. The Raiders featured two top passers in quarterbacks Tom Flores, the AFL's completion percentage leader, and veteran Babe Parilli, along with the leagues second leading running attack, trailing the Dallas Texans by a mere 29 yards. The club now could address its weakness, the defense. Looking to acquire help at the defensive tackle position as well as at outside linebacker and in the secondary, the Raiders involved themselves in the new league's first major swap. In a vote of confidence for quarterback Tom Flores, Oakland dealt Babe Parilli and fullback Billy Lott to the Boston Patriots in exchange for halfback Dick Christy, fullback Alan Miller and defensive tackle Hal Smith.

In trading Parilli, the Raiders gave up the best second-string quarterback in all of professional football, in dealing Lott however, the toll would be much greater. He was ranked first amongst AFL fullbacks in yards per carry with a mark of 5.3 yards per try. They would also be without the AFL's sixth leading receiver with 49 catches and their own receptions leader and an on-field leader. In exchange for the two, they received three Boston starters from the year before, addressing two areas of concern in their defense. Alan Miller, the Patriots' leading rusher and second-leading receiver in 1960 replaced Billy Lott at fullback. Halfback and punt return specialist Dick Christy could also perform as a defensive back. The key player in the deal, Hal Smith, a 6' 5" 250-lb. defensive tackle had served with the Chicago Cardinals and the Pittsburgh Steelers in the NFL, with quick stops in Los Angeles and Denver in the AFL before finding a home and a role in the Boston Patriots' starting line up. Smith caught the eye of Raiders coaches in game films and was expected to make an impact in the Oakland defensive front.

The allure of the Bay Area drew interest from two known football stars as well. Former Cal great Joe Kapp refused to re-sign with the Calgary Stampeders of the CFL, wishing to play out his option and sign with Oakland. Kapp's actions drew the Raiders an unfounded tampering accusation. Bud Hastings expressed an interest in Kapp and encouraged Calgary management to negotiate for his rights. Calgary, in turn, traded Kapp to the British Columbia Lions ridding themselves of their unhappy star. Pittsburgh Steelers defensive back Fred "The Hammer" Williamson returned his contract unsigned, wishing to remain on the West Coast near his wife and infant son and pursue business opportunities in construction, which was far more lucrative in California. Coming off a fine season in Pittsburgh after being traded by the 49ers, Williamson was an outstanding player that would contribute greatly to any team he chose to suit up for. He was best known in the Bay Area for his involvement in a 49ers brawl with the Philadelphia Eagles in the 1960 pre-season, which drew the ire of commissioner Rozelle.

With Lott traded away, Oakland's locker room leadership would be dealt a major blow by the surprise retirement of guard Don Manokian. Beginning to feel his years at age 27, Manokian left to pursue his pro wrestling career. The current Texas Heavyweight Champion and Pacific Northwest Tag-Team Champion had been presented with a rare and lucrative opportunity to tour Japan early in the fall of 1961 and intended to use his earnings to bankroll a real estate and construction business in the Reno/Lake Tahoe Nevada area.

Heading to training camp with sixty-two hopefuls vying for a reduced thirty-three roster spots, coach Erdelatz's first chore was to fill the huge holes left by Manokian and Lott. With thirty-six veterans returning from the campaign prior and twenty-six new players, Oakland coaches were looking for men with that natural leadership ability. With players reporting and practices beginning in Santa Cruz, the void created by the loss of these players was tremendous. A shred of hope would appear with the cancellation of Don Manokian's Japanese wrestling tour. A dozen Raiders veterans, led by all-league center Jim Otto unsuccessfully sought their teammate's return, calling him daily at his home in Portland, begging and even good naturedly ordering him to training camp. Wrestling provided Manokian with a salary triple that provided by football. This, accompanied by an injury bug feasting on these Raiders left the offensive line seriously depleted. Three more offensive lineman were lost when a disc in the back of tackle Paul Oglesby caused him to miss the entire 1961 season. The injury-induced defections of new guards Jim Green and Tom Cousineau left the team with two guards on the roster, elevating the offensive line situation from troubling to crisis.

The defensive line saw the same type of trauma afflicting their offensive counterparts with Ramon Armstrong, Dalton Truax, Don Deskins and Ron Warzeka all informing the club they would not report to camp. Linebacker Larry Barnes fell victim to injury, as knee trouble ended his season before it began. The most crucial ache affecting Oakland was in the back of star halfback Tony Teresa. Having already spent one full month in the hospital, Teresa reported to camp briefly before a sciatic nerve injury ended his playing career. Injuries devoured the Raiders' talent pool, but the most troubling demon the Raiders faced this off-season and throughout the regular season was from the United States government. President Kennedy's speech calling for a military buildup could potentially rob the Raiders of eighteen players. Eleven veterans and seven rookies were military reservists including Alan Miller and Tom Louderback, while six others such as Wayne Hawkins' and Bob Coolbaugh's draft status was classified 1-A.

Management had to move quickly to plug these holes created by misfortune and circumstance. In dealing a draft pick to the San Diego Chargers, Oakland acquired their own draft pick in converted linebacker Al Bansavage with designs on using him at the guard position. Tight end Gene Prebola was dealt to the Denver Broncos for Willie Smith who was expected to contribute on both the offensive and defensive lines. Unfortunately, neither of these new players was available to travel to Hawaii as the Raiders were set to take on the AFL Champion Houston Oilers in their first exhibition game.

Even in a 28-14 loss the week prior to the AFL Western Division Champion San Diego Chargers, the Houston Oilers had shown few changes and much improvement from their championship year. A sharp performance from quarterback George Blanda coupled with an impressive defensive line, made Houston an obvious favorite. Chargers quarterback Jack Kemp was able to exploit the Oilers' one weakness, its defensive secondary. Raiders coaches felt they possessed the best passer in the AFL in Tom Flores, equipped with new weapons Bob Coolbaugh and George Fleming, both starting their first game in an Oakland uniform. These Raiders had three things in mind going into their first contest of the preseason, pass, pass and pass some more.

Houston's defensive line struck first. While not contributing to any point total, they would do damage by knocking Flores senseless early on. Completing only 2 passes in the first half and having trouble focusing his vision and maintaining his balance, Flores was mercifully benched in favor of Fresno State rookie Nick Papac. Already trailing 14-3, after a 15-yard touchdown scamper by Billy Cannon en route to a 15-carry 149-yard performance, Oakland's offensive line woes struck Papac immediately on his first play as a professional as he scrambled for his life and gave up 13 yards to the Houston cause. Punts were exchanged before Papac took over again at his own 43-yard line. After a twelve-yard completion to "Jetstream"

Smith at the Houston 45, a scrambling Papac launched a pass to George Fleming, who was denied a touchdown on an officials ruling that he was downed at the 1. Fullback Alan Miller found paydirt on the ensuing play and Fleming's kick cut the Houston lead to 14-10 at halftime.

A remarkably more clear-headed Tom Flores returned in the second half and led his Raiders to what should have been a 17-14 Oakland lead. Bringing the offense from their own 35, Flores facing fourth and goal from the 11, found Charley Hardy in the end zone. One official raised his arms signaling a touchdown while another ruled that Hardy did not have possession long enough. Houston took over and behind the spectacular effort of Billy Cannon ran the score up 35-10 before Nick Papac, calling the same play which set up the first Oakland touchdown, found Herman Urenda wide open. With the call against Fleming still in mind Urenda went the extra yard, bringing the games' final tally to 35-17 in favor of Houston.

Billy Cannon's big day and a mere 35 rushing yards of their own, coupled with a sore neck suffered by Tom Flores post game, complementing the cob webs he experienced throughout, made one point painfully evident, both Raiders' lines were in serious trouble. In an effort to correct these glaring missteps, coach Erdelatz switched defensive end Carmen Cavelli to offensive tackle and gave study to newly acquired guard and tackle Willie Smith, in an unsuccessful attempt of moving him into the vacancy created by the Cavelli swap. Also moved from offense to defensive end was rookie tackle Dave Williams, who remained there until being waived.

Awaiting them in Spokane, Washington were the even more battered Denver Broncos. With 12 men on its injured list, including 38-year-old starting quarterback Frank Tripuka, the Denver team appeared far worse for wear than their Oakland counterparts. The Broncos' physical condition had Oakland being named two touchdown favorites, serving as a major source of confidence. Despite their own pitiful rushing output, it was more than double that of Denver's the prior week.

Flores led Oakland to a score within the first six minutes, finding newly appointed starting fullback Alan Miller in the end zone for a 4-yard touchdown. This lead was erased immediately. Taking the kickoff on his 5, Jerry Traynham moved ahead to the 15 before reversing to the speedy Al Frazier, who then covered the remaining 85 yards for a score. Denver never looked back. Though being pummeled badly 48-21, Nick Papac showed flash and poise under pressure, which never let up even as the game was hopelessly out of reach midway through the third quarter.

This demoralizing loss to the Broncos only seemed to get worse. Up next for these Raiders was a Chargers team whom Oakland couldn't defeat even if the game was being handed to them. The Raiders looked to stop the bleeding on their defensive line with the addition of rookie Bob Voight, a 275-lb. defensive tackle who joined them after a two-week deployment as an Army reservist. A trade was made with San Diego. In exchange for cash, All-AFL defensive tackle Volney Peters was sent north. Peters, a San Diego native, had always wished for the opportunity to play professionally in his hometown was quite displeased by being sent to Oakland, threatened retirement before donning Raiders Black and Gold. Peters however soon changed his mind after coach Gillman placed him on the Chargers' inactive list. Unfortunately for Oakland, it would be too late for him to face his newly former team. The offense found temporary help, in trading Dick Christy to the Titans prior to the Broncos game. End Dave Ross had finally made the cross-country trek to Santa Cruz and was available for the upcoming contest along with rookie tackle Fran Morelli. Neither would be Raiders come opening day.

Even with these moves the Raiders still stood no chance against San Diego. The competitive phase of the contest was ended in the first three minutes by a 73-yard Paul Lowe punt return, en route to a 26-0 halftime lead. The Chargers went ahead 32-0 before Tom Flores led the Raiders 75 yards in 13 plays, converting on two fourth down situations. The latter of which was a fourth down and nine play, when Flores found Doug Asad on the 1-yard line. Asad broke the plane of the goal line untouched, as the 15-yard strike accounted for all of Oakland's scoring in the contest.

A five-yard defensive holding penalty, called on Chargers defensive tackle Ernie Ladd, as the result of his ripping the helmet off of guard John Dittrich a split second before smashing the stolen equipment into the lineman's forehead, was also a huge help in acquainting Oakland with the scoreboard. This was the real story of the game. Knowing they were out-manned in every aspect of the game, Oakland made the Chargers pay a bloody price for each of their 35 points and every yard they gained. Linebackers from both squads were taking second and third shots at opposing ball carriers. For the equivalent of five Chargers touchdowns, the Raiders maimed one player for each end zone infraction, two of them would suffer season ending broken arms! The Raiders couldn't beat the Chargers on the scoreboard, but on this day, they beat the San Diego club up!

For the first and only time in the 1961 preseason, the Oakland Raiders found themselves at home. In fact a former home, Kezar Stadium, held the Raiders final exhibition game against the Denver Broncos for the Raiders second benefit for Children's Hospital of the East Bay. With former 49ers fullback Charlie Fuller signed and Wayne Crow having reverted to his college position at halfback, Oakland found themselves heavy underdogs to the same Broncos squad that had humiliated them two weeks prior. 6,300 spectators made their way to Kezar for this contest, the third for Denver in ten days and the second in three. Unlike the prior meeting between the two squads, Oakland jumped on Denver immediately. Taking over on their own 31-yard line, Oakland struck quickly as Tom Flores spotted Charley Hardy and 44 yards later Oakland had a 7-0 lead. The Raiders rolled up 468 yards of offense on the afternoon, 34 first downs and 6 touchdowns while the defense added another on a fumble recovery. Oakland ended its exhibition season with a one win, three-loss mark handily defeating the exhausted Broncos 49-12. Raiders coaches couldn't help being pleased by the efforts put forth by the entire squad in their final exhibition game, especially from their new players such as Charlie Fuller, who scored twice, and the defensive efforts of Volney Peters, new defensive end Jon Jelacic and Fred Williamson, handling a Broncos offense, which had run all over them just two weeks prior.

(4)

The euphoria of their victory needed to subside quickly. The schedule makers again had done Oakland no favors in having them face the league's top three teams to open their second season, the first two coming on the road. Of the thirty-three players on the 1961 Raiders squad, sixteen were new and half of them started in the opening contest, with one having been a Raider less than two weeks.

What no one could have predicted was the lopsided outcome of week number one. With the exception of the punting game, the Raiders were outclassed in every way imaginable, as Tom Flores completed just 7 of his 21 passing attempts for 59 yards of offense while 34 of Oakland's 71 rushing yards came on 8 Wayne Crow carries. Houston's big three, Billy Cannon, Charlie Tolar and Dave Smith, on the other hand, had amassed 203 yards on the ground while George Blanda completed 11 of 24 passing with 3 touchdowns in a romp that saw the Oilers executing a successful on-side kick while enjoying a 38-point lead! Houston found the end zone twice more and added a field goal before the carnage subsided and these Raiders learned exactly how good they wouldn't be in 1961, by being crushed 55-0.

With the Houston airport allowing no departures due to foul weather conditions, the team was forced to take a train to Dallas before being able to fly home to prepare for their week-two match up with the Chargers. Having team morale practically executed in Houston, there could be no way they were looking forward to meeting a Chargers team which had once established a league scoring mark (now eclipsed by Houston's outpouring) against them in their previous home game against Oakland. Not to mention the Chargers were none too pleased with the injuries the Raiders had inflicted upon them in the preseason.

As coaches chose to concentrate on their short yardage game in preparation for the Chargers, Raiders public relations found a way to make star center Jim Otto more visible. Nicknamed "Big O" by his teammates. Jim Otto discarded his #50 for the unique #00. Coinciding with the two letter O's in his family name, Otto would be known by fans as "Double O" throughout his career.

Against the advisement of the Oakland press, the Raiders made the trip to San Diego's Balboa Stadium to face the Chargers. In front of 20,000+ Chargers fans and a national television audience, quarterback Tom Flores completed his first touchdown pass of the year on the game's second play. With a poor, hurried and off target throw intended for Charley Hardy, cornerback Dick Harris got his hands under the ball before it fell incomplete and rumbled 41 yards for a 7-0 Chargers lead. San Diego ran the score to 30-0 at halftime and by the games merciful ending, the bloodbath on the scoreboard showed a 44-0 Charger's victory. Upon their return to Oakland, Eddie Erdelatz was fired.

With the exception of George Fleming, who was playing behind Bob Coolbaugh at the flanker position and missed an easy field goal in the second loss of the season, the Raiders had failed to sign any of their top draft choices. With injuries taking a heavy toll and team management not spending to bring in top talent until their reserves were depleted, the reasons for their downfall were apparent. Erdelatz expressed shock at his dismissal even after being outscored 99-0 over the first two weeks. Defensive line coach Marty Feldman was named the Raiders second head coach within an hour of Erdelatz's discharge. With everything going horribly wrong with the Oakland Raiders, Feldman had one thing in his favor. It was unimaginable that the club could get any worse.

(5)

Changes were immediately made. First, coach Feldman released not only one of the Raider's most popular players but also the AFL's leading kick return man, Jack Larscheid. Needing to bulk up at the running back position. Larscheid became expendable with the addition of Charlie Fuller. While not the biggest back himself at 175 lbs., Fuller had 10 to 15 lbs. on Larschied and was placed at fullback. Utilized at both the fullback and halfback positions in the first two weeks, Wayne Crow found the halfback spot his home. To keep such shuffling from being in vain, coach Feldman added 13 new plays to the offensive arsenal without changing any blocking schemes, making them available in the imminent contest against the Dallas Texans, more than doubling the total number of available plays at 25.

As coach Feldman and his charges worked tirelessly readying for Sunday's game, Wayne Valley would be the bearer of bad news. Unless fan support for the Raiders swelled dramatically from the season prior, there would no longer be a professional football team in Oakland. Featuring the lowest season ticket base in the league, Valley claimed the AFL would transfer the franchise. The Raiders had suitors from Portland, Spokane and Memphis, with the latter being well prepared to make the financial investments to move the team eastward. Concerned with Oakland's faltering ticket sales, league officials made no proclamation of a Raiders transfer to any city anywhere. Relocation of any team was at the sole discretion of team owners and not the league. However a team may not be sold without the consent of the league's executive committee. If owners were unhappy, they could also make a case with the executive committee at season's end, relieving themselves of their burden. From there, the committee would examine what was best for the team in Oakland or elsewhere then take the appropriate action.

Finding themselves three touchdown underdogs to Dallas, the Raiders opened their 1961 home schedule in front of just 6,737 fans. While an increase of slightly better than 400 sales from the Denver game three weeks prior, this game's sales would be a mere 53% of 1960's home opener against Houston. The scattered few who made the journey to Candlestick were treated to what, in later years, would be known as a classic AFL shootout. Taking the opening kickoff, Oakland drove to the Dallas 38-yard line before George Fleming put the Raiders ahead for the first time in 1961 with a field goal from 45 yards out. Returning the kickoff to their own 42, Dallas took four plays and 1:25 in claiming the lead, with Randy Duncan (getting the staring nod over and alternating series with Cotton Davidson) finding halfback Abner Haynes in the flat for a 47-yard score.

Defensive end Charley Powell forced Duncan to fumble on the Dallas 21, then five plays later Crow found the end zone and the lead at 10-7. Later in the second quarter, the Raiders fired again as Doug Asad hauled in a 51-yard Tom Flores pass on the 8. Charley Hardy made a leaping grab for Oakland's second touchdown extending their lead 17-7. Dallas' hole was dug a little deeper with a 24-yard field goal from Fleming. Dave Grayson took the kickoff 43 yards and the Dallas offense again made quick work of Oakland's defenders. Led by Davidson, the second 4-play Dallas scoring drive concluded with a 31-yard Chris Burford reception that cut the Raiders lead to 20-14 at the half.

All of 36 seconds elapsed in the second half when a blown coverage sprang Johnny Robinson loose for a 68-yard touchdown with a Cotton Davidson screen pass, relieving Oakland of the lead it had enjoyed for most of the opening half. Later in the period, Oakland moved 80 yards in 8 plays with 26 yards coming on a Crow to Hardy halfback option before Flores scored from the 1 on a quarterback sneak. Three plays and 1:39 later, Jack Spikes went over left tackle, dashing 30 yards for the tying score. Fred Williamson's block of the point after kept the score deadlocked 27-27.

A little more than six minutes had expired in the fourth period as Dallas completed their lone, long drive of the contest with Bo Dickson going over from the 1. Scrambling well out of bounds on the next possession, Flores got a rude introduction to the elbow of a man called "the Beast." The obvious foul committed by linebacker E.J. Holub was not committed in the sanctity of his own sideline but in the hostile territory of the Raiders. A melee ensued, with both squads exchanging punches while Holub received his just rewards from safety John Harris, cornerback Joe Cannavino and former heavyweight boxing contender Charley Powell. Late in the final quarter, defensive back Bob Garner snagged a Cotton Davidson toss returning it 11 yards to the 30. On fourth down from the 28, Flores found Bob Coolbaugh open in the end zone, Crow converted for two points and the Raiders led again, 35-34. The Oakland defense failed them once more this afternoon as Dallas, down only 1, moved 69 yards in 5 plays with Robinson scoring from 13 yards out. Spikes' two-point conversion made the final tally 42-35 Dallas, as two sure Raiders' touchdown passes were dropped in the final two minutes.

Quarterback Cotton Davidson and head coach Hank Stram were first in praising Feldman's Raiders. With a fierce pass rush, Oakland pressured Dallas passers as hard as any team, including San Diego with their feared front four. Stram admitted that if a team were to falter at all in playing these new Raiders, they would find themselves in the loss column in the next day's sports section. Next up for Oakland were the Denver Broncos, who would face the Raiders twice over the next three weeks, with a bye week separating each contest for Oakland. An improved pass defense was vital to any hopes of a Raiders victory over the pass-happy Broncos, who had attempted to move the ball 50+ times through the air in each game of the 1961 season, a telling sign that their own defense was a liability.

With the near miss the week prior, Raiders' morale had been given a boost. The odds makers picked Oakland as its loser by a more respectable five points against the 1-2 Denver squad. The players, however, had far more to say about this game's outcome than any prognosticator. A Garner interception put Oakland in business on the Denver 21-yard line early in the first quarter. Wayne Crow, on his way to a 16-carry 107-yard performance found the end zone on the drives' sixth play. Alan Miller added an 18-yard touchdown reception early in the second quarter before Denver could get going offensively. A Gene Mingo field goal cut the Bronco deficit to 11 at 14-3. Later in the second period, Oakland got two of those three points back when Denver center Bob Hudson snapped the ball high over quarterback/punter George Herring's head. The ball sailed through the back of the end zone for an automatic safety. Though the ensuing Oakland drive stalled out quickly on the Denver 46-yard line, history was in the making. From 54 yards away, George Fleming split the uprights for a 19-3 Oakland lead. In doing so Fleming established a new AFL mark, eclipsing George Blanda's 53-yard kick from the previous season and was just two yards shy of the NFL record of 56 yards set in 1953. A Fred Williamson interception and return to the Bronco 26 enabled a Bob Coolbaugh score. At intermission the Raiders were dominating 26-3. The third quarter saw Crow tear off 62 yards and his heroics paved the way for Alan Miller to score as the

Broncos found themselves buried deeper at 33-3. Denver got on track late in the third quarter, much too little, far too late as the Raiders had their first victory of 1961, 33-19.

Working diligently through the bye week, coach Feldman and his men were busy incorporating new plays before departing for Denver for a rematch with the Broncos. Change occurred in the front office as Raiders' management appointed scout Wes Fry the club's third general manager in 21 months, replacing Bud Hastings, who was departing for other opportunities. In spite of their win two weeks prior and a week of additional preparation, the Raiders found themselves in the familiar role of underdog. This time they were expected to fall short by more than 6 points, the Broncos themselves, with an injury list a yard long struggled to grasp the odds maker's logic. Oakland snagged three interceptions on the day and enjoyed a 24-14 lead halfway through the final period when disaster struck. Charlie Fuller fumbled a kick return on his 30, and after a short return, Denver took over on the 26. On second down, Frank Tripuka dropped back and found an uncovered Al Frazier, bringing Denver to within three. Walloped again, Fuller coughed up the ball, this time on the 15. The Raiders defense held and Gene Mingo, who had recovered the second fumble, tied the game 24-24 with 6 minutes to go. Another Mingo field goal in the final seconds gave the Broncos a 27-24 victory as Oakland's record plummeted to 1-4.

At home, Oakland Mayor John Houlihan was working overtime, rallying support for his city's team for their upcoming game against the undefeated San Diego Chargers. "Beat the Chargers" bumper stickers were found on cars and lampposts all over the city and Mayor Houlihan made a bet with San Diego Mayor Charles Dial. The losing teams' city would provide a live California brown bear to reside in the winning city's zoo. Coach Feldman had just one directive for his squad in light of their loss to Denver and their breakdowns in all of their meetings with the Chargers, "Don't choke." Against a team the had scored no less than 41 points against them in three regular season meetings, "choking" was the last thing the Raiders needed to worry about. With a team as explosive as San Diego's, it was far more probable to drown in an offensive onslaught. Complemented by a bruising defense, it seemed Mayor Houlihan had a pet brown bear he needed to rid himself of.

The injury bug began to gnaw away at both of Oakland's lines again as it had in the preseason with Wayne Hawkins and Volney Peters out of action and defensive end Jon Jelasic missing time due to deployment from the Army reserves. With Chargers owner Barron Hilton making challenges to the rival National Football League for a post-season game against his undefeated squad, the stage was set for another Oakland massacre. Yet Oakland struck first, a Paul Lowe fumble on the kickoff, recovered by Gerald Burch put the Raiders on the San Diego 28. Tom Flores found Bob Coolbaugh for a quick score and an early 7-0 lead. The Chargers fired back hard, running the score to 20-7 by the end of the first quarter and 34-7 at halftime. Beyond the quick score Oakland managed only 30 yards in the air and 2 on the ground. A short punt allowed Oakland into Charger territory once more, but after five plays, the drive stalled and George Fleming's semi-erratic kicking foot hit from 44 yards out. When the dust settled, the Raiders had lost as expected, donating 41 points while collecting only 10.

The injury bug that began its feast on the Oakland club prior to the San Diego contest now seemed to have developed a tapeworm. Jim Otto was injured in the opening quarter and spelled for the rest of the day by linebacker Tom Louderback. A twisted knee and bruised hip hobbled Wayne Crow. Willie Smith would miss action with a knee injury and Hal Smith suffered a broken foot. While thankful to be done with San Diego for the season, the Raiders were set to face a good Titans squad and Dick Christy was eager to prove Oakland foolish for trading him after only one preseason contest.

The New York Titans encountered a courageous Raiders team at Candlestick. A broken jaw had failed to keep Wayne Hawkins out of uniform on Sunday, nor would a debilitating back bruise keep center Jim Otto out of the starting lineup. The Titans went up 7-0 on the opening drive with a 9-yard Bill Mathis run. Through what would be as boring and badly played a game anyone had seen in memory, Fleming kept Oakland in the game with a pair of field goals, one in the first quarter and another in the third. The lone Raiders' highlight of the afternoon came when Wayne Crow, putting his twisted knee and bruised hip behind his powerful foot, punted a team record 77-yard blast into the Candlestick wind. This would be the second team kicking record established in October 1961 that would stand into the twenty-first century.

(6)

With average home attendance in the 8,500-range, the Oakland Raiders were on their knees financially. Losses in 1960 exceeded $300,000 and in 1961, the shortfall was expected to surpass the $400,000 mark. Co-owner Wayne Valley gave Oakland an ultimatum, give the Raiders a home field in Oakland beginning in 1962, or lose the team. A temporary home for the Raiders could be easily constructed with temporary bleachers in Oakland or the surrounding area. A Thanksgiving deadline was given and city officials went scrambling.

Since 1954, Oakland's Port Authority had attempted to sell the city a piece of downtown land for $1. This land, located across the street from Oakland's Exposition Field, was suitable for development and the perfect location for a temporary site. Exposition Field itself, already slated to become a parking lot, provided this vital need for the new facility to be named in honor of retired city councilman Frank Youell. After spending more than 18 years on the Oakland City Council, Youell was one of the first to envision a multi-use stadium for Oakland and through the years had donated much of his time and money sponsoring sports programs in Oakland. On November 16, 1961, a full seven days before an answer was to be given to Raiders' management, construction began on Frank Youell Field and, beginning in 1962, Oakland's Raiders would be wayward no more.

With a 1-6 mark and an undefeated Chargers team poised to wrap up the division crown, the Raiders were set to open a four-game road trek with three of these games in the freezing northeastern United States. The Raiders' defense had improved considerably during coach Feldman's tenure, allowing an average of 12 completions and 168 passing yards over the past five games, Oakland's offense, however, had sputtered and misfired for the past two weeks, even prompting Marty Feldman to accuse some of his players of quitting during the San Diego game.

On the first play from scrimmage, Tom Flores spotted Charley Hardy open on the 24-yard line. Making the reception, Hardy put a move on Bills defensive back Richie McCabe that had him announcing his retirement the following day, before outracing the rest of Buffalo's defenders and taking the early 7-0 lead. A fumble recovery by Fred Williamson on the Oakland 18 and 73-yard return to the Bills 9 gave the Raiders a first and goal. Alan Miller scored from the 1. As quickly as the lead was earned it was taken away. Elbert Dubenion scorched Fred Williamson, taking a 61-yard Johnny Green pass to cut the Oakland lead to 7. An uncharacteristic short punt put the Bills back in business on the Raiders' 44 and three plays later Buffalo hit pay dirt again and a two point conversion gave the home squad a 15-14 halftime lead.

Raiders linebacker Riley Morris put an abrupt end to the Bills opening drive of the second half, grabbing a Johnny Green pass and returning it to the 30. The Oakland offense wasted no time in taking advantage. As they had in the first half, the Raiders scored on their opening play of the second when Flores found Doug Asad for a touchdown. On their next possession, Oakland moved 80 yards in four plays with Alan Miller taking a short pass and dashing 55 yards for his second score. The Bills threatened to make a game of it again early in the fourth quarter when a Glen Bass reception cut the Oakland lead to six. With five and a half minutes remaining, George Fleming put the game out of reach with a 48-yard field goal and the Black and Gold held on to win their second game in eight tries 31-22.

Some old-time psychology was put into place prior to the season's second Raiders/Titans matchup. Assistant coach Tom Kalminar passed out old press clipping to his offensive unit, reminding them of the comments made by Titans' quarterback Al Dorow, who referred to Oakland's offensive unit as predictable and easy to defend. With their second touchdown connection in as many weeks, Flores fired a pass to Charley Hardy. Taking the toss in stride, Hardy waltzed into the end zone for six Oakland points. A block of the point after kept New York down a half-dozen until a Bob Garner muff of a fair catch gave the Titans their first touchdown of the afternoon and a lead they would not surrender. The mistake-riddled affair featured each starting quarterback tossing three interceptions. The Titans' miscues numbered fewer overall, leading New York to an ugly 23-12 win.

Having Billy Lott and Hal Smith out of action for their respective clubs wouldn't diminish the nostalgia felt by Raiders Alan Miller and early season acquisition Harry Jagielski or the Patriots' Babe Parilli. Each was looking to play their best against the team that sent them packing. 18,169 Patriots fans braved the chilly Boston weather for Oakland's second night game in six days and each one of them got their money's worth. The home crowd was first treated to their Patriots moving 76 yards on 9 plays in its opening series and a 7-0 lead. Looking to go ahead 10-0, Boston got a dose of disaster. Babe Parilli's fumbled snap on a field goal attempt gave the Raiders possession on the 28. Eight plays later (five after returning to the game after being dog piled by Boston's defenders on the drives opening play) Flores found his favorite target, Hardy, for 31 yards to tie the score. With their field goal woes resolved, Boston forged a 10-7 lead midway through the second quarter. A recently activated Clemon (Clem) Daniels took the kickoff on his 1 and carried it to his 42. Twenty-seven yards of offense were chewed up by two Hardy catches and a questionable pass interference call gave Oakland a first and goal on the 5, where Flores connected with Doug Asad for a score and a 14-10 lead. Field goals were exchanged, one for Boston just before the half and one for Oakland midway through the third quarter. Boston's offense got moving late in the third before their drive stalled out on the 35. A field goal attempt fell well short and rolled dead at the 4. Unable to move, Crow attempted to punt from the end zone on fourth down. As Raider luck would have it, his punt ricocheted off the goal posts falling back into the end zone. Boston recovered and Oakland went down to defeat 20-17.

While Oakland players and coaches thawed out on the plane to Dallas, AFL owners got a jump on not only the National Football League but also the AFL brass by staging the 1962 entry draft in secret. San Diego would be the first to sign a pick, San Jose State end Jim Cadile, their fifth overall pick, who received $1,000 as a signing bonus. All monies were immediately returned when commissioner Foss declared the draft null and void. The AFL draft again took place on its original date with no surprises as all eight franchises remained true to their original selections with one note worthy exception. Jim Cadile was drafted by Oakland, who in turn signed with Chicago in the NFL.

A major deal had been struck, when Arkansas end Lance Alworth was selected by San Diego with Oakland's second pick, the Black and Gold, in return would get four proven Chargers veterans to be named later. It was a very risky move by the Chargers, because the Raiders would get these players regardless of whether Alworth (who was also drafted high by the 49ers) ever signed with them. Oakland drafted well, selecting North Carolina State quarterback Roman Gabriel with their first pick along with other notables such as 6'5" 225-lb. center/linebacker from Utah Ed Pine and 6'4" 235-lb. Dan Birdwell a center/linebacker from Houston. Published reports in the Bay Area would stir controversy with the Raiders coaching staff over a supposed "revolt." Coach Feldman and general manager Wes Fry immediately dismissed theses reports, and their claims the entire Oakland coaching staff would resign if an additional $100,000 was not made available to sign these new draft choices.

None of this could have sat well with the Raiders' organization with the team in Dallas to face the 3-7 Texans. Charley Hardy fell victim to a knee injury and Dallas felt a sudden urge to play like the contenders they were a year before. Cotton Davidson got rolling for the Texans, finding Johnny Robinson and Abner Haynes who ran up 158 yards and five touchdowns. George Fleming making good on only 1 of 4 field goal attempts and a meaningless Nick Papac touchdown accounted for 11 Raiders' points to the Texans 43. This dejected Raiders squad returned to Candlestick to finish their second season with three games at home.

Their first opponent in Oakland's Candlestick swan song would be the same Buffalo Bills team the Raiders had beaten four long weeks before. Fleming, while continuing his place-kicking duties despite making good just 10 times on 23 tries, would start at halfback for Wayne Crow, who was missing the contest due to his injured knee. Facing a team whom Oakland had scored half of their victories over the seasons first eleven weeks served as a glimmer of hope against Buffalo, which grabbed a 6-0 lead early in the second quarter. The Raiders took their only lead of the day, late in the second when Nick Papac forced a pass to Alan Miller at the goal line through double coverage. Buffalo struck again quickly, rattling off 67 yards in 10 plays, though a failed two-point conversion left Oakland down 5 points at halftime. Gerald Burch, handling the punting chores, booted a ridiculously short 6-yard kick early in the third and the Bills were in business on the Oakland 47. On the strength of their running attack, the Bills extended their lead to 19-7 before Oakland's offense woke from its slumber. Clem Daniels, establishing himself as Crow's main understudy at halfback went around the left side and raced 39 yards reducing the Buffalo lead to five once more. Touchdowns were exchanged early in the fourth quarter, including the second Raiders big play of the half when Flores hooked up with Doug Asad from 43 yards away. After a brilliant stand from the Oakland defense, Flores and the offense had a chance at victory and a season sweep over their rivals from Buffalo when they found another way to lose. Taking possession on their 45, Oakland moved quickly to the Bills' 35. On first down, Flores was dropped for a loss of 8 yards by Bills defensive end Lavern Torczon. Torczon dropped Flores again on second down, setting the Raiders back an additional 12 yards. Now third down and 30 from Oakland's 35, A screen pass to Alan Miller netted only 8 yards and their last gasp was punted away. The Bills ran out the clock, preserving a 26-21 triumph.

This latest loss would have the normally tight-lipped and slippery-tongued Marty Feldman spelling out exactly what was wrong with his team, pointing to five Oakland losses by seven points or less as a sign of immaturity and proclaiming more mature teams find a way to win the close games as opposed to inventing new ways to lose them. Even in this latest defeat coach Feldman found a new star in Clem Daniels who would make his first start at halfback in the Raiders thirteenth game of 1961 when the team from Boston paid a visit to Candlestick Park. Patriots coach

Mike Holovak utilized the ghosts of seasons past against his Oakland foes, a move that would prove inspired. Babe Parilli got the starting nod against his former club and with Billy Lott, now healthy, combined to haunt their former team for each of Boston's five touchdowns. An inconsistent Raiders offense again found themselves tied only once early in the game before a Patriots team could pull itself ahead and into a 35-21 lead keeping their slim postseason hopes alive in the Eastern Division.

The Raiders' 1961 campaign would come to a merciful end against a Houston club that had sent them on their downward spiral with a 55-0 mauling at Jeppeson Stadium. Having been eliminated from title contention in the West by early November, Oakland would be the last obstacle faced by an Eastern Division leading Houston Oilers club looking forward to a championship rematch with the AFL Western Division Champion San Diego Chargers. Only 4,821 Oakland fans made the final journey cross-bay and ascended into Candlestick Park to watch the Oilers abuse the Raiders much the way they had during opening week. Field goals were exchanged during the first period with a safety giving Houston a lead which looked more like a baseball score, 5-3 Oilers, top of the second quarter. Clem Daniels scored on a sweep from the 10 in the midst of an Oilers offensive storm, bringing the Raiders to within ten at 19-9 and a Tom Louderback interception and return for a score brought Oakland to within ten again, midway through the third period. Yet the poor attendance left him no one in those end zone seats to throw the ball to in celebration. George Blanda's masterful 18 of 31 performance for 350 yards, highlighted by three touchdowns along with Billy Cannon running for 145 yards on 21 carries, doomed the Raiders to a 47-16 defeat and a 2-12 mark for the season while propelling Houston into their second consecutive AFL championship game against the Chargers. The Oilers would reign as champions once again, after humbling the high-powered Chargers 10-3.

The AFL paid homage to Jim Otto as he was honored for the second time (along with top honors from both the Associated Press and United Press International) as an All-AFL player. Otto was joined by teammates Alan Miller and Fred Williamson in the first ever AFL All-Star game and all three shone for coach Gillman's squad, helping the Western Division to a 47-27 triumph over the East. Oakland's two top draft choices quickly chose to sign with their NFL suitors, as did many others. Oakland fans, patiently awaiting a winner, were forced to wait until next year. At least...

CHAPTER THREE
A STREAK OF THEIR OWN
1962

The draft day trade that dealt Oakland's second overall pick to the Chargers for four players to be named later, gave the Raiders a great opportunity to steer back onto the success-bound road the club traveled in 1960. This arrangement gave Oakland right of first refusal on all players traded by their in-state rivals (except player for player trades) and those sold for cash. This placed the Raiders hands in San Diego's pockets until early May of 1962. The first new Raider coming to Oakland was Irving (Bo) Roberson. A silver medallist broad jumper in Rome in 1960, Roberson had been timed at 9.4 seconds in the 100-yard dash. The speedster had languished behind Paul Lowe on the Chargers depth chart despite posting comparable statistics.

Quarterback Hunter Enis, initially brought in to back up Tom Flores, was dealt to Denver for former CFL linebacker Jackie Simpson, addressing a need at the position. A pair of tackles finished out the trade, neither of whom ever saw action as Oakland Raiders. Though Roman Gabriel and Ed White decided to play in the NFL, many quality rookies chose Oakland and the AFL. Fullback Willie Simpson, earning praise from his college coach as the best offensive player he ever had, provided a dangerous 1-2 punch with Charlie Fuller on a San Francisco State team that lost only one game during their time together. A pair of first year men from the University of Houston were brought in. Tackle Jim Nixon and fullback Charlie Rieves who was converted to linebacker, joined their former teammate Dan Birdwell in Oakland.

Another collegiate to don Oakland colors amid high praise was Oregon State defensive back Hank Rivera. Selected #5 by the Cleveland Browns, Rivera impressed pro scouts everywhere with his tough, hard-hitting play and was considered one of the most dynamic cover men to emerge from the college level. Joining him in the Raiders defensive backfield was Tommy Morrow. After missing the last half of the Toronto Argonauts' season, Morrow negotiated his release before contacting Oakland officials. Three new assistants, all with NFL experience, joined coach Feldman and assistant Tom Kalminar. Eight-year Detroit Lions tackle Ollie Spencer would mentor the offensive line, while William (Red) Conkright managed the Raiders defensive front and took over for Wes Fry as chief scout. Rounding out Oakland's coaching staff was 32-year-old Walt Michaels; A 10-year veteran linebacker with the Cleveland Browns, Michaels, like Spencer ended his playing career to join Marty Feldman's crew in Oakland. With these new pieces in place, some thought the Oakland Raiders were primed to prove the catastrophe of 1961 a fluke, but those in Raiders management were split in their optimism with coach Feldman leading their franchise.

Troubled by health problems, Robert Osborne, still serving as an Oakland city councilman officially ended his association with the Raiders under doctor's orders to curtail his activities by late spring 1962. However, he found himself embroiled in one more Raiders battle with the City of Oakland. Work on Frank Youell Field was halted due to the reluctance of team management to supply a press box for the new stadium and hesitation to pay rent in advance for seven league games and two preseason contests. The team decided quickly to pay the agreed minimum for the league games and withhold funds for the preseason until the schedule was set. This show of faith from the team was not enough to calm the panic of two city councilmen who proposed a performance bond of $150-$200,000 for the field's use over the next two seasons. For the second time in a year, commissioner Foss and a league attorney were dispatched to Oakland to calm tempers and mediate a resolution. A series of meetings were held between team and city officials upon the commissioner's arrival and the dissention was quickly put to bed. The Raiders agreed to pay the greater of $17,500 for seven league games or 10% of the gate for two seasons and provide an additional $14,000 for an 80-foot press box for the new park. The city, in turn, would order construction to continue and withdraw its ridiculous bond proposal which at its minimum would have enabled the Raiders to easily pay the $1 for the land, $130,000 more for the development and construction of the new field, its press box and have nearly enough to cover a rookie's salary with the remainder.

With the current strife tranquilized and the Raiders moving into their new offices at Oakland's Hotel Leamington, commissioner Foss was off to Baltimore for a real fireworks show, as the AFL's $10,000,000 anti-trust suit against the NFL was about to begin. First to take the witness stand for the American Football League was its founder, Lamar Hunt. In his two days of testimony, the Dallas owner spoke of the Texans and the AFL being injured by the NFL's Dallas entry being part of an established league, able to draw from veteran players from longstanding NFL squads. Hunt also gave testimony of an offer of substantial stock in the Dallas Cowboys to drop his organization of the American League. When he refused, the NFL went ahead with plans to announce its expansion into Dallas and Minnesota with the participation of the AFL's Minneapolis team owner, Max Winter.

Hired by the AFL because of his political connections in Washington, Foss followed Hunt to the stand. His political connections were an item of interest to NFL attorneys, who grilled Foss under cross-examination. Barron Hilton testified that NFL teams could be made available to both Hunt and Oilers owner Bud Adams in Houston and Dallas, upon approval of team owners in the National Football League. Scoffing at his own inclusion into NFL expansion because of a moral obligation to continue forward with the AFL and his Los Angeles team, Hilton also testified of his intense lobbying for the former Minneapolis franchise to be transferred to Oakland to create a natural rivalry with his Chargers. Bills' owner Ralph Wilson told the court he was informed by an official from the Detroit Lions, that the National League was intent upon expansion into warmer climates exclusively, despite the league's move into the frigid elements of Minnesota. The AFL's final witness, Bud Adams testified that he was offered a team outright to drop out of the new league. Adams also offered testimony of his attempts to bring an NFL team to Houston for two and a half years before joining Hunt in the AFL.

Stopping just short of calling their own case weak, AFL attorneys admitted that they offered no proof NFL's recruiting players injured the AFL or demonstrated a conspiracy to kill the new league and conceded the AFL produced no evidence that the Baltimore Colts and Pittsburgh Steelers, in moving their broadcasts to another network (each NFL team was charged with securing their own broadcasts and subsequent revenues) was an attempt to keep the AFL from obtaining broadcast rights. In moving their case forward, AFL counsel stated because the league had not failed did not mean that there were not attempts from the NFL to help its demise or that the NFL was powerless to exclude competition.

Even before calling its first witness, the NFL took to the offensive. Denying allegations of player blacklisting and making accusations of this as an AFL practice, the NFL attorneys proceeded to shoot gaping holes in the plaintiff's claims. Dallas Cowboys owner Clint Murchison refuted Hunt's claims with testimony of his approaching NFL expansion committee head (also Chicago Bears owner and coach) George Halas with his concerns as the original Dallas Texans (an NFL team in 1952) had failed miserably. Murchison also stated that Halas, while intent on expansion to Houston, felt it important to create a rivalry with another Texas team. Halas himself took the stand next for the defense, reiterating Murchison's testimony claiming both Houston and Dallas were leading cities in the Southwest and the NFL was defiantly planning to move in that direction as early as 1958. Denying his assurances to a Twin Cities group was intended to prevent the new league from setting up operations there, Halas testified that local parties had negotiated for teams to be placed there from both leagues and was deciding how to proceed from there. The NFL owners went into their summer meeting jubilant over the judge's decision to dismiss the AFL's claim. Scoring a major victory over their young rival in what was referred to as "a war between the leagues," one question remains unanswered still. If Max Winter was only deciding which way to go, why were commitments made to the AFL for him to operate a franchise in Minneapolis, even up to the November 1959 meetings to draft the American Football League's first class of players, continuing the charade until Titans owner Harry Wismer discovered the ugly truth in the Noverember 22, 1959 edition of *the New York Daily Mirror?*

(2)

Raiders management, settling into their new home, stayed busy rebuilding their team. Rumors were rampant that Oakland would sign away 49ers star receiver R.C. Owens with a contract offer exceeding $40,000 before the disgruntled receiver returned to his team across the bay. Charley Powell retired from football for the fifth time to pursue boxing. Reserve guard Herb Roedel's retirement again downgraded

Oakland's depth on the offensive line. End Gerald Burch and defensive tackle Bob Voight both reported being contacted by officials from the Minnesota Vikings and Raiders' bosses cried foul. Both players had been drafted by Minnesota and, according to both Voight and Burch, had been encouraged to play out the contracts in Oakland so that they may sign with the Vikings. Minnesota officials wouldn't deny contact with these players yet claimed to have given no such encouragement. The AFL had rules barring player tampering, yet they were powerless in keeping teams from other leagues from doing so with their players.

To increase speed in the defensive backfield, Joe Cannavino was dealt to Buffalo for safety Vernon Valdez. A fan favorite in the East Bay for his spirited play and an outstanding rookie season, Cannavino had slowed some through the 1961 season and found himself heading east. A former Los Angeles Ram, Valdez brought great speed and an extra 10 lbs. to the safety position. Film study by the Raiders' new defensive coaches found a replacement for Charley Powell in linebacker Riley Morris. Small for the position at 225 lbs. Morris possessed speed equal to most AFL running backs along with the strength and agility to put tremendous pressure on opposing passers.

Tom Flores developed a strain of tuberculosis that ended his 1962 campaign prior to training camp. With only the inexperienced Nick Papac remaining to call signals, Oakland management made hurried efforts to find an experienced and adequate field general to direct their offense. Packaged with a draft choice, the versatile Wayne Crow was exchanged for quarterback M.C. Reynolds and two-time All AFL defensive tackle Chuck McMurtrey of the Buffalo Bills. In what was probably the most complex arrangement between the hostile American and National Football Leagues, the Raiders bought out the contract of Dallas Cowboys quarterback Don Heinrich. Heinrich, a six-year veteran with the New York Giants was a part of a team that had won four division titles. The former Washington Husky was dealt to Dallas when the Giants picked up 49ers quarterback Y.A. Tittle. Still under contract to Dallas, Heinrich returned to New York to coach the offensive backfield in 1961. His $20,000 contract made him the highest paid player in Oakland. San Jose State quarterback and top ranked NCAA passer Chon Gallegos was brought in to compete for the position.

With his team needing help at several key positions, newly elected AFL president Wayne Valley created a draft plan to bring a competitive balance to the league. Each AFL team would produce a 35-man untouchables list with the rest of their rosters eligible to be drafted away. Oakland, with the league's worst record in 1961, would pick first followed by the Denver Broncos for three rounds. Beginning in round four, the rest of the league would participate in reverse order based on 1961's standings. While no real offensive help was forthcoming from this special draft, Oakland found two unprotected gems from the Houston Oilers. Defensive tackles George Shirkey and Orville Trask who helped stock the Raiders with their strongest defensive line in their brief history and potentially one of the best in of pro football.

With the defense looking stronger than ever, the offense had nearly the number of question marks it did going into their first training camp two years before. Oakland's first trade with Buffalo of 1962 for guard (and original Raider) John Dittrich was cancelled with the retirement of end Doug Asad upon being sent eastward, finding them lighter with pass catchers as well. Second-year passer Nick Papac, seemingly the front-runner to succeed Tom Flores as Oakland's starting quarterback due to his familiarity with Marty Feldman's offensive system, was shown the door less than 10 days into camp. As a result, the Raiders offense sputtered and misfired in practices and was badly outplayed by their defensive counterparts during intra squad scrimmages.

To expand the AFL's popularity throughout the nation, many preseason contests were held in cities without teams from either league, including three of Oakland's five warm up contests, the first of which was held in Atlanta, Georgia against the Texans. M.C. Reynolds, needing snaps at quarterback was sat after their third possession when the offense failed to move with just six running plays and five pass patterns at his disposal. In his place, Heinrich led the squad to the Dallas 12 as Willie Simpson, taking over George Fleming's place kicking duties, gave Oakland its first points of 1962 with a 19-yard field goal. The defense held the lead eleven minutes into the third quarter until a pass interference call gave the Texans possession on the Oakland 13. In relief of former Cleveland Browns reserve quarterback Len Dawson, Cotton Davidson found fullback Frank Jackson for a score and a 7-3 lead. An interception returned for a score ran the final tally to 13-3.

Dallas coach Hank Stram again extended his praise to the Oakland squad, its defenders in particular, but coach Feldman was not so impressed. Blaming mental errors for the loss, despite playing only their first exhibition game, the Raiders boss promised fines for further infractions. Many Oakland players, none gaining great wealth as professional athletes, spent their evenings studying their playbooks hoping to avoid the financial wrath of their coach. Among the many places Marty Feldman chose to lay responsibility for the latest loss was the cool summer weather of the Raiders training facilities in Santa Cruz for keeping his players from achieving top physical condition. Amherst, Massachusetts enjoyed warm humid summer weather and the Oakland Raiders would be calling the facilities at the University of Massachusetts home for the next two weeks.

After doubling the number of plays in Oakland's offensive arsenal, Feldman then named Don Heinrich the starting quarterback after displaying his potential to make something from nothing. A member of the Raiders' injured list would see his first action of the preseason as Dobie Craig's thigh muscle had completely healed, giving Oakland a legitimate flanker as Bob Coolbaugh was not only converted to tight end, but suffered a broken leg in his second practice at the position. Heinrich also found assistance in remaining upright as former Philadelphia Eagles guard Stan Campbell also made his first appearance. Pass protection was key as Boston's secondary was suspect at best. Quarterback Babe Parilli guided his squad to a 10-0 first quarter lead before Heinrich got his team moving, finding rookie Jim Nixon (being tried at tight end) twice for 27 total yards. Alan Miller followed Campbell into the end zone cutting the deficit to three at 10-7. Riley Morris pounced on a bungled exchange on the Patriots' 16-yard line. Attempting a comeback, Al Hoisington gave Oakland first and goal with a leaping third down grab on the 2. Running around right end, thirty-second round draft pick Gene White put the Raiders up 14-10 early in the second quarter.

Boston quarterback Frank Yewsic solved his exchange problems and moved the Patriots offense 53 yards in 10 plays, earning a 17-14 halftime lead. This would be the last touchdown given up by the Raiders' defense. As the Patriots widened their lead with an 18-yard field goal, a fourth quarter punt put Oakland back on their 17. On second down, Heinrich found Charlie Fuller for 32 yards and a Raiders first down on their 49-yard line. Hoisington caught a right fist in the face from a Patriots' defender. The personal foul call moved Oakland to the 36. Heinrich fired to Clem Daniels for the drive's second big play, a 33-yard reception to the 3. Former Patriot Alan Miller reached the end zone for a second time and Oakland held on for their first win of 1962, 21-20.

This first victory of the exhibition season and first of any kind since early November served as a confidence boost for the club and gave hopes of deliverance from the misery of the season prior. How much these Raiders had improved would be known immediately as the same Dallas Texans team that had defeated them in a comeback two weeks before, awaited them in Midland Texas. Again, M.C. Reynolds was given the starting nod over Heinrich under center while Stan Campbell earned the starting role at guard while rookie Pete Nicklas would start at right tackle. The fierce play of Hank Rivera earned him playing time at safety.

Practices through the week were devoted primarily to the ground attack. Seeking a balanced offense where the ground game could open up aerial opportunities, Raiders coaches appeared confident the offense they desired would soon be a reality. Coach Stram and his Texans, however had different ideas. While Clem Daniels and his 81 rushing yards exceeded his teams' production of the previous two games, an intense pass rush kept Reynolds off balance all night as he connected on only 13 of 37 passes for 143 yards. Down 15-0 at halftime, Dobie Craig set up the Raiders lone score with a 50-yard reception. Alan Miller capitalized, going over from the two, but a failed conversion left Oakland with 6 points to the Texans 22.

A game was not the only thing dropped in Midland. Another high draft choice was dealt away to the Texans for Max Boydston. The former All-American tight end joined the Raiders on the trip back to Santa Cruz to prepare for their next contest versus the mighty Chargers of San Diego in the grand opening of Frank Youell Field. The hard-hitting play of rookie linebacker Charlie Rieves had earned him the starting birth on the outside and set the tone for the Raiders' game plan against San Diego, which was to beat the Chargers physically.

While not a sell out, the 17,053 on hand for professional football's inaugural game in Oakland was by far the largest home crowd in team history. Following the offensive failure of the previous week, Feldman again started Don Heinrich at quarterback over Reynolds to give his squad the best chance at winning in their most important exhibition to date. A pass interference penalty late in the first quarter inside the Chargers' 5, gave Oakland the opportunity for an early lead that they seized with a 1 yard Willie Simpson run. Looking to add another touchdown to their lead, Chargers' linebacker Paul McGuire hit Heinrich hard forcing a fumble that was scooped up by fellow linebacker Emil Karns who raced 55 yards, knotting the score at 7. Undiscouraged by their misfortune, the Raiders marched 80 yards in five plays behind the running of Clem Daniels, who chewed up 42 yards on one jaunt before Bo Roberson scurried 25 yards on a halfback draw reclaiming the Oakland lead at 13-7 after a blocked conversion. Emil Karns's second takeaway (also from Heinrich) gave Jack Kemp and the Chargers possession on the Oakland 45. In ten plays the Chargers claimed the lead 14-13 with three and a half minutes remaining in the half. A field goal gave San Diego a 17-13 edge at the break.

Dashing in front of Lance Alworth, Fred Williamson stole a Kemp pass and aided by a vicious block from Jon Jelasic, he completed a 44-yard return in the end zone, taking a 20-17 lead. A field goal tied the game at 20 while two San Diego touchdowns in the fourth quarter put the game away. A 51-yard touchdown march in the final two minutes cut the Chargers margin of victory to six points at 33-27 and ignited the Raiders first Oakland crowd who were proving themselves to be the wildest fans in any pro city.

The exhibition season reached its conclusion five days later, 65 miles east of Frank Youell Field at Stockton, California's University of the Pacific against the Denver Broncos. Any optimism held by the Oakland club quickly dimmed with a 90-yard return of the opening kickoff that instantly ended the competitive phase of the ball game. Performing lifelessly, Oakland's Raiders fell 41-12 in front of the 5,000 in attendance and 100,000 more watching at home on television.

Set to open their third season after their worst exhibition performance, the Raiders featured a remarkably improved defense. Only four players remained from the previous calamity. The offense however, at times explosive the season prior, had ground to a halt. A pair of draft picks were traded to the Houston Oilers for a couple of veterans. Defensive end Dalva Allen, considered one of the AFL's elite at the position, would find his way into the starting lineup immediately and John White, a veteran tight end, found a back up role behind Max Boydston.

Appearing to be exactly what the doctor ordered, the New York Titans were the Raiders' first opponent in 1962 and would face a hostile crowd at Frank Youell Field. Winless in their four exhibitions, the Titans looked to be the Raiders' equal in futility. New York was aided by three missed field goals and a miserable performance by both Raiders quarterbacks, who combined to complete 10 of 29 passing attempts for 158 yards, 81 of which came on one scoring drive. As new Titans quarterback Lee Grosscup led New York to victory. Clem Daniels led the way for Oakland, who collectively gained 184 yards in a 28-17 loss.

A week off could come none too soon. Though the ground attack looked solid in the opening week, the deficiencies caused by the quarterback situation could not be hidden. Having many badly thrown passes destroy opportunities, Feldman and his staff made a hurried search for another passer to spark their floundering offense. Both Heinrich and reserve M.C. Reynolds returned to Raiders' practices following the loss to the Titans as marked men. Never criticizing either man publicly, coach Feldman, when asked of a possible move at the position by the press, pointedly stated "There was no way they could win at the pro level without a passing game, what do you expect?"

The inevitable move was drastic. Waiving both quarterbacks outright, Oakland sent their top draft choice to Dallas for Cotton Davidson, who had lost his starting job to Len Dawson. Having the man they needed starting, NCAA passing leader Chon Gallegos was activated as Davidson's understudy. In spite of Davidson's claim to need time to learn his receivers, he was viewed as a savior after only one practice. Hours with the coaching staff were devoted after practices to learning his new offense, as he would be facing his now former team the Dallas Texans ten days after coming west.

Down 16-3 midway through the second quarter, Davidson surprised his former mates. On second and goal from the 10, he called his own number and took a quarterback draw through a huge hole opened by Jim Otto and Stan Campbell. He then powered his way through the Texans secondary men who had converged on him for the first Raiders touchdown of the afternoon, cutting the Dallas lead to 16-10 at halftime. Chris Burford's third touchdown was followed by a field goal holding the Raiders down 26-10 with time running out. A Hal Lewis punt return gave Oakland great field position on the Dallas 19. Aided by a pass interference call, Clem Daniels grabbed six points on a 2-yard blast but the two-point conversion pass from Davidson and Oakland's hopes of salvaging a tie fell at Daniels' feet. Undeterred nonetheless, Oakland secured possession again as the onside kick was bobbled and dropped by Texans tackle Jim Tyrer. Fred Williamson scooped it up for the Raiders returning the ball to the Dallas 38-yard line. Unable to bring the final score a little more respectability, the Oakland club managed to keep the 12,000 fans in their seats with the late rally, even as the game was out of reach. The defense allowed only 88 yards on the ground all-day and 2 from Abner Haynes on 10 carries. Completing 20 of 41 passes for 248 yards, Davidson's gutsy performance with only a limited grasp of this new offensive system garnered praise from coaches, teammates and fans alike.

The killer of all Oakland optimism lay immediately ahead as the one team the Raiders had never beaten was coming to Frank Youell Field.

The walking wounded known as the San Diego Chargers were 1-2 and with star halfback Paul Lowe out of action with a broken arm, Earl Faison hobbled by a knee injury and quarterback Jack Kemp lost forever as Sid Gillman's gamble of placing him on waivers due to some broken fingers on his throwing hand backfired when the Buffalo Bills quickly paid the $100 waiver fee instantly acquiring him. Now San Diego's offense appeared headless. The Chargers' new quarterback was Dick Wood. His 20 minutes of professional experience made him the most experienced Chargers passer and he led San Diego to an early 7-0 lead. Seconds later, Bo Roberson took the kickoff on his 14 and outraced the San Diego coverage team 86 yards for a 7-7 tie. A fierce Raiders' pass rush knocked Wood out of the game early in the second period and he was replaced by rookie John Hadl. Quickly leading his Chargers into Oakland territory, Hadl threw a pass to Lance Alworth on the 12. A diving Fred Williamson made a spectacular interception, tiptoed along the sidelines until he regained his balance then raced the rest of the way for an Oakland touchdown. In typical Raiders' fashion, everything fell apart. Over the next three minutes, Hadl found Dave Koucourek, Don Norton and finally Lance Alworth for scores and a 28-14 halftime lead. A Willie Simpson field goal punctuated two more Chargers' touchdowns cutting the Oakland deficit to 42-17. With another game hopelessly out of reach, Raiders coaches opted to play quarterback Chon Gallegos who gave the brave suffering Raiders fans that remained something to cheer for. A laser of a pass was wrestled away from Chargers' defensive back Claude "Hoot" Gibson by Dobie Craig and Simpson's second field goal of the half cut nine points away from the San Diego lead. A short pass to Roberson and the ensuing track meet to the end zone ended the scoring as the Chargers left Frank Youell Field with their fifth consecutive victory over the Raiders in as many league games 42-33.

Up next for the winless, hopeless Oakland squad was a much-improved Denver Broncos team. With a record of 3-1 under new head coach (and former Sid Gillman assistant) Jack Faulkner, the Broncos had already matched the number of wins they earned in 1961 and were as formidable an opponent the Raiders would face all season. Under intense pressure from Oakland management to win or else, Feldman watched his Raiders spot Denver a 21-0 lead at halftime. A Jon Jelasic interception on the Bronco 17 gave Oakland the ball and a pass interference call set the Raiders up on the 1. Davidson followed Wayne Hawkins into the end zone for the Raiders lone score in a humiliating 44-7 loss.

Returning to Oakland in the midst of the club's worst start at 0-4 the Raiders were followed home by the same Bronco bullies that had just dominated them. Combined with the losses of the final six contests of 1961, Oakland was caught in a ten-game tailspin that seemed to have no end. The Raiders' misfortunes were also not lost on the fans. A crowd of 7,000, nearly half the size the three previous regular season games, made their way into Youell Field to watch their team face the first-place Broncos. With the help of crowd noise, the defense turned in its best effort of the season. Davidson was ineffective due to a shoulder injury and a pair of turnovers from Gallegos gave the Broncos 23-0 shutout that was wiped away with a Clem Daniels touchdown as time expired. Denver gave the Raiders life twice on the final drive with penalties. A pointless two-point conversion failed and Oakland fell again 23-6.

Claiming he needed to find an offense, as the lack of production from his offensive unit was killing him, coach Feldman instead found himself searching for gainful employment. After amassing 2 wins in 17 league games and losing the last 11, the Oakland Raiders fired their head coach. Joining Feldman in the job market was the last remaining assistant from the Eddie Erdelatz era as Tom Kalminar was also dismissed. Again, the head coaching position was filled by the promotion of the club's current defensive line coach. William "Red" Conkright, also the team's chief scout, became the third Oakland Raiders head coach in less than two and one-half seasons.

With Walt Michaels and Oliver Spencer remaining at their posts, the former Stephen F. Austin coach Conkright closed Raiders' practices to concentrate on the club's latest reorganization and to plan their upcoming game against the Bills in War Memorial Stadium. Dick Dorsey, two weeks removed from replacing Charlie Fuller at halfback, moved to the end position replacing Charley Hardy. Defensive back Bob Garner a fine offensive player at Fresno State undertook double duty as Dobie Craig's understudy at flanker. Going into Buffalo with only two days of preparation and a new formation known as the "Runnin' Gun" designed to give their quarterbacks more time to find their targets, the Raiders faced a Bills team which just a few weeks earlier had been pelted with beer cans by their home crowd but were now treated as kings after winning their first league game the week before against the faltering Chargers. Unlike the previous five Raiders losses, Oakland out-gained their opponents by racking up 290 yards to Buffalo's 252. In the rain and mud of War

Memorial Stadium both teams' passing games were ineffective. Eight-year CFL veteran Cookie Gilchrist carried 19 times for 143 yards and a touchdown to hand the Raiders their twelfth consecutive loss 14-6.

The defeat in the cold, wet elements of Buffalo had Conkright steaming. The two press box phones used by the assistant coaches to communicate with the sidelines numbered only one and failed to work for nearly three quarters. The mandatory 18 game balls were reduced to four and after the first 15 minutes of play, were too rain-soaked to be handled by pass catchers. The Raiders' annual sojourn through the northeastern United States was again marred by controversy back home. According to published reports in Los Angeles, they would be transferred to Kansas City, the San Diego Chargers to New York with the Titans being moved to New Orleans. Wayne Valley, in his role of league president, hotly denied the story, pointing out the efforts San Diego made to accommodate the Chargers and quieting any controversies with his own franchise by admitting their winless 1962 record and the league's worst offense were keeping fans out of Frank Youell Field. With no chance for a division title, the only way the Raiders could attract people from the comforts of their living rooms to their not so humble abode was to play the role of spoiler. The Boston Patriots were next and at 4-2 they were tied for the Eastern Division lead.

As it had the two previous weeks, the sky had dumped heavy amounts of water on the field that the Raiders were set to take. Coach Conkright's "Runnin' Gun" offense was immediately successful in increasing productivity from power back Clem Daniels and speed back Bo Roberson, but the sloppy conditions hampered the still ineffective passing attack. The water poured on the Boston field during week seven, was that of the frozen variety as snow flurries covered the ground. Already down a field goal, Oakland struck quickly with the "Runnin' Gun." A Cotton Davidson to Clem Daniels pass covered thirty yards for a first down in Boston territory at the 34. Dobie Craig split a pair of defenders hauling in a Davidson toss and gave Oakland a quick 7-3 lead. Roaring again after Cappaletti's second field goal, Jack Stone and Stan Campbell cleared Patriot defenders from the path of Bo Roberson, who raced 64 yards to glory. Davidson, now handling the place kicking duties, missed the conversion and the Raiders enjoyed their first halftime lead of 1962 13-6. Any euphoria from this less than stellar accomplishment was washed away when a blown coverage in the secondary allowed Babe Parilli to find

Cappaletti open for the tying score. Field goals were traded before Larry Garron tore off 41 of his 140 rushing yards for six points and Cappaletti's fourth field goal of the night sank Oakland 26-16.

The sweeping changes enacted by coach Conkright continued. Chon Gallegos, along with former Houston Oilers Orville Trask and John White, were released. Quarterback Hunter Enis returned for his second stint as an Oakland Raider in 1962, to spell Davidson, who suffered from a nagging injury to his throwing shoulder. Jim Norris was activated from the taxi squad to relieve defensive tackles George Shirkey and Chuck McMurtrey and Fred Williamson; the best cover man in all of professional football was given a look as a receiver. These desperate and evolving Raiders placed their hopes of a first victory on the New York Titans as Oakland's journey through the frigid Northeast reached its conclusion at the Polo Fields.

Experiencing déjà vu, the Raiders found themselves down 3-0 in the first quarter for the second straight week. A Titans' turnover on the New York 34 led to Clem Daniels scoring from the 2 on the drives' eighth play late in the second quarter. The 39 seconds remaining in the half expired quietly and Oakland enjoyed its second halftime lead in as many games. A Johnny Green (traded to the Titans for Al Dorow) pass was intercepted by Tommy Morrow and was returned to the enemy 4. Daniels found the end zone again putting his team up 14-3. Thinking they had their first victory in hand, the Raiders relaxed and New York made them pay for their overconfidence. Dick Christy grabbed six points on a right end sweep that covered 21 yards; the conversion narrowed the Oakland lead to four points. Three minutes later, a blown assignment placed Titans' end Don Maynard in the end zone without an Oakland defender within twenty yards of him and New York took their first lead of the contest 17-14. On third down and 29 from the Oakland 28 yard line, Davidson launched a missile to the speedy Bo Roberson, who out leaped Lee Riley on the 24 and waltzed untouched to go ahead 21-17. Aided by a spectacular grab from Art Powell and a pass interference penalty, New York reclaimed the lead for good 24-21 on the second consecutive quarterback draw from the 2. An attempt to tie from 49 yards out came up short off the foot of linebacker Dan Birdwell and the Titans took over on the 11. Bill Mathis secured a Titans victory with a two-yard run that concluded a 14-play drive at 31-21 and the Raiders secured an unwanted place in history, setting a new professional football standard for futility by losing their fourteenth consecutive game.

Though *The Oakland Tribune* newspaper was finally gracious enough to print a scoring recap for the first time in 1962 when the Raiders found some offense under the new regime, Red Conkright, like Marty Feldman before him, was not so excited with his men, pointing out that the squad held the lead at halftime the past two weeks yet never managed to post either of them in the win column. Blaming inexperience on five of Oakland's eight losses in 1962, the comebacks allowed over the past two weeks proved that under Conkright, the Raiders had improved greatly on offense but were not playing football for a full 60 minutes.

Suffering a series of injuries against New York, Conkright was forced into more lineup changes than he liked. Defensive tackle Chuck McMurtrey was slowed by a foot injury. Running back Hal Lewis endured a muscle pull. Stan Campbell was ill, Dobie Craig had an impacted wisdom tooth, and Vernon Valdez would play in spite of a muscle tear. Willie Simpson returned from injury none too soon as both Alan Miller and Clem Daniels suffered knee strains. Raiders' management signed 43-year-old Kicker "Bootin' Ben" Agajanian, a 19-year veteran of 11 pro teams. "Bootin' Ben" was nearly forced to retirement when an elevator accident claimed four toes on his kicking foot in 1941. The tenacious kicker had a cobbler make him a special shoe to minimize the pain and he soaked his foot in brine to toughen it. According to Agajanian, it improved his kicking game enough that he advised an inquisitive father to cut his son's toes off if he wanted him to be a good place kicker. Claiming to have another seven or eight seasons remaining in his career "Bootin' Ben" had become quite the sight on the field wearing no pads and streaking immediately to the sidelines after kicking off to avoid hard physical contact with opposing players.

The Houston Oilers came to Oakland next to take on the Raiders and their quirky new kicker. A resurgent team with Billy Cannon returning from injury and George Blanda finding his passing game needed a win to stay a half game back of the Patriots in the Eastern Division. Tommy Morrow snagged a George Blanda pass and returned it 30 yards to the Houston 36. Bo Roberson, proving to be one of the most exciting players in the AFL, took a handoff around the right end and went untouched into the end zone giving his team the early 7-0 lead. Cotton Davidson, completing only 9 of his 32 passes, returned the favor by being intercepted by Tony Banfield on the Raiders' 39. Six plays later Billy Cannon knotted the score at 7 with an 11 yard sweep around the left. As three minutes remained in the half Oakland secured their third straight halftime lead as Dobie Craig stole Tony Banfield's sure second interception and raced

30 yards for a touchdown. Agajanian's kick was blocked and Oakland led 13-7. Seven more Oakland points were added when Bo Roberson took a 7-yard Davidson toss in the flat and broke away for a 67-yard touchdown romp to begin the second half..

Missing his first field goal attempt in Black and Gold, Agajanian kicked short from 36 yards away. From their 20, Houston drove 80 yards before Charlie Tolar was awarded a touchdown after clearly being stopped short of the goal line in clear view of everyone at Frank Youell Field with the exception of the officiating crew. Crawling into the end zone, Tolar carved seven points from the Raiders' lead. Playing a more complete game, Oakland held onto the six-point margin midway though the fourth quarter but found another way to lose. Agajanian's second missed field goal, kicking short once again from 22 yards, gave the Oilers possession. A pass interference penalty dug them out of their hole with a first down on the Raider's 35. Blanda fired over the middle to Tolar, who needed no breaks from the referees this time; Blanda's conversion claimed the lead for Houston at 21-20. The backs of the Oakland club were broken a minute later as Davidson airmailed a pass to linebacker Gene Babb, who returned the errant toss 31 yards for a score giving Houston a 28-20 win.

Raiders coaches had a simple game plan for the incoming Buffalo Bills, A smothering defense, the electrifying Bo Roberson and the toe of Bootin' Ben's kicking foot. The toe, with a little help from the wind, struck first with a 49-yard blast near the end of the first quarter for the 3-0 lead. Toward the end of the second quarter, Raiders defenders were helped by an unseen source, Bills fullback Cookie Gilchrist. Stopped a yard shy of the end zone, Gilchrist lashed out at Fred Williamson for having the audacity to deny him the score. The punch thrown cost the Bills 15 yards. A disgusted Oakland crowd then drew an obscene gesture from Gilchrist for voicing their disapproval of his conduct. The officials voiced their displeasure with a penalty flag, tacking on another 15-yard penalty for unsportsmanlike conduct. Instead of a first and goal on the one, Buffalo began on the 31 and settled for a field goal of their own and a 3-3 tie at intermission. Picking off a Warren Rabb pass, Jackie Simpson put Oakland in the driver's seat. Agajanian's second kick, this time hitting from 36 yards gave Oakland the lead at 6-3. The Bills' offense failed to budge and the Raiders beat themselves to lose for the sixteenth consecutive time. Blowing an attempt at a fair catch, Bob Garner's blunder gave Monte Crockett a live ball to recover on the Raiders' 33. In his first action as a Buffalo Bill, Jack Kemp moved the ball to the 16 by scrambling before finding Wayne Crow open for the winning touchdown and a gift 10-6 victory.

For the final time in 1962, the Raiders took their winless act on the road. First up for Oakland was a Dallas Texans' squad looking to lock up their first ever AFL Western Division title. Dallas established its dominance on the game's first play, a 42-yard Curtis McClinton gallop up the middle set the tone for the day and helped the Texans to a 14-0 first-quarter lead. A Tommy Morrow interception enabled his offense as Hunter Enis (starting for an injured Cotton Davidson) found Dobie Craig for a 16-yard touchdown and Oakland's lone score. The Raiders defense, in its weakest effort of the season, allowed McClinton 109 yards on 12 carries and Abner Haynes 112 more in 18 tries, condemning Oakland to a 35-7 defeat.

A wait-and-see approach was utilized for the 1963 entry draft. With its first five picks dealt away trying to sail their sunken ship, the Raiders selected only two players who ever saw action for the club, defensive tackle's Dave Costa selected in the seventh round and twentieth round choice Rex Mirich, who eventually made the squad in 1964. In an effort spearheaded by Mayor Houlihan, two county governments and twenty-six Bay Area cities came together to guarantee 12,000 season ticket sales for the 1963 season. It was a move which had Oakland management suspending all negotiations to sell the club, that garnered interest from investors in New Orleans who pledged 12,000 season packages of their own.

This news of domestic stability served as a major morale boost for Raiders players even as they headed into San Diego to face a team they had still never beaten. Earl Faison was still hobbled after the previous meeting with Oakland and Paul Lowe was out of action for the year, crippling the mighty Chargers, sending the division champions to a 3-8 record, and losing their last five. Enis was unable to move the offense and San Diego opened up a 21-0 lead midway through the third period. Forced into action, an ailing Davidson took over and launched a 48-yard bomb to Roberson for a first and goal at the Chargers 5. Clem Daniels took it over on his second attempt and Oakland was in business trailing only 21-7. A quick San Diego scoring drive set the Raiders back again early in the fourth quarter, only to be answered in one play with another Davidson bomb. Dick Dorsey scored for Oakland from 65 yards out. A San Diego punt pinned the Raiders back on the 15 and Roberson being dropped for a loss of five yards dug the hole even deeper. A toss to Dorsey in the flat turned into a footrace won by the Oakland end earning the approval of the Chargers fans on hand and bringing his club to within seven, 28-21. The defense dug in again forcing one final San Diego punt. Davidson, looking for one more miracle to bring the score to a 28-point tie, was picked off by Faison in Raiders territory. An easy 12-yard field goal sent Oakland to their eighteenth loss in a row 31-21 and twelfth of 1962.

The ill-fated Raiders returned to Texas to finish out the road schedule against Houston. Hoping to play spoiler against a team set to win their third division title in as many years and defend a league championship that had never been held by another team. Without the presence of coach Conkright and assistant Ollie Spencer, who were away scouting, Oakland made it easy for the Oilers. A pair of Raiders' turnovers gift-wrapped a 20-0 Houston lead early in the second quarter. Clem Daniels ripped 72 of his 187 rushing yards for Oakland's first score and Tommy Morrow's league leading ninth interception created a scoring opportunity and an Agajanian field goal cut the difference in half at 10 points. Moving 75 yards in 10 plays, Davidson sliced seven more away from the Oilers' lead with a quarterback sneak. If it weren't for bad luck the Raiders would have none in 1962 as evidenced by Agajanian's 50-yard field goal attempt, which was blocked by Ed Hussman, who recovered the kick and was escorted to the end zone by Tony Banfield as Oakland looked to tie the score. An 11-yard field goal from Blanda and a safety on a punt return as Bob Garner was buried in the end zone trying to run the kick out sent Oakland to their nineteenth loss in a row 32-17.

Coming home to Oakland knowing this final contest would be his last as the Raiders head coach, Red Conkright had only the game to lose. The former Stephen F. Austin coach had a simple game plan in mind for Boston at Frank Youell Field; hit the Patriots with everything Oakland had, including *The Oakland Tribune* tower! With Raiders Appreciation Day and the new DRIVE (Damn Right I'm for Victory in the East Bay) campaign in full swing to sell the promised tickets for next year and to support the Raiders against Boston, the Oakland team had full community support in its quest for success. 8,000 Raiders fans braved rainy weather to root for the home team against a Patriots team that needed a victory to unseat Houston as Eastern Division champs. Finally, mercifully, Raiders fans wouldn't leave Frank Youell Field disappointed. Fooling the Boston team with an onside kick on the opening kickoff, Fred Williamson's recovery in the mud gave the Raiders possession on the Patriots 41. A 19-yard Agajanian kick gave Oakland its first lead in a month. Finding themselves in a third and 17 situation from the 25, Davidson found Daniels by himself along the sidelines at the 40 on a busted play. Making two Boston defenders miss, Daniels raced the remaining 60 yards for a 10-0 Oakland lead.

Striking quickly to open the second half, Davidson found Max Boydston for 23 yards then connected with Roberson, who was stopped on the Patriots 4-yard line. Losing three yards to the 7, an incomplete pass brought up third down. Following a Jim Otto block, Daniels found the end zone for a 17-0 lead that was beginning to look like a runaway. Jim Norris recovered a fumble on the Boston 37. As the ensuing drive stalled on the 14, Agajanian added the final score of the day with a 21-yard kick. Dalva Allen's fumble recovery and Tommy Morrow's interception on the Oakland 4 with less than a minute remaining gave Oakland it's only victory of 1962 and the first shutout win in franchise history. The crowd that counted down the final 30 seconds of Oakland's first triumph in 20 games rushed the field embracing their muddied heroes and giving them congratulatory slaps to the rear. As the longest losing skid in professional football died in the mud of Frank Youell Field, a new era was set to begin in its place.

CHAPTER FOUR
UNDECLARED CHAMPIONS
1963

There is only one word to describe what the Oakland Raiders had become, *pathetic*. The promise first shown in 1960 had diminished in the darkness of 25 defeats in 28 games over the past two seasons and 33 losses in only 42 contests overall. The grimmest reaper appeared over Frank Youell Field, looking to lead Oakland football forever into the black unknown. Rumors circulated quickly that the AFL had granted permission to move the Raiders to Portland, Oregon at their earliest convenience. Hotly denied and eventually put to rest by the Raiders themselves, this along with offers to purchase the team from suitors in New Orleans and reports of a move to Kansas City caused enough unease in the Alameda County Board of Supervisors that completion of the new coliseum was now scheduled for the 1965 season. Repeated assurances were eventually able to calm nerves just enough for the project to receive another final go-ahead.

The DRIVE campaign, coordinated to acquaint new fans with the American Football League, the Oakland Raiders and to ensure the established fans that the club was not only there to stay, but to win as well, sold nearly half of the guaranteed 12,000 season tickets instantly. Interest in the Raiders was strong despite their mammoth shortcomings. The general partners knew that they would have to put a winning product on the football field if they were to have any hopes of maintaining their popularity.

Between the AFL's winter meetings in San Diego and deflecting innuendo regarding the teams' future, Wayne Valley and Ed McGah began their search for someone, anyone who could guide their mess to respectability. With the surprise dismissal of Paul Brown as head coach of his namesake team in Cleveland doubling the number of available professional head football coaching positions to two, they were afforded the luxury of being choosy. However, one man stood high above all other candidates both real and speculative, 33-year-old San Diego Chargers offensive backfield coach Al Davis. With one of the brightest young football minds of his time, Davis was already a 13-year coaching and administrative veteran and was considered a near genius by many of his peers. His prowess as a recruiter was unrivaled, signing many of the Chargers' top players including (now Oakland's) Bo Roberson, Earl Faison, Ron Mix, Bob Hudson and Lance Alworth proving Gillman's gamble in obtaining his rights to not be the risk it first appeared to be.

With an abundance of physical and mental energy and a keen mind for the game, Valley and McGah saw Davis fit to succeed not only Red Conkright but also general manager Wes Fry. The Raiders had their man now and their man had his mission, to turn pro football's biggest disaster into the finest, most respected organization in all of professional sports. Two tasks lay immediately ahead for the young dynamo, reorganize the front office and find players who could score points quickly and often.

Still employed in Oakland until Davis' ascension to their posts, Fry and Conkright had begun another Raiders rebuilding process. Draft rights for Oregon State All-American quarterback Terry Baker were obtained from San Diego, despite his announced intention to play for the Rams in the NFL and Alabama running back Cotton Clark, whose 92 points the year earlier ranked him second in the nation while his 42.5-yard punting average graded him third in the country in that regard. An offensive weapon of Clark's caliber fit well into Davis' plans, yet with the return of Tom Flores from his ailment and a strong-armed veteran in Cotton Davidson, a bidding war with Los Angeles for Baker's services was unnecessary. These two, along with center Jim Otto, halfback Clem Daniels and cornerback Fred Williamson formed the foundation on which these new Raiders would be built. Much like the two remaining assistant coaches, the rest of the Oakland roster's future with the club was very much in doubt with the announcement that the remainder of the squad was on the trading block. While the league inked a developmental deal with the United Football League giving Oakland seasoned help from the Louisville Raiders, Davis went out and found some real help in the form of New York Titans' end Art Powell. With his talents being sought by a pair of AFL and CFL clubs and several NFL squads, this move drew loud gasps from throughout the football world, though none could compete with the screams coming from Titans' owner Harry Wismer. Claiming Powell had been tampered with by Wayne Valley, Wismer alleged the league's former president had been in collusion with Powell for a full year and influenced his decision to leave New York, a charge that was quickly dismissed by the league as Davis was given verbal permission to negotiate with the receiver although he had played out his option and was a free agent, able to negotiate with anyone of his choosing in any league.

Dismissing these allegations with a laugh, the club began its frantic restructuring of its coaching staff and front office. Former New York Yanks (of the old American Professional Football Association) and Georgia Bulldogs quarterback John Rauch filled the first opening on the coaching staff assuming the duties of offensive backfield coach, a position left vacant since the ousting of Tom Kalminir and Marty Feldman following 1962's fifth week. Like Davis, Rauch was a fine recruiter with an innovative football mind who had developed Army's famed lonesome end system. The new assistant, sold on Oakland's potential as a football town with its rabid, knowledgeable fans and on Al Davis himself, was joined by incumbent offensive line coach Ollie Spencer, who had survived an extensive search to fill his position.

Tom Dahms, a three-year Dallas Cowboys assistant, was brought aboard to coach the defensive line. An NFL veteran with stints in Los Angeles, Green Bay, Chicago with the Cardinals before finishing his playing days as a San Francisco 49er, Dahms was eager to return to his native California and was the last assistant hired in the short term. No announcement had been made regarding the future of Walt Michaels or his position as defensive backfield coach; the team instead chose to devote time to a front office face-lift. J.I. Albrecht, another top recruiter who served as director of player personnel for the Montreal Alouettes, came to Oakland as the Raiders' new business manager. Joining him from the San Diego Chargers was George Glace to handle the duties of ticket manager relieving Jack Hennessey, who was shuffled to an interim appointment to the new special promotions post, charged with stimulating fan interest and allowing tackle Jack Stone to concentrate on football. Twenty-five-year-old UCLA Bruins assistant coach Jim Dawson, with an outstanding record as a coach and excellent reputation as a recruiter, was named director of player personnel. Further shuffling finished out the front office realignment for the time being with former sports writer Bill Tunnell shifting from director of publicity post to public relations director.

(2)

For the first time in three years Oakland went without a visit from commissioner Foss to iron out internal issues or those arising between the club and local political leaders. Instead, Foss could again proclaim Oakland's potential as a great AFL city and the plausibility of the Raiders to become one of professional football's best teams. To this end, Davis and his assistants Dahms, Spencer and Rauch followed player personnel director Jim Dawson on a month-long scouting expedition covering more than 100 schools in search of the best collegiate talent and bring them back to Oakland as Raiders. A pair of former draft picks found their way to Oakland. Originally picked eighteenth as a halfback from Illinois, Joe Krakowski opted for the NFL, being drafted #6 by the Dallas Cowboys before winding up in Washington where he was converted to safety. Krakowski stole four passes as a Redskin then retired in 1962 to go into business in his hometown in Illinois. His name found its way into Al Davis' consciousness by way of a Chargers' prospects list. The thirteenth pick from 1962, George Pierovich chose to play in San Francisco before being sidelined by injury was given an opportunity at fullback. To complete a trade from the season prior, the Raiders acquired a pair of Texans, guard Sonny Bishop and Dick Davis, a defensive tackle who alternated to the defensive end position throughout the 1962 Dallas championship run.

A roster released by the team in May containing only 40 names gave Oakland fans their first glance at the Al Davis version of their Oakland Raiders. Safety Vernon Valdez, unable to recover from injuries incurred in an auto accident the previous November, hung up his cleats. Accompanying him in retirement were veterans Stan Campbell and Max Boydston. Many players such as Riley Morris, Ben Agajanian, Mel Montalbo, Willie Simpson, Gene White, Jackie Simpson, Hal Lewis and Glen Hakes were released, leaving barely the shell of what was the 1962 club that had lost their first thirteen games. A few would make their way back to Oakland in training camp but for now what remained was the rough draft of the new-look Oakland team featuring four quarterbacks: Cotton Davidson, Tom Flores, Hunter Enis and Dennis Spurlock, one halfback, Clem Daniels, three fullbacks with Bill Strumke listed as the starter, George Pierovich as his backup and Alan Miller listed third as talks of trading him back to Boston warmed. Art Powell was named the starter at left end with sprinter Dick Dorsey as his understudy; on the right Bo Roberson was the top man with Dobie Craig eager to spell him. The offensive line was deep in some cases and thin in others. Charlie Brown held down the left tackle spot with Pete Nicklas and Jim Norris in line to replace him. Dan Ficca was the lone left guard. Next to him was only center the Raiders had ever known, Jim Otto, who himself had no one listed to cover him in case of injury. New acquisition Sonny Bishop found a home behind original Raider Wayne Hawkins and Jack Stone handled the right tackle position with George Hogan and behind him. Making a comeback from a broken leg, Bob Coolbaugh was the sole tight end with all of one practice in training camp the year before his complete professional experience at the position.

The defense had as many questions that would need to be addressed in camp and the impending exhibition season. Dalva Allen was by himself at left defensive end, while on the right Jon Jelasic and Joe Novsek would battle for the starting spot. With Chuck McMurtry on the left and rookie Dave Costa on the right had the defensive tackle positions sewn up tight with former New York Titan Proverb Jacobs, an offensive tackle getting a look on defense, and the returning George Shirkey in reserve on the left with Tony Discenzo behind Costa on the right. The Raiders now featured just three linebackers, Dan Birdwell on the left and Bob Dougherty in the middle with Charlie Rieves on the right. Bob Garner had the right cornerback position to himself while All-Star Fred Williamson owned the left corner spot with "Hatchet Man" Hank Rivera listed as his relief. Though proclaiming the need for offensive firepower, Davis saw something in Cotton Clark and moved him to strong safety. Starting him in front of veteran George Boynton while Tommy Morrow and Joe Krakowski were left to compete for the free safety position.

A special league meeting in New York resulted in a plan to help the perpetually rebuilding Raiders and New York (former Titans, who were now renamed) Jets. The six other clubs were allowed to protect 25 players currently under contract, with an exemption for new rookies and a free agents. A stipulation in the agreement of Sonny Werblin's purchase of the New York team from Harry Wismer guaranteed New York the first pick in this draft as the Jets were unable to sign any draft picks in the off season and lost Art Powell to Oakland. The $15,000 price tag placed on the Jets' first pick and $7,500 for any other selections for either club made drafting the allowable twelve players for either squad unrealistic. With a record of 5 wins and 9 losses with two victories coming against Oakland, the Jets' entitlement to the first overall pick, despite the doubled fee for the players' services cast a shadow of disbelief over the Raiders organization and a late ruling by the league had Al Davis calling the entire plan "a joke." Despite the vast majority of AFL players in the military being reservists on short duty and able to wear their football uniforms by the start of training camp, the league saw fit to give these players a special exemption, allowing the coaches from the other clubs to protect other players making the already slim talent pickings, anorexic. Jets' coach Weeb Ewbank found no one left worthy of the agreed $15,000 drafting price giving Oakland its well-deserved first choice. However Davis found only one player available worthy of a $7,500 price tag, two-year veteran Claude "Hoot" Gibson from the San Diego Chargers. Slated to play the right cornerback position, the 6'1" 193-lb. cover man was tied with Fred Williamson for the league lead in interceptions giving Oakland arguably the best corner tandem of the time.

Both franchises were in line for help again with the first refusal draft in which Oakland and the Jets were given right of first refusal on players cut from NFL squads in training camp. Instead of waiting around for table scraps to befall him, Davis again went out and found choice talent in the form of three-time All-AFL linebacker Archie Matsos. Smallish at 6' and 212 lbs. Matsos compensated for his lack of size with agility, speed and smarts, and he excelled against both the run and pass. Unfortunately for Davis and his Raiders, this prize came at a heavy price as defensive tackle George Shirkey, offensive tackle Pete Nicklas and defensive back "Hatchet Man" Hank Rivera were sent to Buffalo to complete the swap.

More trade activity loomed on the Oakland horizon, but not until Davis and his young coaching staff (Davis, now 34, Spencer, 31, Dahms, 35, new defensive backfield coach Charlie Sumner, 36, and John Rauch, age 37) had a chance to evaluate the talent they already had at their new $50,000 training facility at the El Rancho Motel in Santa Rosa. Located 60 miles northwest of Oakland, an entire court of the hotel facility along with a banquet room were to be used by the team for living and office space along with a 3,000-square-foot field house to be used for locker room, training room, weightlifting and storage facilities along with two full-sized practice fields surrounded by an eight-foot fence to allow closed practices yet open some to public view.

Guests at the El Rancho Motel were normally treated to luxurious accommodations, but for the 26 new rookies and 9 new veteran players these Raiders, along with the returning vets were to be treated no such luxuries as the televisions were first removed from their rooms followed by orders to remove the telephones. With more than 30 new players, 4 new coaches, new offensive and defensive systems to install, Al Davis' three-year plan to mold the pitiful bunch known as the Oakland Raiders into contenders was underway.

Immediately the Raiders' toughest training drills to date went into full swing. Davis first directed his attention to the deficient passing attack that, until the last portion of the 1962 catastrophe, was an utter failure. The addition of Art Powell and the conversion of Bo Roberson locked up the starting end positions. The tight end position was still a matter of grave concern. With only the inexperienced Coolbaugh to handle these duties, rookie linebacker Ken Herock was moved to the offense to compete for the position. More reinforcements were brought in on the offensive line as young Dan Ficca was dealt away to the Jets for another three-time All-AFL player, guard Bob Mischak, while safetyman Cotton Clark was given a look at his natural halfback position and linebacker Charlie Rieves was returned to fullback where he excelled in his blocking early on, upending charging defenders from their pursuit. Contact that stressed blocking and individual attention from the coaches was given to their charges to ensure these athletes knew precisely what their assignments were and what was expected of them.

After the first scrimmage, which didn't displease the coaches, more were ordered to iron out deficiencies, primarily in the running game. Fifteen to twenty minutes every morning were devoted to scrimmage work for the offensive linemen and backs to enable them to pound the ball through the middle with authority. While too many passes were dropped to suit coach Davis, pass protection held up well and the defense was ahead of schedule with their two new coaches installing brand new schemes. Coach Sumner stressed run support from his secondary defenders, which the season prior was poor at best.

The AFL equalization plan had managed to, once again, prove itself a bad joke as the first refusal rights to players cut from half of the NFL squads was ignored, as the Broncos signed former Los Angeles Rams quarterback Ron Miller. Players from the Rams, one of seven NFL teams Oakland had draft rights to, were subject to a 30-day waiting period for the Oakland team to sign them. Commissioner Foss ruled arbitrarily that Miller should play in Denver when Jack Faulkner made claims of quarterback problems despite having Frank Tripuka and George Shaw in camp, while Oakland had a returning Tom Flores, who missed the previous season with an illness and Cotton Davidson, who suffered through injuries throughout the entire 1962 campaign.

(3)

More moves were made to shore up the improving offensive line. Securing waivers from every National Football League team and from the AFL offices, former Detroit Lions and Green Bay Packers tackle and Oakland Raiders offensive line coach Ollie Spencer was activated to the roster. Referring to Spencer as a blue-chip athlete, Davis later announced that it would be Cotton Davidson receiving most of the protection from player/coach Spencer and his cohorts as Tom Flores, as a part of the plan for his rehabilitation would only play the final quarter to a third of the opening preseason game. This was the plan for the early exhibition season only; after that the job was up for grabs and the starting job for the regular season would be earned in practice and through the exhibition slate. Guard Bob Mischak, the three-time All Star who had earned All-American honors at West Point as an end and defensive back was moved behind Ken Herock at tight end, who held the position all to himself after the release of Bob Coolbaugh.

A new sense of confidence was evident in the Raiders' locker room. With new pro style offensive and defensive schemes in place, the players worked tirelessly in practice, some through painful injuries without missing time and in meetings and studies to master their new system. Enduring more contact than in any camp before, veteran tackle Jack Stone claimed to have gained more knowledge in this camp than any he'd been through before. Wayne Hawkins stated simply the Raiders were more prepared for the exhibition slate than they were a year before on opening day against the Titans and made promises to surprise their competition in the upcoming season. Immediately ahead were the only team Oakland had surprised in a very long time, the Boston Patriots. More heavy scrimmages were ordered to prepare for the team Davis referred to as the AFL's most solid in each aspect of their game. The Patriots provided a stern test for Davis, who was undefeated as an assistant coach in the preseason, and his new squad, who considered themselves genuinely lucky to not be run out of the park on Sundays.

These new Raiders took the fight to Boston midway through the second quarter. Moving 85 yards in 7 plays. Art Powell hauled in a 23-yard Cotton Davidson pass over Patriots' defender Jimmy Fields in the corner of the end zone and the new Raiders enjoyed a 7-0 halftime lead. In his first action since the end of the 1961 season, Tom Flores fired an ill-advised pass into the arms of Patriots linebacker Ronnie Loud on the Boston 36, forty yards later Tom Yewsic began on the Oakland 24 and the game was knotted on first down with a pass to Art Graham. Undeterred, the Raiders found themselves in striking distance after a 33-yard Davidson (back to spell Flores after his misfortune) to Clem Daniels pass set up a Durward Pennington field goal try from the 46. Kicking true on his second attempt of the afternoon, the Raiders went ahead 10-7, only to have Boston answer with a 16-yard kick from Gino Cappaletti. Davidson, in retaliation, directed the offense to the 1-yard-line with passes to Powell and a hobbling Bo Roberson (who picked up 92 yards on 4 receptions) before calling his own number and recapturing the lead on a quarterback sneak as time ran out in the third period. It was Babe Parilli's turn to lead the Patriots against his former team, starting from his 26; the Patriots found themselves on the Oakland 44 and suddenly facing the Raiders of old. Converging on Gino Cappaletti on the 30, a collision between Bob Garner and Tommy Morrow left the pair lying as Cappaletti waltzed uncontested into the end zone for the tying score. Punting away their opportunity to regain the lead after three plays to the Patriots. Parilli discovered misfortune of his own as his pass found its way directly between the numbers of middle linebacker Arch Matsos playing in a zone defense on the Patriots 40 and the errant toss was returned 23 yards to the Boston 17. Gaining a first and goal at the 2, Davidson called Alan Miller's number and the fullback delivered the decisive score and the Raiders first ever, exhibition-opening victory, 24-17.

Seldom the scene of a victory celebration, the winning locker room couldn't have been more jubilant had they won the AFL championship. Davis spoke as the voice of reason pointing to the limited play calling from both teams but his players took the next step. A beaming Hawkins, who earlier in the week promised surprises for Oakland's foes now boasted his team would win more than a few games in 1963 and gave reporters permission to quote him. Davidson heaped praise upon his protectors after being reached only twice by the ever-blitzing Patriots, even accepting responsibility for one encounter for his holding onto the ball too long. The quarterback then lauded his teammates on defense for their efforts as Art Powell took time to hail coach Davis and made a promise to win a lot of games for him.

Davis himself softened his stance about the victory after viewing the game films. The smiling coach refused to share in his charges' excitement but he was obviously pleased with his team's showing. Staying true to his claim to need more players Davis plucked tackle Dick Klein from Boston for a player to be named later. A starter for the Patriots since joining them early in 61, Klein needed to earn his way onto the Oakland roster after the stellar performance of the Raiders' front line against Boston and he had to learn fast, as the usually tough Denver Broncos had made the journey to Frank Youell Field.

Expected to be a far tougher task with the Broncos, as coach Davis' plan was to use more reserve players to better evaluate them. The Oakland defense also found themselves shorthanded with Chuck McMurtry and Bob Dougherty (the first of four Raiders players in the exhibition season to be) missing time to mourn the loss of a loved one. Regardless of the odds and inconveniences against them, the Oakland team came to Frank Youell Field to win, something AFL Coach of the Year Jack Faulkner's club helped early on with a 17-yard pass interference call setting Oakland up with a first and ten on the Denver 34. Clem Daniels took the handoff from Davidson, made a defender miss, then broke to the right sideline and put the Raiders up 7-0. Two Gene Mingo field goals cut the Raider lead to one at 7-6 as the first period wound down, though Daniels was able to move the ball running around the tackles. Another penalty, this time for roughing the passer, gave Oakland's drive life on their 25. In a second and 27 situation from the 42 after Davidson was sacked for a huge loss by linebacker Tom Erlandson, the Oakland passer spotted Bo Roberson between a pair of defenders on the original line of scrimmage; using his world-class speed, Roberson ran away from his pursuers and Oakland took a 14-6 lead.

Taking the helm on offense to begin the third quarter, Tom Flores immediately looked to improve on his 4 of 6 performance against Boston, passing to the Denver 5 before Pennington missed the first of his three field goal attempts on the afternoon. Quickly forcing a Bronco punt, Oakland took over again on the 41. In the Raiders' second display of big-play magic, Flores found Roberson alone along the sidelines. Falling to the ground, Roberson, after making the reception jumped up and ran into the end zone untouched for a 21-6 Raiders lead. The Oakland defense halted Denver and gave possession back to their offense on their 35. A 6-yard scamper from Daniels followed by a 20-yard catch from Powell and another 12 yards from Roberson gave the Raiders a first down on the Denver 39. Three brilliant faking moves from Powell and a perfectly thrown ball from Flores ended the competitive phase of the game with the score 28-6. Though the ensuing kickoff was returned 99 yards for a score by fleet running Al Frazier and a fumble by Daniels on the Raiders' 16 gave Denver on opportunity to pull within a touchdown, Bob Dougherty swatted a Tripuka pass down keeping the Broncos at bay. A wobbly George Shaw blunder into the flat as time expired found its way into the hands of new Raiders fan favorite Joe Krakowski, who stumbled into the end zone, the final slap to a tough Bronco team that had handed Oakland two of its worst defeats the season prior.

The 35-19 conquest of Denver added further to the Raiders' swelling confidence as they departed the friendly confines of Frank Youell Field for the next four weeks to finish their out their practice slate and begin the new campaign on the road. First to the University of Washington's Memorial Stadium to face the reigning AFL champions. Relocated from Dallas to Kansas City with a guarantee of 25,000 season ticket sales and renamed the Chiefs, Lamar Hunt's ball club would give Oakland its toughest test to date.

In addition to preparing a game plan and schooling his players for their date with the champions and the upcoming season, Davis now worked with a smaller office staff. Absorbing the duties of business manager into his own, coach Davis saw no further need for the services of J.I. Albrecht while newly hired assistant talent scout Ron Wolf took over for Jim Dawson in revamping the Oakland roster for 1963 and beyond.

With time for only one extended practice during the week prior to their departure, coach Davis' admitted plan for the powerful Kansas City franchise was remarkably simple, to see how well his squad could play some old-fashion football. Still improving from week to week, the Raiders' running game hadn't met Davis' expectations and his improving defense would meet the AFL's best running combo, Curtis McClinton and Abner Haynes head on. Staying true to his tactics of telling the press one thing and sending his Raiders onto the field to do another, the 13,500 who found their way into Memorial Stadium were witnesses to an air war. Connecting on a combined 17 passes in 41 attempts on the afternoon for 252 yards, 81 of which were gained with a Davidson toss to Daniels that put Oakland up early 7-0. The lead was brief. Quarterback Ed Wilson, taking a large majority of the snaps for coach Hank Stram's club, moved 75 yards in 10 plays, capping the drive himself with a quarterback sneak from the 1-foot line for a first quarter tie at 7-7. Two Wilson scoring tosses to Chris Burford, the first for 9 yards and the next covering 11, closed out the first half with Kansas City dominating 21-7. Following a Chiefs punt early in the third quarter, Flores took the helm of Oakland's attacking unit. Moving downfield quickly with passes to Powell and Roberson, the Ice Man (a nickname given Flores for his cool in the pocket in the face of intense pressure) found the latter in the corner of the end zone from 22 yards away. Showing why they were the AFL's top club, the Chiefs roared back immediately. Marching 67 yards in 8 plays, then capping the drive with a 5-yard toss to Fred Arbanas, the Chiefs reclaimed their 14-point cushion. Oakland caught a break however as Abner Haynes mishandled a punt from Cotton Clark and linebacker Dan Birdwell secured the loose ball. Flores sent Powell across the middle from the 10 and cut the Kansas City lead to 7 again early in the fourth period. Dalva Allen laid into Haynes hard at midfield forcing his second fumble of the half. Bob Dougherty scooped it up and brought it to the Kansas City 43. With time and a prime opportunity to tie, the Raiders imploded. A pair of five-yard penalties and three incomplete passes found the Black and Gold in a fourth and 15 situation at the 49. After punting away their last chance, Abner Haynes redeemed himself by tossing a halfback option pass to Frank Jackson. The 49-yard strike put the game away at 35-21.

Remaining positive despite their shortcoming, coach Davis and his staff went to work addressing needs highlighted by this loss. Linebacker Clancy Osborne was brought aboard and veteran kicker Mike Mercer was added to heal a woefully inadequate kicking game that had succeeded only once in nine preseason field goal tries. Cotton Davidson reassumed punting duties with the release of Cotton Clark but the most pressing need to be satisfied in the short term was how to replace talent such as Art Powell, Fred Williamson, Bo Roberson, Gene White, Clem Daniels and Proverb Jacobs. These six players, accounting for every African-American on the Raiders roster wouldn't be making the trip to Mobile, Alabama to face the Jets in protest of Ladd Memorial Stadium's segregated seating policy.

Only three short years before, this same team from Oakland crossed a picket line formed by the National Association for the Advancement of Colored People (NAACP) to capture their first ever regular-season victory against the Houston Oilers at the segregated Jeppesen Stadium only to return a year later and play despite the black players' being asked to sit out in protest. Now, the players had the full support of their coach and management and very quickly from the mayor of Mobile, though he had no direct control over the stadium's policies as it was privately owned and operated. Seating integration was a condition of AFL football being brought to Mobile and, at best, was being honored half-heartedly. With only the corner end zone seats (typically the worst seats in a football stadium) made available to people of color, with two or three vertical rows of seats alienating them from their fellow man there were no restrooms in the facility allowed for their use. Taking less than kindly to the protests of the Oakland ball players and the public pressure applied by Mobile's mayor, Ladd Stadium management instantly halted their insincere efforts to integrate, breeching their contract with the AFL. In turn, the league immediately cancelled the game.

Praised was heaped upon them for their stand by Oakland civic leaders who then made a plea for support of the Raiders to a sympathetic public, however the six players and their coach were deeply disappointed. While split on the accomplishments of their deeds, each wanted to participate in the first ever, professional game in Alabama in front of an integrated audience. Now it was not to be. The game was rescheduled for the following Sunday afternoon at Frank Youell Field in front of 8,317 Raiders fans that grabbed these seats as tickets for this surprise game went on sale only four days before kickoff. They were rewarded greatly.

Jim Norris' block and recovery of a Jet punt on the New York 9 in the first period put the Raiders in position to strike with a first and goal. Unable to move more than a yard, Mike Mercer connected from 15 yards out for a quick 3-0 lead. From their 20, the Jets marched 80 yards in 16 plays with tough running from Dick Christy and Bill Mathis, who went the final yard. After a fruitless Raiders series, New York took over again and disaster struck, a Lee Grosscup pass to Don Maynard was picked off by rookie safety Warren Powers; 52 yards later, Oakland regained their lead at 10-7. Another errant pass, this time picked off by Arch Matsos gave Oakland possession on their 41-yard line with two minutes remaining in the half. Thirty-nine yards were chewed up with short passes to Dobie Craig. With 10 seconds remaining in the half Mercer connected for his second field goal and Oakland headed for the locker room up 13-7.

Flores opened the second half with an interception to Lee Riley who was stopped three yards shy of tying the game and the chance for a New York lead with a conversion. Bill Mathis was stuffed for no gain on first down and Tommy Morrow threw Marshall Starks for a loss of 8 yards on second down. The third down encore saw Jim Norris planting Johnny Green 7 yards further back and faced with a fourth and goal from the 18, New York settled for a field goal. Another Mercer kick gave Oakland back its 6-point edge, but not for long. Their next possession saw Clem Daniels cough up the ball up on the Raiders' 14. Lee Riley grabbing his second takeaway of the period, would not be denied the end zone a second time, the score was deadlocked at 16 and remained so through the third quarter as Fred Williamson raced in and tackled the holder before the extra point could be attempted.

What through three quarters had been the most exciting Raiders exhibition of 1963 became their biggest blowout as soon as the fourth quarter began. A clipping penalty set Oakland back on their own 6 to begin the period. The Raiders dug their way out three passes to Powell covering 12, 13 then 21 yards, Alan Miller took a Flores toss for 7 and Dobie Craig caught one for 25 more, moving the Raiders into Jets' territory. Fifteen yards were donated by the Jets with an unnecessary roughness call and a Daniels catch on the 2 and step towards pay dirt covered the last 15 yards of a 94-yard journey in less than 3 minutes. A 1:22 was all that were required for the next Raiders strike, an interception by "Hoot" Gibson on the 30 and 20-yard return gave Oakland possession at midfield. A stumbling Daniels took the handoff up the middle, regained his balance and outran the Jets' defense for his second score of the young quarter and a 30-16 Raiders' lead. The third Oakland tally of the period drained another 1:51 off the clock. Flores' pass to Craig brought the Raiders to the 9 after Dave Costa's fumble recovery on the 35; Mike Mercer connected on his fourth field goal of the day. A stout defense held and the Jets were forced to punt from their end zone. Playing in kind, the Jets defense slowed the Raiders but allowed the fifth Oakland field goal of the day to widen the Raiders' lead to 20 points at 36-16. With less than two minutes remaining in the game, new linebacker Clancy Osborne nabbed Oakland's fifth interception on the Jets' 29 and returned it 5 yards. Advancing to the seven and with only two seconds left, Flores waited for rookie tight end Ken Herock come open and delivered his first professional touchdown, sealing Oakland's third exhibition victory, 43-16.

Their courageous stand against social injustice brought them further into the public's consciousness, and their fourth quarter fireworks show made believers out of the skeptical Bay Area football fans who were now looking to the East Bay for their first gridiron championship. Yet before any of these glory-filled aspirations could be realized, the new heroes in Oakland needed to finish the exhibition season against a seemingly invincible foe known as the Chargers. A 16-yard field goal from Mike Mercer gave the Raiders a quick lead in the opening quarter that was quickly matched by San Diego's George Blair. Further heroics came from Blair at the linebacker position, stealing a Cotton Davidson pass (the first of his two and Oakland's four interceptions) on the Oakland 42. Seven players later, fullback Bob Jackson went over from the 1 giving the Chargers a 10-3 halftime advantage en route to a 13-3 victory. This latest loss closed out the Raiders' first winning exhibition season with a mark of 3 wins and 2 losses and only these same Chargers outperformed the Oakland club in the AFL's fourth exhibition season with a 4-1 record.

(4)

With the final cuts, four starters from the season prior handed their walking papers. Both starting tackles, Jack Stone and Charlie Brown, were let go as coach Davis and his staff added bulk to the position with Frank Youso getting the starting nod along with Proverb Jacobs. Player/coach Ollie Spencer saw relief duty along with tackle Dick Klein. Fullback George Pierovich was also waived as were linebacker and converted offensive lineman Dan Birdwell, flanker Dobie Craig, rookie defensive back Warren Powers and Charlie Rieves having been switched back to linebacker, the latter four all found their way to the Raiders taxi squad and back into Oakland uniforms by the seasons end.

The uniforms they would wear as Raiders upon their return would no longer feature white pants with a gold and black stripe down the legs, black jerseys with rounded white numbers and gold trim with three gold stripes on the arms and a black helmet with a gold stripe down the middle (the stripe was added for the 1962 season as the helmet was plain black for the first two seasons). Instead the Oakland team would wear a silver helmet with their shield logo emblazoned on the sides, a black jersey with square, silver numbers for home games and white with the same silver numerals for the road and silver pants with a black stripe down the legs.

Three remarkable occurrences happened opening week. The first was the four fumbles recovered and six passes intercepted by Oakland defenders, three by Tommy Morrow. The second was the AFL record 237 yards in penalties amassed by both squads, 158 belonging to Oakland for

17 infractions. With the defense allowing only a pair of field goals from George Blanda in the first half, quarterback Tom Flores took over on his 44 after a brilliant Bo Roberson return to open the second half. Clem Daniels bulled over from the 2 on the drives seventh play giving Oakland the lead 7-6. More flash from Roberson gave the Raiders' a first and goal at the 5 though a tough Houston defense held and Oakland settled for a Mercer field goal. The Raiders' defense controlled the game throughout the third quarter and into the fourth when the Oilers' defenders showed life of their own as blitzing linebacker Mike Dukes hammered Flores for a 13-yard loss on the Raiders 15. In response, Flores dropped to his 5 and found Art Powell in double coverage on the Oakland 30. The Oilers' defensive backs collided; Powell outran rest of the Houston defense (with a pulled leg muscle that was to limit his availability) the remaining 70 yards for an 11-point lead at 17-6 and tying a two-year-old Oakland record for the longest pass reception. Houston watched helplessly as their hopes of an opening week victory slipped away as Ken Herock scooped up a fumbled punt on the Oilers' 15 and was escorted into the end zone by five teammates. Trailing 24-6 Jacky Lee came in to spell Blanda after his fifth errant throw. Lee tossed a meaningless 34-yard touchdown to Charlie Hennigan before time expired and the day's third remarkable event was official, the Oakland Raiders had won their first season opening contest.

None of the historical happenings were lost on the men in Silver and Black. While Al Davis' squad were becoming adept in locker room celebrations, original Raider Bob Dougherty gave warning to the rest of the league, these Oakland Raiders were nothing like the club that opened the 1961 campaign in Houston only to be bludgeoned 55-0. The linebacker gave assurances that this Raiders team would be in the hunt for the American Football League title at season's end. The confidence exuded from Dougherty and his mates was also shared by an eager public who filled a regular season record 17,568 seats to watch their Oakland Raiders, a 10-point underdog face Buffalo Bills.

Deflecting questions of a quarterback controversy by informing the press that he coached to win football games, Al Davis started Davidson and used Flores sparingly later on as the pair combined for 397 yards. Three Clem Daniels receptions covered 172 yards combined with his 76 yards on the ground brought his total to 248 yards on the afternoon. With the defense silencing Cookie Gilchrist, holding him to only 19 yards on 10 carries, Buffalo passer Jack Kemp was forced to the air for 355 yards. Scoreless through the first quarter, Oakland took over after a Wayne Crow punt fell dead on their 39-yard line. Nine plays later, Art Powell caught a 1-yard Davidson toss for a score. The defense halted the Bills' drive on their 25 but Mack Yoho put Buffalo on the scoreboard, carving three away from the Raiders lead with a 33-yard field goal. One play was all that was required for Oakland to reclaim its lost margin and add four additional points as a scrambling Davidson made a three-yard pass to Daniels from the 27 that the explosive back cashed in 70 yards away, launching Oakland ahead 14-3. An intense blitz from linebacker Arch Matsos, jarred the ball loose from Kemp who more resembled a tackling dummy with butter fingers than a top professional quarterback; Dalva Allen recovered on the 24. On the third play from the two, Alan Miller followed tackle Proverb Jacobs and Ollie Spencer (subbing for an injured Sonny Bishop) into the end zone with 1:41 remaining in the half for a 21-3 Oakland lead. Kemp and the Buffalo Bills wouldn't back down from these Raiders under any circumstances; going 88 yards with less than 100 seconds remaining in the half, bringing the score to 21-10 as time expired.

As it was in the first half, the Raiders defenders were unrelenting; Matsos, along with left side linebacker Jackie Simpson, forced Kemp's second fumble which was recovered on the 5 by defensive tackle Chuck McMurtrey. A perfectly executed chop block from Bo Roberson sprang Davidson on first down and the Raiders led once again by 18 points, 28-10. Following suit, it was the Bills' turn to pressure the quarterback, forcing a Davidson fumble on the Oakland 43. On first down Elbert Dubenion got behind Joe Krakowski and the newly acquired Jim McMillin for a 57-yard score. To begin their next possession Buffalo was pinned on their 4 as Mike Mercer rolled a punt out of bounds. Kemp first threw incomplete. Taking to the air again, Kemp's second down attempt was batted by both Matsos and Allen and fell into the hands of Jon Jelasic on the 5. An easy return added the Raiders fifth touchdown and put on exclamation point on a dominating performance as Oakland grabbed their second victory in as many tries 35-17.

For the first time since 1960 the Oakland Raiders were enjoying a winning streak. Also for the first time since that same year, the odds makers chose these same Oakland Raiders as their favorites to win an AFL game. The three points given to Oakland seemed fair to some in light of their recent success considering the contest would be in the home confines of Frank Youell Field. As Clem Daniels sat out with a deep muscle bruise, the odds makers drew stern criticism from Al Davis himself, who labeled their logic ridiculous. When his third contest as Oakland Raiders head coach ended he only had slightly more to say about his own ball club calling their performance, "lousy period." After watching his offense lose 100 yards attempting to pass and going into the fourth quarter down 20-0 to the Boston Patriots, they finally seemed to have prepared for the game, properly executing their blocking assignments and allowing Tom Flores to throw a pair of scoring tosses, a 33-yard strike to Art Powell and to Bo Roberson for 52, making the score appear far more respectable at 20-14 than it actually was.

With the odds makers favoring them the week before despite their disappointment, it now seemed to be the AFL schedule makers turn to favor the Oakland franchise. Taking their 2-1 record on the road for their annual swing through the northeastern United States, only now the tour was to begin in late September and run through the early weeks of October, allowing the California club to play in warmer weather than they had experienced in November and December in the seasons past. Daniels returned and Jim Otto used pads in his cleat to relieve his jammed toes, only Bob Dougherty was sidelined for the first game of the eastern swing against an also reorganized New York Jets squad that had just defeated the Houston Oilers for the first time in their history. Favored on the road despite only three days of practice in a short week, the Raiders took the field and quickly moved 63 yards in 7 plays gaining an early 7-0 lead with Davidson scoring on a 2-yard quarterback keeper. Despite an interception from Jim McMillin and a pair from Joe Krakowski and Tommy Morrow extending his league-leading total to eight after only four weeks, it was the Raiders' secondary that blundered as the new Jets' and former Chargers' passer Dick Wood found Bake Turner open for a 51-yard scoring play that tied the game at 7 later in the opening quarter. Ineffective offenses played out the remainder of the contest with the Jets managing a single third-period field goal that proved the difference as Oakland fell to the Jets 10-7 and a record of 2-2.

The New York side of Niagara Falls became the Raiders home for the next week and a half. Coach Davis was forced to reactivate Dan Birdwell as Frank Youso was sent home to Oakland with a badly strained knee that ended his season. This minor bit of shuffling was nothing compared to the full rearrangement performed by his Buffalo counterpart Lou Saban, making the team the Raiders defeated handily in the second week at Frank Youell Field almost entirely different. Despite work on Oakland's lackluster offensive performances of the past two weeks, a 3-0 halftime lead was all the winless (0-3-1) Bills needed to hand the Raiders their third straight loss though a 24-yard Bill Miller touchdown reception and a safety in the third quarter were added in a 12-0 defeat, the first shutout suffered by Oakland in over two years.

Despite a hard-hitting defense that had yielded an average of 14.4 points over the seasons first five weeks, the offense had slipped badly averaging only a touchdown per game in their current three-game skid. Changes were made on both sides of the ball. A youth movement found the number of original Raiders remaining on the Oakland roster trimmed to three as Bob Dougherty was waived and the versatile Charlie Rieves was returned to defense in his place. The sputtering offense was given a minor facelift. Tom Flores would start his first game of 1963 against Boston, while Bob Mischak was returned to the guard position in front of Sonny Bishop, leaving the tight end spot to the able rookie Ken Herock. Trailing 3-0 early on, it was the tough Raiders defense that took control with Jim McMillin thieving a Babe Parilli pass intended for Gino Cappaletti on the Oakland 47-yard line and his 53-yard return captured a 7-3 lead. Cotton Davidson (in for Flores who was knocked cold completing a pass to Dobie Craig to the Boston 10) scrambled 11 yards behind the superb blocking of a reshuffled line, capping an 80-yard scoring drive, raising Oakland's tally to 14. Babe Parilli, completing only 5 passes in 20 tries cut the Oakland lead to 14-10 early in the third period before Boston defensive end Larry Eisenhauer displayed his own brand of heroics, recovering a Flores fumble on the Raiders' 25. The Patriots' offense, unable to move, settled for a field goal. On first down after the ensuing kickoff, Eisenhauer again struck for Boston, forcing Bo Roberson to fumble on the Raiders' 24. The 6-yard return by Ross O'Hanley gave Parilli the chance to capture the lead. Finding halfback Tom Neumann on the five, Parilli's strike ensured Oakland it's fourth consecutive loss in an encore of the 20-14 defeat that started their month long string of futility.

It would be nine full days from the Friday night self-destruction in Fenway Park until the Oakland Raiders faced their next opponent, the New York Jets at Frank Youell Field. Nine badly needed days of preparation and healing as the AFL's 33-man roster limit left little room for depth in case of injury, as was the case with Clem Daniels, who, for the last month had been hobbled on his best day by a deep thigh bruise that refused to heal, costing Oakland the league's leading rusher and crippling its offense. Still ranked ninth overall among AFL ball carriers, Daniels started against the Dick Wood-led Jets the current owners of the lead in the Eastern Division race with a mark of 3 wins and 2 losses. New York seemed poised to run away with their second victory over Oakland in a month after a quick 34-yard scoring toss from Wood to tight end Gene Heeter. Only performing for a quarter, Tom Flores completed 4 of his 8 attempts and shattered the first of four Raiders records to fall this day, with a 93-yard bomb to Dobie Craig the sailed 55 yards in the air to tie the score. Daniels got underway breaking two records of his own ripping off 74 of his 200 rushing yards on the day to give Oakland the lead for good at 14-7, 21-7 at the quarter's conclusion and 35-13 at the half as Davidson found Alan Miller for 8, Ken Herock from 38 and Daniels for 56-yard scores. A relaxing Raiders defense allowed six Jets points in the third quarter while the offense outscored them by one. Keeping more than enough distance between the clubs as Oakland matched two meaningless touchdowns in the fourth quarter, snapping their losing slide at home, 49-26.

This victory over a team that Jets coach Weeb Ewbank criticized for playing a lousy game moved Oakland into not so familiar territory, placing them alone in second place in the Western Division. However a mark of 3-4 put them a full three games behind the first-place Chargers, who were waiting for them at Balboa Stadium. Coming off a 4-win 10-loss season, as a series of injuries had handicapped the Southern California club. The Chargers were again healthy and, at 5-1, proving themselves not only to be the best team in the AFL, sweeping the league champion Kansas City Chiefs for two of their early victories, but one of the best in all of professional football in the process. Even to the most amateur prognosticator, San Diego seemed a sure bet to extend their lead to four games over the Raiders who hadn't played close to the Chargers late in a contest since 1960. Not even a psychic could have predicted anything other than a complete Chargers domination of the upstate rivals, including San Diego's mayor who declared this Sunday would be "Charger's Day" in his city, while television cameras for the first time in 1963 beamed a signal back to Oakland so the fans at home could witness the bludgeoning in the comfort of their living rooms. Instead, they witnessed an Arch Matsos interception on the Chargers' 38. A quick lateral to "Hoot" Gibson and a 13-yard return to the 25 set up the Oakland offense nicely three minutes into the contest. Two runs by the current AFL Player of the Week, Clem Daniels, created a third down and five situation on the 20. Eyeing Art Powell, Flores fired into the end zone for six points with his end sealing the deal with a catch over defender Dick Westmoreland and the Oakland Raiders quickly owned a 7-0 lead over the "unbeatable" San Diego Chargers. Answering quickly, San Diego returned the kickoff to their 48 then handed off to the AFL's rushing leader Paul Lowe for 17 yards and to Keith Lincoln for 13 more. Oakland's defense clamped down on the Chargers attacking unit, forcing a 23-yard George Blair field goal to preserve the lead at 7-3. San Diego's defenders reciprocated, forcing the Raiders to punt deep within their territory and securing excellent field position on their own 42. On the heels of a 10-yard run from Paul Lowe and a 15-yard catch and run from Lance Alworth, Tobin Rote spotted the former Arkansas All-American cutting in front of his former teammate "Hoot" Gibson and hit him for an easy score. Looking to avoid further failures in pass coverage, Davis ordered Fred Williamson to cover Alworth no matter where he lined up. It was a move that paid immediate dividends as Williamson stole a Rote pass and Oakland took over again, this time at the Chargers' 30. Daniels picked up twenty yards on the ground for a first and goal at the 10. Flores called on fullback Alan Miller who responded by picking up six yards on the ground and the final 4 through the air when Flores spotted him open under the goalposts, giving Oakland the lead once again, 14-10. John Hadl, wearing Dalva Allen like a bathrobe, fired low down the middle to Jacques McKinnon, who plowed through a Fred Williamson tackle on his way to a 69-yard touchdown and a Chargers lead at 17-14.

Two plays into the second half, Dick Harris stepped in front of a Davidson pass on the Oakland 10 and waltzed into the end zone adding six to San Diego's point total. A bad snap kept the Chargers from adding a seventh point but down 23-14, these Raiders, instead of folding, made their own breaks as Gibson picked up a failed lateral attempt from Lincoln to Lowe and Oakland had the ball again on the Chargers' 39. A slant pass to Dobie Craig brought the Raiders right back into the game; Mercer's conversion left Oakland trailing by two at 23-21. A San Diego field goal put them up by five and forced Oakland to shoot for the end zone to reclaim the lead and they did. Launching the ball 65 yards in the air to open the final period, Powell outfought Harris and Westmoreland for the Davidson pass and the lead again in this seesaw battle. Lincoln reclaimed the advantage for the Chargers after three and a half minutes, sweeping around the left end and outracing Fred Williamson for a 51-yard score to go ahead 33-28. The defense slowed San Diego well enough to force a punt, then Oakland's offense took over on their 37 with less than four minutes remaining, making a last-ditch effort to finally slay the mighty Southern California goliath. Daniels brought them 41 yards closer to history with a sweep to the left. Davidson scrambled for 14 more and a

Raiders' first and goal at the Charger 9-yard line. Daniels lost a yard on first down then dropped a pass on second. On third and goal from the 10 Davidson dropped back and stunned the 30,182 in attendance and a national television audience by finding reserve halfback Glenn Shaw utterly neglected in the end zone for a 34-33 lead. A two-point conversion attempt failed and the Chargers had one final gasp of their own with less than two minutes to go. Oakland's defense smothered San Diego's attackers, and exorcized the mighty demon called the Chargers

The three remaining original Raiders huddled together in a corner of the visitors' locker room, where the first tears of joy were shed by center Jim Otto, quickly followed by Wayne Hawkins and Flores who had all scraped the bottom of the AFL barrel for the past two seasons with their trio of victories and just past the half way point of the 1963 season, they had surpassed that win total.

(5)

Coach Davis rewarded his Raiders with an extra day off after their emotional win over San Diego; the young mentor spent his time deflecting the good deal of praise befalling his coaching abilities after only a few wins, yet the press and the public agreed that the Raiders' rebuilding process was well ahead of schedule and Davis reorganization of the franchise as a whole was a resounding success. Instead, the coaching prodigy (as he was beginning to be called) and his staff found themselves in another unusual yet very comfortable position, two full games ahead of the defending AFL champion Kansas City Chiefs. Yet if they were to maintain this illustrious distinction they needed to beat Kansas City in consecutive games. To complicate matters, the Oakland coaching staff was again forced to shuffle their already thin line up due to injuries incurred by Tommy Morrow and Sonny Bishop against San Diego.

Concentrating the team's practices in the areas of special teams, particularly punt returns and blocking kicks and defense to return the Raiders to their dominating ways of the season's beginning. All three would factor heavily in Oakland's ninth game. A defensive struggle ensued with the league champion Chiefs having a death grip on a 7-3 lead going into the fourth quarter. A punt to the Raiders' 15-yard line was fielded by "Hoot" Gibson. Running up the middle where Kansas City players were blocked out masterfully by his teammates, Gibson cut to the left sideline at Frank Youell Field where he outraced Chiefs punter Jerell Wilson to the end zone, establishing a new AFL mark for the longest punt return and elevating Oakland into the lead at 10-7. Len Dawson and the Chiefs offense wouldn't go down quietly; after a dropped pass in the end zone by Abner Hayes, Kansas City lined up to tie the game with a 30-yard field goal with 8 seconds remaining. Forcing his way into the Chief's backfield, Arch Matsos deflected the kick locking up Oakland's third straight victory and establishing another Raiders' team record for the longest winning streak.

Another short week, five days between contests accompanied by a trip to Missouri that prevented another day of practice. The only thing favoring either squad was that they had seen each other the Sunday before in Oakland. Hot on the heels of the first-place San Diego Chargers though still trailing by a game and a half, Al Davis' men found themselves the underdog to the league champion Chiefs. Remarkably healthier after their win against Kansas City than before it, only Warren Powers was promoted to the starting line up in relief of cornerback Jim McMillan, who was sidelined with a sprained ankle. This recent health epidemic and never-say-die approach had transformed Oakland's football franchise into the exact opposite of the club very few East Bay residents supported in seasons prior and had many convinced the Raiders were currently the leagues best team. Some of the new believers were members of the Kansas City Chiefs themselves who, unlike the week before, were dominated by these Raiders from beginning to end. Len Dawson's 6 completions in 25 attempts for 49 yards told only half of the story, the other is told in the number of yards lost by sacks, 71, leaving him with 22 fewer yards passing on the season than he had coming into the Friday night contest at Memorial Stadium. Already trailing 6-0, Jerell Wilson punted short and out of bounds on his side of the field at the 36. Flores and the opportunistic offense scored on the drives third play as Art Powell beat the single coverage he had publicly wished for a few weeks prior, pulling away from Bobby Ply then hauling in the pass in the corner of the end zone. Excellent kickoff coverage had Dawson opening deep in his own territory. A stingy defense sacked Dawson on his 6, forcing Kansas City to kick from their own end zone and into the second costly kicking error of the quarter. The ball left the punter's foot and traveled directly into the back of the goal posts then shot backward into his arms! Rewarded for his sure handedness, Wilson was crushed for a safety by Glenn Shaw and Arch Matsos.

A 15-0 lead for Oakland and possession of the ball led quickly to the three touchdowns Davis said were necessary to defeat Kansas City as Powell took a Flores rifle shot between his usual double coverage on the goal line for a 22-0 lead. Although Kansas City scored after a muffed punt by the previous week's hero "Hoot" Gibson, it would be their lone highlight as the AFL's hottest team cruised to a 22-7 triumph, extending their longest win streak into a well earned week off.

The time off from their AFL schedule gave the players ample time to heal their bumps and bruises, yet it was possibly the busiest time of year for coach Davis and his staff. Between laughing off criticism of Oakland's success being the result of the poorly executed equalization draft, the Raiders preparing for another trip eastward to Denver to meet the floundering Broncos, co-owners of last place in the Western Division with the Chiefs after their meetings with Oakland and the upcoming entry draft. Oakland's coaches worked as frantically away from the field as they had in practice and on the sidelines all season long.

All of these grand concerns were forced to take a back seat while the Raiders prepared to depart for Denver. In Dallas Texas, an assassin's bullet claimed the life of President John Fitzgerald Kennedy, who was riding in a motorcade with his wife and Texas Governor Connelly, who was also wounded in the attack. President Lyndon Johnson, sworn to his new post an hour after the shooting, immediately called for a national day of mourning upon taking office. In response, the AFL postponed all four games scheduled that weekend, while the NFL played on despite protests from hundreds of fans and in front of smaller, somber and for the most part silent crowds across the grieving nation. The Raiders-Broncos clash in Denver was rescheduled for Thanksgiving Day with all of America at home watching their televisions, badly needing a distraction as images of the tragedy were broadcast endlessly. The remainder of the league's games were rescheduled for the following Sunday.

In front of a national television audience, John McCormick fumbled in his own end zone. It was recovered by rookie half back Billy Joe who was instantly smothered by Dalva Allen and Arch Matsos, giving Oakland an early 2-0 lead from the Bronco miscue for which they were truly thankful that it wasn't a touchdown. A battle of defensive wills ensued, with Denver's Gene Mingo kicking true from 52 yards away. At halftime, the Raiders trailed 3-2. Hoping to build on the slimmest of leads, the Broncos moved into Oakland territory when a healthy Tommy Morrow stepped in front of a Don Breaux pass on the Raiders' 13 and returned it 35 yards to the 48-yard line. Davidson, again starting the second half, found Bo Roberson, who beat rookie cornerback Willie Brown for 39 yards and the game's first touchdown. On Denver's next series, Breaux again turned the ball over to Oakland's swarming defenders, fumbling while being crushed by Dave ("Fidel") Costa (a nickname given to him by teammates in training camp as he never took time out from studying his playbook to shave and his bearded appearance began to resemble Cuban dictator Fidel Castro) and the relentless Dalva Allen on the 18-yard line. The Bronco hole deepened with an opportunistic Jon Jelasic scooping up the loose ball and bolting untouched for a touchdown. Not content with a lead of 16-3, Oakland padded their lead further first with a 16-yard Mike Mercer field goal. Fights erupted throughout the next Raiders' drive that saw Alan Miller gain 35 yards on a draw play. Glenn Shaw tallied the final Raiders' score going over left tackle to bring the score to 26-3. Again, with the outcome well in hand, Oakland's defense relaxed and Denver moved 80 yards in four plays for a meaningless touchdown in a 26-10 defeat.

With Oakland's victory they found themselves with a record of 7 wins and 4 losses, guaranteeing them the best record in their history with three games remaining and ranked second overall in the American Football League, trailing only the Chargers. For the first time since the 1962 entry draft Oakland did not have the dishonor of picking first overall; that distinction now belonged to the Broncos, whose loss to the Raiders earned that right away from the floundering league champion Kansas City squad by a half game. Al Davis, assisted by Ron Wolf, easily selected Oakland's best draft for their fifth season first selecting Tony Lorick from Arizona State University, a bruising 210-lb. fullback who enjoyed contact enough for his coaches to use him as a linebacker and cornerback. Lorick had a history of getting into the end zone and could provide a dual threat in the Oakland backfield with Clem Daniels. Other notables such as Dan Conners, a defensive tackle from the University of Miami, was selected second, Boston College linebacker Bill Budness was taken fourth, another linebacker John Robert Williamson from Louisiana Tech was drafted in the ninth round along with George Bednar of Notre Dame, John Sapinsky of William and Mary and Mickey Babb of Georgia. These players, along with the others chosen and the foundation laid in Oakland, gave notice that the Raiders were only beginning a run of success by building a talent-laden ball club for seasons to come.

Having everything go right for the Raiders couldn't change the harsh reality that they still lagged two full games off the pace for the Western

Division title with first place San Diego scoring a victory during the Raiders week off prior to President Kennedy's assassination. Two things favored Oakland, their last three games of the regular season were at home in Oakland, and the first of which was against the first place team from Southern California. As the monster Al Davis helped create was set to take on his latest creation at Frank Youell Field, a new kind of beast prowled the facilities perimeter, the scalpers who were selling the normally $4.50 tickets for as little as $8 and as much as $15. The importance of the game with the home Raiders needing a victory to avoid elimination from the division race against a class outfit that was the odds-on favorite to capture their first AFL title was lost on no one. 20,249 souls braved the rain to watch not only their own Clem Daniels chase Cookie Gilchrist's single-season rushing mark of 1,096 yards but also the AFL's close second and third of Keith Lincoln and Paul Lowe. An estimated equal number of fans hoping to catch the home team's biggest game in their history thus far were turned away. This first sellout resulted in the games' local broadcast, only the third Raiders' game to be viewed by a local television audience, sending many fans into a frenzy back to their homes, homes of friends or into drinking establishments where there were televisions to witness this all-important contest. Blows were exchanged early with San Diego going up 7-0 with Don Norton hauling in a 32-yard Tobin Rote pass for the opening score. A Bob Jackson run from 14 yards away widened the gap to 11 at 14-3. Although down so quickly, the resilient Raiders' offense fooled an entire stadium, save those in Silver and Black uniforms, with a fake handoff and pass to a wide-open Art Powell who was understandably lonely without a San Diego defender within 15 yards of him to keep him company. The neglected receiver quickly covered the remaining 45 yards to glory shedding seven points of deficit to trail 14-10. With the late October upset still in mind, Rote passed the Chargers into a 20-10 lead with a Jacques MacKinnon touchdown reception from 5 yards out (Blair's extra point missed) to close out the first half and a 15-yard pass to Alworth ran the score to 27-10 halfway through the third period.

Looking to make a statement against these Raiders while wrapping up their third division title in four seasons, San Diego's offense was driving to put the game out of reach early in the fourth quarter only to have Bob Jackson hammered and lose control of the ball. Tommy Morrow recovered for Oakland and Clem Daniels gave them a quick first and goal from the 4 with a 35-yard sweep. The awakened and drenched crowd rose to see Davidson lose six yards on first down then throw incomplete on second down before finding Art Powell for his second score of the afternoon. Now down 27-17, with a shade less than 13 minutes remaining, the rejuvenated Oakland fans wondered if there was enough time to come back against one of professional football's most explosive clubs; one that would now have possession, free to burn time and possibly score again. On the drive's second play it was Paul Lowe's turn to be crushed and fumble the ball away. Joe Krakowski recovered on the San Diego 23, adding fuel to the Raider's comeback fire. The Chargers defense held and with 11:36 to go, Mike Mercer kicked a 30-yard field goal and Oakland now trailed only 27-20 erasing any doubts of a possible comeback. Oakland forced the Chargers to punt after only four plays. The snap was low and Paul Maguire kicked it on a bounce! The ball was downed on the San Diego 43. With nine minutes to go there wasn't the hurry to score anymore, yet Oakland did on a 9-yard quarterback draw that climaxed a 5-play drive tying the score at 27. With 7:54 to go, this game belonged to the Oakland Raiders and everyone in the tiny Frank Youell Field facility knew it, including the San Diego Chargers. 2:21 after the tying score Powell grabbed his third touchdown of the day taking a jump ball away from Dick Harris for a 41-yard score and the Raiders finally led 34-27.

Gillman replaced Rote with John Hadl, who managed one first down before throwing short on a fourth and 10 play on the Chargers' 38 that was intercepted by Clancy Osborne, who raced toward the end zone before being dragged down at the 12 as the fans at Frank Youell Field exploded. Roars of approval echoed until Alan Miller ended the comeback carnage with a two-yard run behind Wayne Hawkins that climaxed 31 fourth-quarter points and the Raiders pulled to within a game of the division lead with a 41-27 triumph.

The jubilation ended quickly. While Oakland was able to attract more top draft choices than before with Bill Budness and John Robert Williamson quickly coming to terms with the Raiders, Oakland's first pick, Tony Lorick, had not only agreed to be a Raider but also a Baltimore Colt very soon after. Al Davis delayed announcing Oakland had signed Lorick as Arizona State was in line for a bowl bid. However, after being signed to a deal by Los Angeles newspaper editor Brad Pye on behalf of the Raiders and accepting cash and a check as partial payment of his signing bonus, Lorick obtained the existing three copies of his deal with the Raiders from Pye, his own copy, the ones belonging to the team and to Pye claiming a desire to show them to his college coach. With Oakland now holding no evidence of this agreement, Baltimore signed him quickly. Believing

Lorick to be confused and under pressure, Davis left the legal wrangling to the league office feeling the conflicting, ever-changing stories told by both Lorick and the Colts were direct evidence of an airtight claim for Oakland should the matter be heard in court.

Sporting a mark of 8 wins and 4 losses, Oakland ranked as a heavy favorite as the AFL's worst team came to visit. In spite of public optimism, several Raiders players were again nursing more than their fair share of bruises and abrasions after another brutal physical battle with San Diego. Davis was quick to point out these ailments were slowing his squad and the physical and mental energy expended by his men against the Chargers left them exhausted leading to poor practices throughout the week. The Denver Broncos found themselves in a fine spot to assume the role of spoiler. Fielding an awful 19-yard punt on the Denver 32, the tired Raiders began to put the game away with their first offensive play. Flores found Roberson open on the 20, the sprinter reversed his field and made three Denver tacklers look foolish on his way to the end zone for the Raiders' first touchdown of the afternoon. A half-dozen minutes later, Flores led a six-play drive that featured a 35-yard reception by Ken Herock and another for 18 by Clem Daniels that was equaled by Art Powell's 18-yard scoring reception. The Broncos retaliated immediately. A screen pass to Donny Stone covered 60 yards giving Denver life at the Raiders' 17. In two plays, rookie halfback Billy Joe swept for 9 yards cutting the Oakland lead in half at 14-7. The Broncos were on the move again in the second quarter when the miserly Raiders' defense forced a field goal attempt. "Fidel" Costa batted the 48-yard Gene Mingo attempt back into Denver territory where Krakowski covered it on the 33. Flores again found his man in the end zone as Clem Daniels added 7 points to the Oakland point cache, extending the lead to 21-7. A 35-yard field goal from Mingo cut the margin to 21-10 at the half. Needing to close the door once and for all, Bo Roberson's brilliant 55-yard return got the offense started on the Denver 40. A two-yard loss by Daniels on first down sent Oakland's red-hot Flores to the air again, spotting Clem Daniels open for his second touchdown of the contest and a 28-10 lead. Finally, fatigue set in. Midway through the third quarter, Denver returned a punt to their 37, Slaughter connected with ex-Raider Gene Prebola for 58 yards for a first and goal on the Oakland 5-yard line. Losing 9 yards in two plays, Slaughter again hit Prebola, who made a circus catch over Krakowski for seven Bronco points. Playing up to their competition, Denver forced Mike Mercer to punt the ball away and the

Broncos started near midfield on their 46. Hewritt Dixon soon took it over from the two and in less than three full minutes an eighteen-point Oakland advantage had dwindled to four at 28-24.

Starting from the 20, the Raiders burned 5 minutes of precious time away with a 9-play drive that ended with Powell's second touchdown reception from three yards out. Down by 11 once more, Denver outdid the Raiders efficiency by moving 76 yards themselves in 7 plays as Lionel Taylor brought his team to within four with a 29-yard touchdown. Denver tried for the lead again twice more this day, the first opportunity resulted in a punt and the second was intercepted by Fred Williamson on the Oakland 18. This final bit of misfortune ruined the Broncos' chances and the Raiders hung on to win their seventh consecutive contest, 35-31.

Still a game off the pace with one more to be played, Oakland's hopes of capturing the Western Division crown were turning to a whisper and a prayer with San Diego hosting the AFL's cellar dwellers from Denver to finish off their slate with the Raiders playing host to the three-time defending Eastern Division champion Houston Oilers. Sporting a passing attack capable of dousing crude on any title contender in their way, Oakland needed to fend off this challenge and get help from the Broncos to force a playoff game against the Chargers in San Diego (the site for this potential tie-breaker was decided by a coin toss at the league offices) despite the Raiders sweep of their in-state rival. Al Davis, the unanimous choice for Coach of the Year honors led his four offensive (Jim Otto, Clem Daniels, Art Powell and Wayne Hawkins) and four defensive (Fred Williamson, Arch Matsos, Tommy Morrow and Dave Costa) AFL All-Stars into battle at Frank Youell Field for a wild exhibition of aerial warfare. Though George Blanda was held on Houston's first possession, "Hoot" Gibson supplied the first shot of lightning by returning the ensuing punt 58 yards for the afternoon's first score. Blanda quickly responded with a pair of touchdowns. A pass to Charlie Hennigan and another quick drive that ended with a Dave Smith touchdown run from the 2, closing out the opening stanza with a 14-7 Oilers' lead. Blanda's third scoring pass, connecting with Willard Dewvall for 12 yards extended the Houston lead to 14. The resilient Raiders fired back with two touchdown passes from Flores, the first a 7-yard toss to Ken Herock followed by a 56-yard strike to Clem Daniels to knot the score again. Touchdowns would be traded twice more in the opening half as Houston reclaimed their lead with Dave Smith's second touchdown, a 25-yard reception, only to have the Flores-Powell connection strike again with an 81-yard bomb matching Houston at 28. Attempting to slow the Raiders by keeping their defenders on the field, Oilers coach Pop Ivy instructed George Blanda to run time off the clock, calling running plays and short passes, controlling the ball until 1:09 remained in the half when Charlie Tolar joined the scoring orgy giving Houston the lead again 35-28. Not to be outdone, Flores moved his Raiders to the Oiler 20, with six seconds remaining, the quarterback found his favorite target as Powell worked himself open in the end zone and brought the Oakland club back yet again. As time expired the exhausted scoreboard read Oakland 35, Houston 35 and George Blanda could be heard complaining on his way to the locker room "we've scored enough points to win two games but we're still tied with these sons of bitches!"

The Raiders got the ball to begin the second half. Clem Daniels who collected all but three of the yards he needed in the opening half to reach 1,000 yards on the season, started with a 27-yard gallop to set up Oakland's sixth touchdown of the day, a 46-yard Flores to Powell laser between two defenders in the end zone. Powell's third touchdown gave Oakland its second lead in the wildest of ball games at 42-35. Houston required only four plays to place themselves in position and a fifth to erase the Oakland lead again with Willard Dewvall's second touchdown reception, this time from 26 yards. With more than seven minutes on the clock in the third quarter one was certain in this game. The offensive onslaught on display through its first 38 minutes had yet to run it course. Houston was first to show a flash of defensive prowess in the second half forcing Oakland to punt and rewarding themselves by being the first team to reach the 49-point plateau with 2:22 remaining in the third period. Flores was intercepted, as was Blanda by All-Star linebacker Arch Matsos on the Houston 24. Everyone in attendance knew the pass was coming to Art Powell, everyone except the Houston Oilers, who again were made to look foolish by Powell's mastery and record setting fourth touchdown reception to tie the score again, at 49 points. Houston drove deep again but "Hoot" Gibson's second interception halted the Oiler drive on the goal line. Taking over at the 20 after a touchback, Daniels, who had been quietly amassing big yardage underneath the 98 points residing on the scoreboard, was called on often in this drive, running his club to the Oilers' 32. Mike Mercer split the uprights from 39 yards earning Oakland the lead again at 52-49. The Raiders' best defensive effort of the day followed, halting Houston, who chose to punt away on their last drive.

As Clem Daniels remained 1 yard behind Cookie Gilchrist for the AFL single-season rushing crown, he took the handoff from Davidson on the games final play picking up four more yards for a grand total 1,099 for the season and earning his place as the league's all-time single season rushing champion and finally unseated the Houston Oilers as Eastern Division champions. Inside the locker room post-game, Raiders' players and staff huddled around a small transistor radio and transformed themselves into the most ardent supporters the Denver Broncos had ever known. With their new favorites trailing 33-20 some optimism arose as the Broncos at least had a chance to come back, however this was not to be as the Chargers pulled away first at 36-20, then 42 and finally a 56-20 ending, clinching the AFL's Western Division championship for the third time in four years. The Chargers went on to crush the Eastern Division champs from Boston 51-10 for their first league crown. With the locker room almost empty except for coach Al Davis, his young son Mark and a couple of lingering reporters, Davis summed up his rookie campaign eloquently, stating "It's been a hell of a year."

CHAPTER FIVE
SOPHOMORE JINX 1964

The Oakland Raiders record setting nine-game turn-around in 1963 went unnoticed by virtually no one. Pulling a clean sweep in being acknowledged as Coach of the Year by the AFL, the Associated Press, United Press International and the Sporting News, Al Davis, in his first year as an Oakland resident, was also named Oakland's Outstanding Young Man of the Year by the Oakland Junior Chamber of Commerce, who proclaimed he had done more in the final half of 1963 to promote Oakland as a big-league city than their civic leaders had done since the turn of the twentieth century. Welcomed by standing ovations for his accomplishments at awards ceremonies throughout the Bay Area, the Raiders dynamic young leader informed the press and public alike that it was unrealistic to consider his squad a contender for a Western Division title in 1964, saying his greatest accomplishment was developing a sense of pride in the organization and remaining poised no matter what the scoreboard read or the time remained. As local leaders and fans were asked to adopt his "pride and poise" posture, Davis found several eager takers among his new draft picks.

Following the lead of Bill Budness, Dan Conners and J.R. Williamson, eight of Oakland's top ten draftees quickly inked their deals, accepting Oakland as a sound team in a legitimate league. However when Davis went to deal for veteran ball players who could contribute immediately, he found himself an unwelcome commodity in the trade market as teams, especially the talent-rich Chargers and Chiefs, were unwilling to have their castoffs spun to gold in their own division by Oakland's Rumpelstiltskin.

Instead, he would rely upon his returning veterans, featuring eight members of the AFL All-Star roster, including the league's second ranked passer Tom Flores and the AFL's Most Valuable Player Clem Daniels, who himself became the target of trade talks with Buffalo's Cookie Gilchrist demanding a trade and expressing his desire to be an Oakland Raider. Though admitting to be interested in the Buffalo powerhouse if an equitable trade could be arranged, there was no way the Raiders would part with Daniels. Art Powell, planning to relocate his family back to Toronto suggested himself in trade for the disgruntled Bill. Buffalo was less than 100 miles from his preferred Canadian home where Powell had several off-season business opportunities. This was vetoed first by Davis then squashed once and for all by Buffalo coach Lou Saban, who made it clear that Gilchrist would remain a Buffalo Bill through 1964 and beyond.

It was the Bills who finally made a deal with Oakland at the league's summer meetings. Leroy Jackson, a reserve halfback and former #1 draft choice of the Cleveland Browns in 1962, would reunite with Lou Saban, his former college mentor at Western Illinois for tackle Ken Rice, a two-time All-American tackle at Auburn and 1961 Rookie of the Year runner-up. Surprised to be dealt, the 255-lb. Rice fit well into Davis' plans to add bulk to his offensive line and was a potential starter with Ollie Spencer serving only as an assistant coach. In the absence of Tony Lorick, Oakland also dealt away their eighth overall draft choice to Houston for fullback Bo Dickinson. A four-year veteran of three AFL squads, Dickinson was a pass-catching threat hauling in 60 tosses in 1962 for 554 yards and four Denver Bronco touchdowns.

The final bit of player business other than the lingering Lorick mess was Davis' useless protest of the New York Jets' signing of kicker/quarterback Jim Turner. The league's hierarchy again ignored Davis' claim that the Jets needed Oakland's approval to sign any player entering the AFL after being discarded by the Washington Redskins as they had when players with rights held by Oakland signed elsewhere in the league. An East Bay native, Turner remained a New York Jet as current Raiders players from all over the country were setting down blue-collar roots in the East Bay.

Clem Daniels AKA coach Daniels found off-season employment at Oakland's Skyline High School, teaching physical education and mentoring the schools' wrestling program. Fred Williamson worked as an architect designing a beautiful park in the city of Fremont with a manmade lake (known as Lake Elizabeth), adjacent swim lagoon, picnic, and elaborate play areas. Broadcaster Bo Roberson, whose weekly radio sports talk show was heard on the Raiders flagship station KDIA Radio, was enrolled in Wells Fargo Bank's management training program, while others such as Tom Flores learned the real estate developing trade. Arch Matsos served as a sales representative for a glass company and penned a booklet titled "Inside Pro Football" as a part of his sales pitch. Others accepted jobs distributing liquor, sales and rentals of heavy equipment, cement sales and other types of industry throughout the area.

The construction business in Oakland was set for a major boom. The Oakland city council approved the addition of nearly 4,200 seats to Frank Youell Field, contingent upon the Raiders' successful negotiation of a new lease for the facility. With delays and legal wrangling mercifully out of the way, construction was set to begin on the new multi purpose Oakland Alameda County Coliseum and Arena, scheduled for completion in the spring and summer (for the adjacent arena) of 1966 and available to the Raiders beginning that season. While expressing a sincere interest in relocating his team to Oakland, Kansas City Athletics owner Charles O. Finley was forced into a 4-year agreement in his current home under the threat of franchise revocation. Enthusiastic Oakland officials went scrambling to accommodate the Athletics at Frank Youell Field until the American League's heavy-handed action. Now should the A's still choose to come west when their new lease expired, they would reside in a new, state of the art facility capable of holding 45,000 baseball fans, while a few thousand more seats could easily be added for the original, intended occupants, the Oakland Raiders, with scaffolding and some of the 12,000 extra seats Coliseum Inc. had purchased from Frank Youell Field for $96,000.

(2)

It was an exciting time for the American Football League. A new broadcast agreement with the National Broadcast Company (NBC) worth $36 million dollars payable over five years was to take effect in 1965, with each of the AFL's eight franchises assured nearly $900,000 in annual revenue, enabling them to operate at a profit, compete with the NFL in signing draft picks and established veteran players and afford the leases on the new, state of the art facilities being erected for their use. This new deal was equitable with the NFL's, whose new broadcast deal with CBS worth $28.2 million over two years, brought the NFL's fourteen clubs nearly $2,000,000 each over that time.

Now on par with the older National League financially, many in the AFL felt they were equal to them on the field. Immediately following the Chargers 51-10 desecration of the Boston Patriots in the AFL championship game, coach Gillman made a challenge for a game between his squad and the Chicago Bears. Commissioner Foss spoke optimistically about a playoff between the leagues saying many NFL owners and players were in favor of a system similar to that of Major League Baseball, whose American and National League teams played within their respective leagues through out the regular season and playoffs, with the champions from both leagues meeting for one final contest to decide professional footballs' ultimate champion.

With the AFL's impending financial success, the league voted unanimously to recognize the AFL Players Association, agreeing to provide the players a pension, life insurance and a hospitalization plan for the players and their families. The teams themselves grew in 1964. First looking to raise squad limits to as high as 40 players, the AFL instead chose to match the NFL again by allowing each club a 35-man roster as their rival raised their limit from 35 to 37 men. The number of 35-man rosters was also examined. Investors from across the United States and a pair in Canada had designs of AFL franchise ownership. Feeling the time wasn't right for league expansion, the door for future growth was left open while Dave Dixon, a New Orleans investor who sought a franchise initially, lobbied the American League for an All-Star game in his city between the AFL's top talent against the finest from the NFL. As players and owners from both sides sought unity, NFL commissioner Rozelle quickly dampened their hopes, declaring there would be no inter-league play of any kind, adding tension between the leagues at the executive level that would only increase.

The Raiders themselves had already suffered casualties in this struggle as recently as the entry draft. As usual, Davis was left to handle the matter himself. Seeking a meeting with Tony Lorick and Baltimore Colts management to resolve the issues surrounding the fullback's double signing, he ultimately found himself dealing with commissioner Rozelle. First tabled for several days, while Davis found himself involved in another double signing snarl with coach Vince Lombardi of the Green Bay Packers over the services of recently signed Jan Barrett, whom Lombardi claimed was "loaned" to Oakland. When the commissioner finally addressed the Lorick matter, news for the Raiders was expectedly bad. Because Lorick had regained and allegedly destroyed all copies of his agreement with Oakland, none were available to be presented to the NFL's head-man, who, in turn, declared Tony Lorick property of the Baltimore Colts. In a telegram sent to Rozelle from Brad Pye, the Raiders representative blasted the commissioner for setting a precedent that could destroy professional football. Pointing to statements Lorick made to the press, the returned bonus checks from the player were ample evidence of his agreement with Oakland. Rozelle dismissed the matter once and for all, charging the Raiders as unethical by using a newspaperman to represent them, leaving the matter between the Baltimore Colts (who later that summer were banned from the campuses of all eight AAWU schools, including the Universities of Southern California and Washington State, over their signing practices of red-shirted players), the Oakland Raiders and the courts.

The Billy Cannon double signing, first a predated agreement with the Rams of the NFL, (with Pete Rozelle serving as their general manager) and then with the Oilers after Bud Adams agreed to double his salary had set precedent. Upon learning of the Louisiana State fullback's intentions, Rozelle warned Cannon at the Sugar Bowl that the Rams would take legal action against him and the Oilers if he we're to sign again. Already under contract to Houston at this time, Cannon put on a show for the fans in attendance and those watching on television after LSU's 7-0 victory over Clemson, where Cannon threw for the game's only score. Walking into the end zone immediately following the contest, he signed another contract with Houston and informed the world he was now professional football's highest paid player with a $100,000 salary to be paid over four years, a $10,000 gift for his wife and the possibility of business opportunities in the Houston area. The judge who heard the matter as brought forth by Rozelle and the Rams, sided with Cannon feeling the player should be entitled to as much as possible for his services. With this in mind Oakland let the matter go and Lorick became a Baltimore Colt. Barrett remained a Raider.

With their star defector lost, the Oakland Raiders opened their second summer training session at Santa Rosa's El Rancho Motel with 55 bodies looking to fill 35 roster spots. The lineup started taking shape as the new veterans and rookies reported to camp first. Charlie Rieves and rookie fullback Doug Mayberry were let go in an early wave of player cuts. The Oakland Raiders opened their fifth camp without two vital cogs in their offensive machine. Fullback Alan Miller would miss the entire 1964 season to pursue his law degree at Boston University (where he was the editor of the school's law review and eventually graduated second in his class) and receiver Art Powell. Having requested a trade, Powell was reportedly reminded that he was under contract to Oakland by the Toronto Argonauts of the Canadian Football League. Powell reported, eight days later than mandated. A late-night meeting with coach Davis was held to iron out any issues arising from his absence while Powell relocated his family. Dismissing his tardiness in the press the receiver promised to build upon his 16 touchdowns the season prior by hauling in 20 scoring aerials in 1964. A confident Clem Daniels also reported with his goal of amassing 1,500 yards in 1964, feasible with his record setting 1,099 yards in 1963 coming despite his missing or seeing limited action in four games the year before. Davis was more cautious about his club's chances to repeat the 10-4 heroics of the season past and his odds were dealt a major blow by the surprise retirement of guard Bob Mischak. Claiming to have lost the desire to play, the former three-time All-AFL guard ended his playing days to spend time with his family and return to the teaching trade or reinstate his registry on the New York Stock Exchange. Unfortunately for Davis and his Raiders, Kansas City had loosened their belts and offered a trade for Mischak, offering linebacker Sherrill Headrick for the guard a few weeks earlier. The deal was vetoed when Mischak assured Davis he intended to both play and remain a Raider. Mischak returned to Oakland in a few weeks following a change of heart.

Moving forward with those remaining, Raiders coaches trained players at new positions in case the starters in those spots fell to injuries or unforeseen events such as the Mischak retirement. Dick Klein drilled at the center position should the indestructible Jim Otto be unavailable. Herculean linebacker Dan Birdwell was given a look at the defensive tackle spot behind McMurtrey and Costa while kicker Mike Mercer took snaps as the teams third quarterback behind Flores and Davidson. As injuries occurred throughout the Raiders roster, primarily on the offensive line and throughout the linebacking corps, the result early in the preseason was an Oakland team that was not up to task with a Kansas City Chiefs club that resembled their championship form of two seasons prior than their 5-win, 7-loss, 2-tie encore. A 33-yard Cotton Davidson pass to

Powell put Oakland up 7-6. But an interception, followed by a pair of receptions, first by Solomon Brannan to the one-yard line before a Jack Spikes catch reclaimed the Chiefs lead at halftime 13-7. Fifty-seven yards were consumed over 11 plays to begin the second half as Brannan hauled in an 11-yard Ed Wilson scoring toss. Another pass, fielded by Fred Arbanas, added two more to the Kansas City total and the Chiefs were the proud owners of a 21-7 lead. Pitching three second half interceptions and having four passes batted by Buck Buchanan, Kansas City's cushion became insurmountable as Oakland's lone scoring drive in the second-half came so late in the contest there was no chance for them to repeat and the Raiders dropped their opening exhibition at Youell Field 21-14.

Blaming mental breakdowns for the loss, coach Davis had only one day of practice to prepare his squad for a Friday-night exhibition against the Broncos at Bear Stadium. It was a game, which featured a pair of Clem Daniels touchdown receptions, from Cotton Davidson for 11 yards in the first quarter to put Oakland ahead for good at 7-0 and a third period bomb from Tom Flores that covered 62 yards and brought the score to 17-0 in Oakland's favor. Hewritt Dixon's 1-yard touchdown reception from Mickey Slaughter got Denver on the scoreboard in a 20-7 Oakland victory. But instead of preparing for football, Davis and his coaching staff arguably should have given their charges karate lessons to combat the cheap shots and foul play which had Broncos coach Jack Faulkner apologizing post game. Four players, a pair from each squad, were ejected during the fracas. First Ken Herock and Denver's Tom Erlandson were ejected for trading forearm shivers in the first quarter. Then, in his last act as a professional football player, Chuck McMurtrey was ordered to shower early for retaliating against Denver center Jerry Sturm who himself was ejected later on for decking linebacker Clancy Osborne from behind, a full 20 seconds after the previous play had been whistled dead while he spoke with an official. The act drew condemnation in the press box from Colorado area sports writers who suggested openly that someone repay him in kind. "Hoot" Gibson would, after another cheap shot against a teammate, igniting a sideline-clearing brawl that lasted several minutes.

Except for a shoulder injury suffered by Dave Costa that was unrelated to the on-field fisticuffs, the Raiders came out of their surprise battle royal relatively unscathed. They returned to their Santa Rosa training facility with nine days to prepare for their next contest against the Bills. This long layoff gave Davis a prime opportunity to try his magic in the trade market once again. Bob Jackson arrived in Santa Rosa from the fullback rich San

Diego Chargers before the announcement of his acquisition could reach the press. The 6'3" 228-lb. Jackson was thrilled with the deal that sent him north as he eagerly awaited some playing time, which he lacked on Sid Gillman's squad behind Keith Lincoln. Jackson's size and blocking ability provided some much needed pass protection for Flores and Davidson, who had spent a great deal of time on their backs in the exhibition season's opening loss to the Chiefs.

Chuck McMurtrey's retirement following the Denver debacle cleared the way for Dan Birwell to assume his duties on the defensive line. Unfortunately in the short term for coach Davis and his Raiders, Birdwell would soon depart the team to tend to a family emergency in Texas missing practice all week and Dave Costa, hospitalized with a shoulder injury, left them skeletal at the defensive tackle position, just in time to face the Buffalo Bills with a scrambling quarterback in Jack Kemp and a pair of bruising backs in Gilchrist and Wray Carlton, who wore down the league's best defensive fronts when they are 100% healthy. This gave the Bills an evident edge over the Raiders in Oakland. Gilchrist scored first for Buffalo midway through the first period from a yard out and the Hungarian refugee Pete Gogolak, who reestablished Cornell University's kicking records, was now threatening to revolutionize the pro football kicking game with his soccer-style kicks was true only once in the first half on three attempts into a swirling wind for a 10-0 halftime lead. Nearly perfect as he opened the second half, Tom Flores moved the offense 82 yards in 10 plays. Slamming over from the 6-inch line, Glenn Shaw cut the Buffalo lead to 10-7. The Bills responded by opening the floodgates, scoring three touchdowns in five minutes. First on a 1-yard quarterback sneak from relief passer Daryle Lamonica that capped a 69-yard, 8-play march. Oakland then chose to contribute to the Bills' fortunes first with a Bo Roberson fumble of the kick off on the Raiders 10, setting up Leroy Jackson's run to glory on first down. An errant toss from Flores was fielded by rookie defensive back Butch Byrd, who raced 54 yards to give the Bills a 31-7 lead with less than six minutes remaining in the third quarter.

Byrd's interception was the only blemish on Flores' outstanding 13 of 16 outing as Oakland's field general ignited the offense again as he had to begin the half, directing a 91-yard, 9-play march that ended with the quarter as Art Powell made a spectacular 36-yard catch in the end zone that drew the accusation from Buffalo coach Lou Saban, that he was the planet's best receiver. Still down 17 as the final quarter began, the Raiders' defenders halted Buffalo forcing their kicking game to again face the whipping Oakland wind and Paul Maguire's punt sailed only 15 yards. Taking over in Bills' territory, Flores, on second and 6 found Powell open again deep, this time from 41 yards as coach Saban's argument of Powell's greatness was made stronger as Oakland chiseled another seven from the Buffalo lead and trailed by ten, 31-21 with less than two minutes gone in the final period. The wind was again a factor as Gogolak's 39-yard kick came up a yard shy and was returned a yard beyond its point of origin to the 40. Following a 20-yard Jan Barrett reception Oakland pulled within a field goal as Flores again found Powell for a score, his third in less than seven minutes.

The Raiders' defense held for the remainder of the contest forcing two punts. Both Raiders' possessions resulted in Mike Mercer's field goals. First a career long 46-yard boot to tie the game with 3:47 remaining despite the wind that haunted Buffalo's kickers the entire day and one from 32 yards to earn Oakland a slim 34-31 victory over the astounded Buffalo Bills and astonished the 10,243 Raiders fans on hand who, 15 minutes of game time earlier, had resigned themselves to a loss. Playing like the red-hot club that tattooed the scoreboard for 31 fourth-quarter points for a comeback victory over San Diego the past December, the Raiders took their show on the road to one of the few places on earth that could be as hot as they seemingly were, the Nevada desert, to face the Houston Oilers at Las Vegas' Cashman Field. The Oilers, wanting to evaluate their rookie talent, started seven first-year men against Oakland including Scott Appleton, the 250-lb. All-American from the University of Texas and beneficiary of a $140,000 signing bonus while the AFL's former highly compensated rookie Billy Cannon spent most of the game on the bench having fallen out of favor with the new Oilers coach Sammy Baugh. Despite being Houston's leading rusher in the exhibition season Cannon reported to camp weighing 228-lbs. and, according to his new coach, was unable to carry it.

With the kickoff time pushed back to 8:30 pm local time for the desert weather to cool and to lower the player's risk of heat stroke, the 90-degree temperature when play commenced did nothing to slow the black wearing Oakland Raiders. Clem Daniels tore off 68 yards of real estate late in the opening period. Aided by the opening created by Jim Otto and sprung by a thunderous block from Bob Jackson, Daniels beat Houston's final pursuer at the enemy 30 and captured a 7-0 lead. Having seen enough of rookie quarterback Don Trull by the halfway point of the second period, coach Baugh replaced him with his reliable veteran

George Blanda, who promptly threw the first of his four interceptions and the first of two by Tommy Morrow, who returned this first theft 7 yards to the Oilers' 39-yard line. Unable to get a first down, Oakland settled for a 38-yard field goal and a 10-0 lead that grew again quickly. Joe Krakowski intercepted another ill-advised toss from Blanda and set his offense up near midfield. Moving in close, the officiating crew overturned a 3-yard Fred Gillette touchdown catch and Oakland settled for three more points from Mercer's foot only to have their lead expand again in two plays. Blanda's third interception of the quarter by Fred Williamson, who returned the ball to the Houston 20, preceded a 20-yard scramble from Cotton Davidson, whose downfield receivers provided him with excellent blocking for a 20-0 lead at halftime.

The neutral site spectators, split in their allegiance during the opening half rekindled their love affair with the underdog, became Houston fans as the game's second half began and the turncoats were rewarded with a 12-play, 73-yard drive that culminated in a 21-yard Charley Tolar touchdown reception. A poor snap sent kicker George Blanda back looking to pass for two points instead of the intended one, only to be crushed back on the 25-yard line by rookie defensive tackle Rex Mirich. Daniels roared again in response to the Oiler uprising, rambling for 44 yards in one run on the ensuing drive as the Raiders advanced 80 yards in seven plays before he reached the end zone for the second time from four yards out. Utilizing short passes to Charlie Tolar and the bench warming Billy Cannon, Houston found success again in thirteen plays with the former LSU Tiger Cannon scoring from the 1 to bring the Oilers to within 27-13 as the third quarter reached its conclusion. The Houston defense played up to its competition in the game's latter stages, pitching a fourth-quarter, shutout but any hopes of the now Oiler friendly crowd seeing a miraculous comeback were thwarted as Blanda threw his fourth and final interception. Tommy Morrow returned his final theft 32 yards for another Raiders' touchdown extending the lead to 34-13. With Jacky Lee traded to Denver, Don Trull returned to action for the Oilers as Blanda found himself benched for his poor showing. Trull took full advantage of his second chance and moved Houston for one final score en route to a 34-20 defeat.

With the next game billed as the "Nothing Bowl" by the Oakland press, the 3-1 Raiders made the trip from the sweltering desert to the sunny and still quite warm Southern California, to square off against the San Diego Chargers. It was a game coach Davis would love to have skipped altogether as the typically fierce Raiders/Chargers battle took its toll in injuries right before the 1964 season was set to begin. Rookie linebacker Dan Conners, starting his third exhibition game, was rushed to the hospital in the second quarter with a shoulder injury. Rex Mirich suffered an injury to his foot while Wayne Hawkins sat out most of the contest with an ailment, which added to the injury woes of an Oakland team that was already missing Arch Matsos, who was hospitalized in Oakland with a viral infection. The warriors from Oakland asked no quarter and the enemy from San Diego obliged as Tobin Rote passed for two touchdowns to Don Norton while Gerry McDougall gained 128 yards on the ground to counter the opening Mike Mercer field goal that gave the Raiders a fleeting 3-0 lead, which they lost on the next Chargers' possession and never regained. Trailing 21-3 in the second half, Davidson replaced Flores, who was given the starting call in this contest and moved the offense 64 yards in 5 plays going the final four yards himself on a rollout play that served as Oakland's lone highlight. The Chargers added another field goal and sent Oakland into the regular season hobbling and on notice that their main competition was as ferocious as ever.

With the regular season set to begin within a week and the league-mandated final cut downs a mere two days ahead, coach Davis in a matter of speaking made the necessary trim easier by first sending three players, flanker Dobie Craig, guard Sonny Bishop and fullback Bob Jackson to Houston in exchange for Billy Cannon. With Cannon, Oakland added a potent fullback to complement halfback Clem Daniels in the offensive backfield. Having both a size and speed advantage over Daniels, the Raiders plans for their new #33 was to involve him in the passing game, drawing coverage away from the often double and triple teamed Art Powell as well as bolster the Oakland ground game, which had faired poorly at times during exhibition play. The following day Davis made a deal with Buffalo that more resembled highway robbery as a draft pick was sent east for receiver Bill Miller whose 69 receptions in 1963 were second in the AFL to Art Powell's 73.

With the headline grabbing moves made leading up to the regular season opener the always cautious Davis gave the Oakland media a brief history lesson, the Oakland Raiders had never won a single game in the papers and warned the Boston Patriots were inclined to keep it that way.

Despite the optimism from his players and a nod from the odds-makers, the Raiders were down six men with injuries and three more familiar with Oakland's schemes were dealt away in the Cannon swap. Davis instead fielded a shorthanded team at Frank Youell Field with his new fullback seeing limited action as a blocker and the aching Bill Miller took in the seasons' first contest from the sidelines. A prime spot to observe his new team, which was pinned deep in their own territory, march 95 yards in 10 plays with the aid of two major Boston penalties accounting for 37 yards. A pass interference penalty committed in the end zone gave Oakland a first and goal from the 1. Glenn Shaw followed a push from Jim Otto and Bob Mischak and the Raiders took their first lead of 1964 at 7-0. The lead held until midway through the second quarter, when journeyman quarterback Babe Parilli caught his former mates sleeping on a third and 17 play from his 28 and placed a perfectly thrown ball into the hands of Art Graham on the Oakland 25. Graham had a step on Joe Krakowski, and widened the gap post reception and the game was knotted following a Gino Cappaletti conversion. Parilli struck again through the air in the third quarter, locating tight end Tony Romeo, whose diving touchdown catch gave the Patriots a lead they would not relinquish. Following a Cappaletti field goal, Oakland's pride and poise surfaced and the offense made a spectacular drive of its own, including Billy Cannon's first carry in silver and black that gained 18 desperately needed yards. Powell's diving 33-yard touchdown catch pulled Oakland to within a field goal at 17-14. Though the Raiders' offense created opportunities for victory, misfortune plagued them as Mike Mercer's game-tying field goal hit the cross bar and bounced back into the field of play. The next Oakland drive failed on the Patriots' 3-yard line as Clem Daniels, enduring the worst game of his football life in a −1 yard performance committed his fourth fumble taking the handoff from Flores. In their last gasp, coach Davis played to win instead of tie by calling a pass play to Powell (which was batted down by Boston's Ross O' Hanley) instead of attempting a 42-yard field goal. Aiming his criticism at the play of his MVP halfback and at himself, neither Davis nor his players made any excuse for the loss owning up to their failures by admitting "we blew it."

After releasing cornerback Jim McMillin and placing five of his thirty-five players on various injury lists, Davis and his assistants took their Raiders on their annual journey to Jeppeson Stadium to face the Houston Oilers. These various ailments, were coupled with the benching epidemic on the Oakland sideline that saw Cotton Davidson coming in before his normal second-half appearance as Flores had two passes intercepted and returned for touchdowns. Reserves Ken Rice and Dick Klein took over on the offensive line, likewise for Glenn Shaw at the fullback position as Houston handed the Raiders their worst defeat of the Al Davis era.

Ahead 14-0 at the end of the opening quarter and 28-14 at halftime, the Oilers made quick work of Oakland in the third quarter as halfback Sid Blanks tore off 68 yards running to his right giving Houston a first and goal on the Raiders 4. Bob Jackson reacquainted himself with his former club on third down taking a handoff and scoring from the 1. Rookie safety Bennie Nelson stole a Flores pass on the Raiders 45 and raced in for a Houston end zone encore. The scoreboard reflected a 42-14 Houston lead with 3:45 remaining in the third quarter. With Flores sitting, Cotton Davidson mounted two scoring drives, the first covering 85 yards in 9 plays, all passes with 6 completions, three to Ken Herock and the final 19 yards by Daniels with almost 10 minutes remaining in the contest. One final scoring reception by Daniels from 22 yards away in the final minute brought Oakland to within two touchdowns as the Raiders fell to Houston 42-28 and to 0-2 on the season.

Upon their return to Frank Youell Field the Oakland team was beginning a season long re-shuffling process, as three veteran players, Glenn Shaw, cornerback Mark Johnston and linebacker Jackie Simpson were released while three others were moved. Guard Ken Rice was moved out to tackle in relief of the injured Proverb Jacobs; Rex Mirich resumed his role at left defensive tackle while Dan Birdwell was shifted left for a spot at defensive end. Behind him, replacing the departed Simpson was rookie Bill Budness, making way for Arch Matsos who had finally recuperated from the viral infection that had him hospitalized as the season began. Buffalo's 30-3 drubbing of San Diego the eve of the week three Oakland-Kansas City clash raised the stakes in this contest as the winner would gain no less than a tie for the AFL's Western Division lead while the loser would find themselves the sole proprietor of the division cellar. Playing like a pair of winless clubs, Oakland answered a 7-0 Chiefs' lead with three Mike Mercer field goals for a 9-7 advantage at the end of the third quarter. Shifting gears from a double tight end running offense to a high-octane passing attack, Hank Stram's squad reclaimed the lead four plays into the final period. Len Dawson unloaded a 56-yard bomb to Abner Haynes, who cut past linebacker Clancy Osborne for the go-ahead score. The Raiders managed two more first downs before punting away to Kansas City, who took over deep in their territory on the 6. Dawson's bombs were falling into the hands of his receivers with two aerials covering better than 35 yards, including Haynes' 39-yard touchdown, condemning Oakland to a 21-9 loss and at 0-3, the league's worst record.

Winless months, such as September 1964 were a familiar occurrence to the Oakland Raiders' organization, however it was an unfamiliar and unwelcome circumstance for their coach, who moved Ken Rice back to his natural guard position, switched Frank Youso from right to left tackle while Dick Klein covered Youso's former position at right tackle while a pair of new faces, 6'8" 270-lb. defensive end "Big" Ben Davidson (who would soon be dubbed "The Tree" by the press) and rookie defensive back Howie Williams showed well enough in practice that they would face the Buffalo Bills in War Memorial Stadium on the first stop of Oakland's yearly three-week sojourn to the Northeast. The 36,451 on hand at "The Rock Pile" by far constituted the largest audience ever assembled to witness the Oakland Raiders. Perhaps it was the large crowd, or the new blood in the lineup, or the gift airmailed to Tommy Morrow on the Oakland 7-yard line he returned 77 yards before the safety was dragged down from behind by the face mask by Joe Auer, that added 15 yards to the return to give Oakland a first and goal from the Bills' 8-yard-line. For a brief, flailing moment, the Raiders appeared to have life for the first time in their fifth season. Penalties and dropped passes nullified two touchdown plays on the opening drive as the Black and Silver team settled for a quick 18-yard field goal. The undefeated Bills came right back with a 67-yard drive to the Oakland 13-yard line before Cookie Gilchrist was met hard by four defenders on a fourth and 1 play, lost a yard and the possession on downs. This second sign of life was squashed as Flores' struggles continued with his deep pass stolen on the Buffalo 8 by Booker Edgerson and returned to the Bills' 27. Ten plays later Buffalo found themselves on the Raiders' 9-yard line as Jack Kemp, rolling to his right, found daylight and put his squad ahead 7-3. Cotton Davidson took the reigns of Oakland's offense in the second half and maneuvered 85 yards in 6 plays. Displaying his own magic on a 6-yard quarterback draw, Oakland had their second lead of the afternoon at 10-7. Pinned deep, Kemp threw his second interception to Morrow on the Bills 18, however linebacker Harry Jacobs picked off a poor toss by Davidson in the end zone for a Bills' touchback. Coach Saban took his turn in benching a quarterback and with Daryle Lamonica at the helm, the Buffalo offense accelerated. A 19-yard pass to Ernie Warlick and another to Cookie Gilchrist for 29 more put Buffalo on the Raiders' 1-yard line. Lamonica scored on a sneak and Buffalo reclaimed the lead 14-10. Billy Cannon sparked the Raiders with a 44-yard kickoff return and the offensive unit moved to the Bills 12-yard line. Stalling, Mercer connected and brought his squad to within a point. Looking to recapture the lead with a single stroke, Davidson fired a missile to Art Powell that was intercepted by rookie phenomenon Butch Byrd. A short return and a facemask on Powell gave Buffalo the ball on the Oakland 41. Striking on the third play, Lamonica connected with Elbert Dubenion for the Bills' third touchdown and the Raiders trailed by 10 when Davidson was hammered in the end zone for a safety. Buffalo was looking to add to the Oakland deficit with a Pete Gogolak field goal, when the Raiders fortunes changed as Rex Mirich put a hand on the ball, batting it down with less than five minutes to play. Oakland was in business just beyond the enemy 40. Pulling to within a field goal in just five plays, Davidson spotted Jan Barrett open in the end zone with 2:33 to go. As time was running out Oakland's defense forced a critical three and out series and Paul Maguire's punt sailed into the end zone for a touch back. 80 yards from victory with a little more than a minute remaining, Davidson threw to Powell for 22 yards, to Billy Cannon three times, once for 6 yards, then for 5 following an incompletion and for 14 on the games' final play where Cannon turned inside to gain additional yardage instead of out of bounds to stop the clock, enabling coach Davis to decide to go for a 40-yard field goal to tie or run one final play in an attempt to capture the elusive first victory of the season. Instead, time ran out and two things remained constant, the Buffalo Bills were undefeated and the Oakland Raiders winless, falling 23-20.

Collectively, 48 fewer spectators were a part of the Oakland Raiders' record-setting crowd in Buffalo than the one assembled at Oakland's next stop, New York's Shea Stadium. The entirely partisan Jets crowd and the home squad had a ball at the expense of the visitors from California. Rookie fullback Matt Snell set two Jet rushing records, the first for attempts, 26, and for yards gained on the ground, 168, shattering their mark of 127 yards by Bill Mathis set against them in 1961. Oakland errors and misfortune contributed to a 35-0 lead enjoyed by the former Titans as the third quarter expired. As Jets fans filed out of the stadium heading for warmer surroundings in light of this no contest, the home team's defense relaxed, allowing the clock to run and two Raiders touchdowns, the first by Billy Cannon from a yard out (the two-point conversion attempt failed) and the second a 13-yard Davidson to Daniels connection that garnered the final 7 of Oakland's 13 points as they fell for the fifth consecutive time, losing 35-13 to the Jets.

The final leg of the northeastern expedition came against the Boston Patriots at Fenway Park. To slow the always-blitzing Patriot defenders Cotton Davidson was given the starting nod over Tom Flores for his scrambling ability, abandoning their two-quarterback system by handing Davidson the reigns for the full 60 minutes. Ahead midway through the opening period on Mercer's seventh field goal in 9 attempts, Oakland saw its lead vanish as the old gunslinger Babe Parilli put the ball in the air for better than 60 yards on the opening period's final drive that culminated in a Ron Burton 2-yard touchdown run on the second quarter's opening play. Davidson then directed a 6-play, 56-yard trek to the end zone capped by a screen pass to Clem Daniels, who was freed by a crushing block by Billy Cannon 26 yards from glory and Oakland reclaimed the lead 10-7. Taking an easy gamble on fourth down and less than a yard from the Oakland 49-yard line, Tommy Morrow threw Larry Garron for a yard loss. Davidson made Boston pay immediately. Finding the lightning-quick Bo Roberson open on the 5-yard line and 10 yards from the nearest Patriots defender, Oakland went up by ten points 17-7 as fast as the former silver medalist could cover 50 yards. Answering in kind, the Patriots roared right back as Parilli threw over Fred Williamson for a 36-yard scoring strike to Jim Colcough on the drive's third play. Taking over on the 20 the Oakland track meet chewed up 80 yards of real estate of their own in only five plays; first Cannon and Daniels gained 20 yards on the ground between them followed by a pair of Davidson strikes, the final 39 yards were picked up by Art Powell, who faked himself free from Chuck Shonta's coverage and Oakland took a 24-14 lead into the locker room at halftime.

The Raiders' machine rolled again as the second half got underway, Cannon switched to halfback temporarily, while Daniels recuperated on the sidelines after a tough hit, and ran 34 yards behind the blocking of Wayne Hawkins and Jan Barrett. This followed by Mercer's second field goal of the day, put Oakland ahead by 20, 34-14 just past the halfway point of the third period. Throwing complete seven times in as many attempts, "the Sweet Kentucky Babe" moved his Patriots 84 yards in 9 plays as Larry Garron made his final scoring catch from 10 yards away. With Garron's second touchdown and Art Graham adding another, Boston came from virtual extinction, rallying midway through the final period to lead Oakland 35-34. A second bomb to Roberson netted 54 yards putting Oakland in scoring position and another pass to Art Powell from the 10 brought Oakland back from behind again to lead 40-35 after a failed 2-point conversion.

With time running out, Parilli, in a desperation move, fired for 30 yards to Colcough, who lateraled to Cappaletti, who in turn lateraled (whether either of these laterals in fact were or illegal forward passes was debated) to Garron, who ran 11 more yards. Only 48 seconds remained as Garron took a swing pass from Parilli and outran three Raiders defenders for his third touchdown. The two-point conversion was good and Boston kicked away with a field goal advantage leading 43-40. Daniels took the kick off 30 yards to the Oakland 38. A pass interference call put Oakland in Boston territory on the 42. An alert fumble recovery by Hawkins preserved Oakland's possession and Davidson quickly fired to Powell for 17 yards on Oakland's final offensive play of the contest. Splitting the uprights from 35 yards out with only 5 seconds remaining Mercer secured a 43-43 tie. A squib kick failed to run off the game's final five seconds giving the Patriots the ball on their 38-yard line and a final shot at victory. "Hoot" Gibson intercepted Parilli's final pass on the Raiders' 24. Returning the ball along the sidelines hoping for the winning score, Gibson was planted on his 44. Despite his protests that the tackle was made by a player who came off the Patriots' bench (a fact not in evidence in the coaches' game films), the Raiders settled for their first tie in team history and, for the first time in 1964, managed not to lose.

Returning home to Oakland's Frank Youell Field the Raiders greeted a familiar face. Back from his six-week exile in Houston, fullback Bob Jackson was re-acquired to shore up the Oakland offense's deficient backfield blocking. To clear roster space for Jackson, Proverb Jacobs was waived midweek as improved play from Ken Rice made him expendable. Cotton Davidson remained at the helm of Oakland's offense after his performance against Boston elevated him to the second overall ranking among AFL passers. With the former Cleveland Brown Mac Speedie taking over for deposed head coach Jack Faulkner, the Denver Broncos came to Oakland high off a stunning 33-27 triumph over the Kansas City Chiefs the week before. They would exit Frank Youell Field humbled and in the Western Division cellar. With the superb running of Daniels, who returned to his MVP form of the season past, more than doubling his season output of 119 yards and a 1.9 yards per attempt average. He alone racked up 168 yards on 19 carries placing his average for the afternoon at 8.8 yards per try, and Oakland moved the ball at will. With a pair of Billy Cannon touchdown receptions from 33 and 11 yards, punctuated by a field goal, the Raiders' opened up a 17-0 lead in the first quarter. A 65-yard missile fielded by Hewritt Dixon brought Denver within striking distance and Jackie Lee called his own number and scored the Broncos' lone touchdown with a 1-yard quarterback draw. With Davidson completing 23 passes for 419 yards setting the first of two Raiders records and the 628 yards of total offense shattered the AFL mark established by Houston against Denver in 1961. The Broncos quick strike was the sole glimmer in a day as dark as the jerseys worn by their opponents. Finding the end zone the next four times they owned the ball, Davidson's aerial surgery of the Broncos' defense saw him find Powell twice for scores and Jan Barrett for his fifth and final scoring toss from 11 yards out as Oakland carried a 38-7 lead into the fourth quarter. The Raiders drove one final time, but Denver's defenders held, taking the ball away on downs at their own 2-yard line. Reciprocating the tough defensive play, reserve quarterback Mickey Slaughter chose to run out of the end zone to avoid the oncoming avalanche of Rex Mirich, Ben Davidson and Dalva Allen, all three having infiltrated the Bronco backfield as if they had lined up there to begin the play. The Raiders' 40-7 bludgeoning of Denver was as welcome as air to a suffocating man but if they were to have any hopes of capturing a division title, they desperately needed an encore of their pride-and-poise heroics of the year past.

If not for Oakland's passing attack, the Raiders offensive backfield would be dead quiet. Except for the previous contest against the Broncos both the reigning league MVP, Clem Daniels, and former Heisman trophy winner Billy Cannon with his 5-yard plus average per carry were both held out of the league's top 10 in terms of yards gained prior to the meeting with Denver. To add depth to his running attack, general manager Davis traded 4-year veteran Stan Fanning, the newest member of the Raiders taxi squad, to Denver for rarely utilized running back and kicking specialist Gene Mingo. With Mike Mercer kicking true on 13 of 16 attempts at the season's midpoint, Mingo's duties would be solely in Oakland's backfield, adding fuel to a fire that finally started to spread over the past two weeks.

The AFL's West Coast war between Oakland and the San Diego Chargers began as the Raiders' plane landed in Southern California as Sid Gillman announced former Raider "Bootin" Ben Agajanian had been activated by the Chargers. While Davis himself wasn't rattled by the event, another Raiders official blasted Gillman for tampering the day after commissioner Joe Foss forced Gillman to give up a CFL castoff Bill Frank, who was drafted by the Chargers before his signing in Canada. A clause in Agajanian's pre-Davis agreement didn't bind the kicker to Oakland in the event of his retirement and the Raiders were forced to give up their claim to the kicker. Despite six interceptions, Oakland only trailed San Diego by a touchdown heading into the fourth quarter. Matched evenly in most statistical categories the Chargers added a final touchdown to this forgettable Oakland outing and dropped the Raiders to 1-6-1 with a 31-17 defeat.

Assured of being home for the holidays as the AFL's regular season schedule ended for Oakland on December 20 and their sixth loss in eight outings eliminated them from post-season competition. In making their yearly pilgrimage to Kansas City, the Raiders delighted Chiefs fans by suffering their worst loss since their week-four visit to Denver in 1962. Watching the first Oakland road game beamed back to Bay Area televisions, Raiders fans back home bore witness to five Oakland turnovers and four touchdown passes from Len Dawson, who completed only 8 passes on the afternoon in 17 attempts. Ken Herock's 6-yard scoring catch from Davidson shielded them from the embarrassment of a shutout as Kansas City buried their visitors 42-7.

The six-game losing slide currently endured by the Houston Oilers made them single-point underdogs in their visit to Frank Youell Field against an injury depleted Oakland squad. Wayne Hawkins would start in spite of a concussion that left him unable to recognize his teammates in Kansas City, while rookie Bill Budness was lost for the season following knee surgery. Dan Birdwell was returned to his collegiate position in relief. Trailing 3-0 at halftime and facing the wrath of their coach during intermission, the Raiders' defense emerged from the locker room and forced Houston to attempt a long field goal that came up wide and short. Bo Roberson's return netted Oakland 35 yards in field position and the Raiders quickly tied the contest at 3. In a second-half performance that had the Oakland press suggesting he be given the deed to Frank Youell Field, Art Powell took a pass from Davidson on the Oilers 10 and sauntered into the end zone to put his squad ahead 10-3. Adding to his kicking troubles, George Blanda was hammered by Ben Davidson. Coughing up the ball, Dalva Allen smothered the loose pigskin in Oilers' territory on the 43 and Powell stuck again, snaring Davidson's toss as he slid into the end zone for his second score in six minutes. Mercer connected for his second field goal bringing the Oakland lead to 17 at 20-3. With their second victory finally in hand the defense relaxed, allowing one final drive with less than two minutes to go that culminated in a 6-yard scoring toss from Blanda to Bob McLeod, as seven seconds remained to bring the final score to 20-10.

Pleased for the first time in 1964 with his team's efforts, coach Davis expressed his hopes to finally build momentum and achieve the full potential of his squad in the coming weeks. As the ground game misfired in 1964 it was seemingly given a face-lift as the troublesome Cookie Gilchrist was claimed off waivers from the Buffalo Bills. The signing of their second "troublemaking" running back (Gene Mingo being the other) of the season was short lived as Gilchrist, finding himself near the AFL basement, apologized for the behavior that led to his dismissal, asked for the forgiveness of his teammates and Bills management just before he was to clear waivers and become an Oakland Raider for good.

(3)

As Matt Snell set Jet records and Wahoo McDaniel established himself as the AFL's premier middle linebacker (over the often-injured Arch Matsos) in their week-five 35-13 domination at Shea Stadium, the Jets of New York were poised for a week-eleven encore in Oakland by opening up a 17-7 lead early in the second period. Cutting the lead to three as Davidson found Billy Cannon in the clear for a 10-yard touchdown pass, the Silver and Black would trail at halftime by six, 20-14 following another New York field goal.

An interference with the opportunity for a fair catch penalty against the Jets gave Oakland possession on the New York 32-yard line and a shot at taking the lead. Billy Cannon scored his second touchdown on a handoff on the eighth play from a yard out. Ahead by a point, a poor snap was juggled by New York's place kick holder Curley Johnson and Dave Costa blocked Jim Turner's kick. Pulling away and running precious time off the clock with a 14-play drive to begin the fourth quarter, Cotton Davidson completed 7 of his 8 passing attempts and Billy Cannon scored for the third time after a faked pass to a triple covered Powell opened the fullback up for a 10-yard reception that put the Raiders ahead by eight, early in the fourth quarter. Regaining possession quickly, Oakland found themselves within striking distance on the Jets' 7-yard line. Calling a roll out to the left, Davidson fooled everyone at Frank Youell Field, himself included, by making a mental error and rolling to his right. Receiver Art Powell spotted Davidson's goof and spared his teammate from humiliation and possible injury with a crushing block on linebacker Larry Grantham, clearing the way for his quarterback to put the game out of reach at 35-20. New York flashed one final bit of lightning as Don Maynard outran Fred Williamson to a 48-yard Dick Wood touchdown pass but the two-point conversion pass to Snell was swatted down by Clancy Osborne with five minutes to go and Oakland sailed to a 35-26 triumph and their first winning streak of the season.

Already featuring more legitimate running talent than any squad in professional football, the Raiders addressed their deficient ground attack in the 1965 entry draft by selecting a pair of tackles in the first three rounds. The first of Oakland's new blockers was Harry Schuh from Memphis State, a 6'3" two-time All-American selected in the first round, and Bob Svihus, a 6' 4" 235-lb. Bay Area product from the University of Southern California. Adding depth to the linebacking corps, Gus Otto from Missouri was chosen in the fourth round. Despite his announced intentions of joining the Dallas Cowboys, who selected him first in the NFL draft, California quarterback Craig Morton was chosen to be a Raider in the draft's tenth round. Other than Morton, second round pick Fred Biletnikoff from Florida State, scheduled for an appearance in the Gator Bowl was the only Raiders high-round selection to remain unsigned within 24 hours of the draft.

Current AFL Player of the Week Cotton Davidson, injured in the Jets game was spelled by his understudy Tom Flores, who along with the remaining available Raiders embarked upon a quest to erase a particularly ugly blemish upon their disappointing win-loss total. Winning 3 games to a pair of losses at Frank Youell Field, Oakland's ghastly road record featured no wins, five losses and a tie. With the only team in the Western Division whose won loss mark was worse than the Raiders awaiting them at Bear Stadium, Oakland fans knew their last chance for a victory away from the East Bay was at hand and they were encouraged by their Raiders' 40-7 October demolition of the Broncos. Matching Raider misfortune with strategy, Broncos' coach Mac Speedie sat quarterback Jacky Lee in favor of understudy Mickey Slaughter and in this battle of backups, the Denver head man threw every conceivable defensive element at Flores while the Raiders defense turned in a hard-hitting effort, beginning with the game's opening play as Dave Costa hammered halfback Charlie Mitchell, who promptly fumbled. After Dan Birdwell recovered on the 34, Clem Daniels took a handoff around the right side on third down and a yard and raced 25 yards for a 7-0 lead. Two of Oakland's 10 penalties on the afternoon, contributing to 111 enemy yards, came on the ensuing drive. A 65-yard, 7-play effort tied the contest at 7 with a 2-yard blast up the middle from Billy Joe. Denver surged ahead on their second attempt at a field goal (Dick Guessman connected only twice in 6 attempts bringing his total to 4 in 17 tries after the Mingo trade) that was matched by the far more reliable Mike Mercer; the score was tied at halftime. The sole Bronco possession of the third period was a demonstration of ball control, consuming nearly 11 minutes, moving 80 yards over 17 plays, the last of which was a 2-yard sweep around the right end by Charlie Mitchell, who redeemed himself for his early miscue by waltzing past fallen defender Howie Williams who was leveled by the lead block of guard Ernie Barnes. Ahead 17-10 heading into the fourth period the Broncos received a pair of breaks, the first stopping Billy Cannon at the Oakland 42 on fourth down and inches. Unable to move, the Broncos punted away and former Raider Jim McMillin recovered the bouncing kick after it touched Tommy Morrow on the Raiders' 32. Guessman's final field goal put Denver ahead by 10 at 20-10.

Only 28 seconds elapsed between Denver's field goal and Oakland's answer. Off the heels of Bo Roberson's 59-yard return Flores connected with Powell short and then fired long toward the end zone to have the pass tipped by John McGeever into his receiver's hands, slicing the Raider deficit to three. Oakland's hopes were nearly cancelled, until Slaughter was hit low by Arch Matsos and high by "Hoot" Gibson on fourth down and dropped on the Raiders' 1 yard line, inches short of a first down and goal. Flores led the offense onto the field 99 yards from victory and with time running, fired to the Bronco 44 on third down into the reliable hands of Art Powell who was finally forced out of bounds on the Denver 12. Clem Daniels swept right for the go-ahead score, which was nullified by a holding penalty. Pushed back to the 32 after another 5-yard infraction, Mike Mercer tied the game with a 40-yard shot. The 20-20 decision, while not a loss, doomed the Raiders to a winless season on the road and stagnated the Oakland franchise to a 3-win, 7-loss, 2-tie mark after 12 weeks.

Arriving back home to finish the 1964 campaign, the Raiders were again embroiled in another draft pick signing controversy. Larry Todd of Arizona State University, the Raiders first-round selection in the red-shirt draft, had agreed to sign with the Oakland Raiders' despite a year of remaining eligibility. Knowledge of Todd's intent to turn pro after his junior year due to financial concerns was widely known throughout the football world. Securing him was the work of Brad Pye, acting again on behalf of the Raiders. In a carefully worded statement, Todd spoke of how he was approached by an ASU assistant who offered to show Todd how to get out of his new agreement even after Todd informed him he had no interest in what the coach had to say. Todd simply explained to the media "I don't intend to be another Tony Lorick."

Looking to lock up the AFL's Eastern Division and earn a birth in the league's title game against the San Diego Chargers, the 11-1 Buffalo Bills, neck and neck with the Baltimore Colts for professional football's best record, needed a single victory to eliminate the Boston Patriots, who trailed them by a game and a half going into the league's final three weeks. Oakland drew first blood scurrying 74 yards in 4 plays, capped with a 35-yard pass from Flores to Clem Daniels in the second quarter and a 39-yard kick from Mercer put Oakland ahead 10-0 early in the third before Buffalo's offense got on track with Daryle Lamonica under center. Hitting Elbert Dubenion with a 38-yard strike with 33 seconds remaining in the third quarter pulled the Bills to within three at 10-7. A pair of field goals from Pete Gogolak gave Buffalo the lead with two minutes remaining in the contest. Taking over on their 25-yard line after a Roberson return, Flores made a point of utilizing the former Olympian's speed by connecting with him on two straight plays, the first for 11 yards and the second for 28. A holding call moved Oakland back to their 46 where the firing Flores found Daniels for 10, then Art Powell on three consecutive plays covering 4, 24 and 8 yards. A pass interference call against defender Charley Warner, who draped himself all over Bo Roberson, gave Oakland a first down and goal on the 1-yard line with only seconds remaining. Flores lofted a high pass into the end zone's left corner as time expired that Art Powell brought to his chest and stole a victory from his biggest admirer and his Buffalo Bills. A wildly enthusiastic crowd rushed the field, scooped Powell up, giving him a victory ride on their shoulders. The raucous group prevented an unnecessary extra point from being attempted and Oakland had their fourth victory of the season 16-13.

Taking their jubilation into a long overdue week off, the Oakland Raiders came crashing back to reality at home in front of their television sets as they watched the Chargers suffer a demoralizing 49-6 loss to the Kansas City Chiefs. The Chiefs' victory assured them of second place in the Western Division over the Raiders ending the only divisional race remaining in the West. Though some considered a show placing respectable for a club that enjoyed victory only once in their first nine outings, a far more horrid prospect now loomed on the horizon, a powerful San Diego team looking to right their ship before attempting to defend their AFL Championship against a 12-2 Buffalo Bills team that had sewn up the Eastern Division the morning of the final Raiders-Chargers clash. Having survived retraction in their bye week when the league rejected an NFL olive branch that would have merged six AFL teams into the older

National League (the Jets were also asked to be retracted to not have two ball clubs playing in one market) 20 of the 29 former Oakland Raiders who remained in the Bay Area witnessed a familiar site on Raiders' alumni day. San Diego jumped out to a 10-0 lead early in the second quarter only to have their former teammate Tom Flores lead the current Raiders back with a pair of touchdown strikes, first to Powell for 26 yards and a 10-yard toss to Gene Mingo that capped a 55-yard, 7-play drive in the final 2 minutes of the opening half, that gave Oakland its first halftime lead over the Chargers in their five-year history. The lead found its way back into the capable hands of Sid Gillman's club exactly 3 minutes into the second half as Paul Lowe took a pitch out around his right end and raced 28 yards for a score. A pair of major penalties further aided San Diego, helping them into field goal range and extending the Charger lead to six at 20-14.

Pinning Oakland on their 4-yard line, the Chargers were poised to win a battle of field position and run out the clock, earning a sweep over their in-state rivals, yet Oakland's ground game, dormant the entire year, came to life as Oakland maneuvered out of their well dug hole and toward the glory of the end zone. First Clem Daniels ran off right tackle for 37 yards, then for 17 more on a sweep to the same side. Billy Cannon galloped for 20 more on the right side before the usually stout Chargers' defense halted Daniels after a three-yard gain. Flores was rushed hard and coughed up the ball on a second and 7-play from the San Diego 17; fortunately, Oakland's second consecutive comeback bid was saved by tackle Frank Youso, who scooped up the ball and gained 4 yards. On third and 3 from the 13, Flores dropped back to pass, fired to an open Billy Cannon on the goal line and for the second time in as many games, the Oakland Raiders mounted a fourth quarter comeback against a division champion. Oakland's defense kept their worst nemesis on their side of the field throughout the remainder of the game until the retiring Tobin Rote fired a bomb to the Oakland 25-yard line that was intercepted by Warren Powers. With 1:25 to go, Oakland held on to win 21-20 over the Chargers, who faced the same Bills team Oakland had bested 14 days before. Having righted their ship with a division clinching victory over the Patriots during Oakland's bye, the Buffalo Bills used the momentum gained from victory and rest with a bye in the final week to breeze by the Chargers 20-7 for their first league championship.

Wayne Hawkins (65) leads the way for Buddy Allen (24) in the Raiders first game against the Dallas Texans on 7/31/1960.

Wayne Crow (22) leaps to try and stop Howard Ferguson from tying the contest in the first Raiders/Chargers meeting 8/19/1960

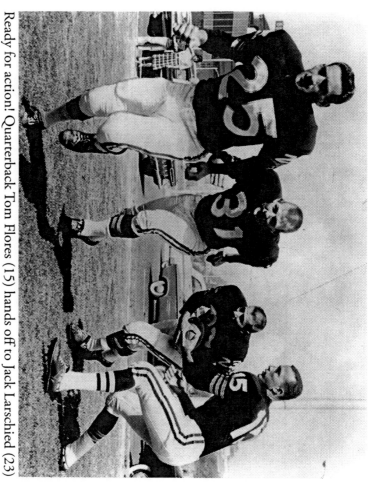

Ready for action! Quarterback Tom Flores (15) hands off to Jack Larschied (23) in downtown Oakland while Tony Teresa (25) and Billy Lott (31) lead the way in front of some curious onlookers and passing motorist just two days before opening their first season against the Houston Oilers at Kezar Stadium.

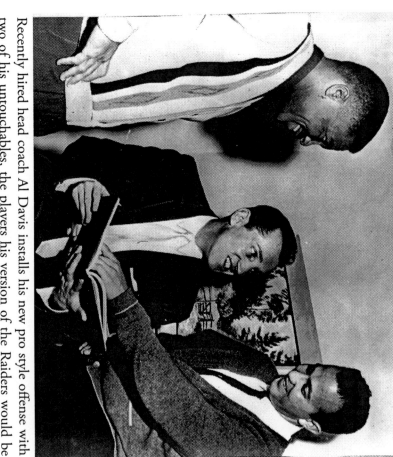

Recently hired head coach Al Davis installs his new pro style offense with two of his untouchables, the players his version of the Raiders would be built upon, Tom Flores and Clem Daniels.

ALAN MILLER   FULLBACK   OAKLAND RAIDERS

Team captain Alan Miller in a publicity photo, circa 1965

Setting down roots in the community as Clem Daniels gives a lesson to a Jr. High School class in Oakland.

Ben Davidson and Ike Lassiter proudly display the banner they earned for a 13-1 regular season record and a 40-7 desecration of the Houston Oilers to win the American Football League Championship.

A quarter of originals, George Blanda (16), Billy Cannon (33) original Houston Oilers are honored next to their teammates and original Raiders Wayne Hawkins and Jim Otto (00) for their 10 years of on field service to the American Football League.

Gus Otto (34) prepares to drop Chiefs quarterback Len Dawson in the American Football League's final championship game 1/4/1970.

The pain of losing and the disdain for the Kansas City Chiefs are clearly written on the face of center Jim Otto, who made no bones about his feeling that the American Football League's best would not be representing the league for the last time against the Minnesota Vikings in Super Bowl IV.

CHAPTER SIX
IN THE BLACK 1965

Oakland Raiders fans awoke New Year's morning to find they had been blessed. The team's second-round draft selection Fred Biletnikoff of Florida State, found Oakland's passing-style offense more suitable to his game than the one utilized by the NFL's Detroit Lions, who had taken him with a third-round pick. Just before what was lunchtime in the East Bay, many Oakland fans were afforded their first look at Biletnikoff as he and his Seminoles teammates took the field against a highly touted Oklahoma squad and squashed the mighty Sooners 36-19. Years later, the award for the nation's top receiver was named to commemorate Biletnikoff's collegiate career, which concluded this day with a brilliant 13-catch, 192-yard, 4-touchdown performance. Fans across the country who witnessed his Gator Bowl pass-catching clinic would find the honor well deserved, along with the two-year agreement tendered by the Raiders, with its value rumored to be between $100,000 and $150,000. Biletnikoff endorsed this pact, as promised, on the Florida State sideline when the Seminole victory was well in hand.

This signing meant that for the first time, the Oakland Raiders had secured their first five draft choices over the National Football League and removed any remaining doubt in the football world that the AFL had the necessary ingredients to become a top-flight professional football league. In obtaining the rights to the league's championship and all-star games, NBC pledged another $850,000 in revenue for 1965 with the amount to increase gradually over the remainder of the decade to $2.2 million following the final contest in 1969. Most of these new monies from post-season play would be contributed to the AFL players' pension fund. As the new television contract was set to take effect, pouring badly needed funds into the league's eight operations; rookies entering the professional arena found themselves far wealthier than their predecessors in years past. Leading the way was Sonny Werblin and his New York Jets club tendering $600,000 in contracts to a pair of first-year quarterbacks, Heisman Trophy winner John Huarte of Notre Dame collecting $200,000 and Joe Willie Namath of the national champion Alabama Crimson Tide, commanding a record $400,000 salary. Namath was the proud owner of a set of knees that required off-season surgery before he would ever wear a Jets uniform, fueling speculation that he may never play professionally. Without spending the unprecedented amount on raw talent as the Jets, the Raiders added to their entire roster. Draft rights for two new men were dealt away to Houston for Nebraska halfback Kent McCloughan. With the glut of talent in the Raiders offensive backfield, McCloughan was moved to the defense, where his sprinter's speed would be counted upon to cover the AFL's top pass catchers as they ran their routes both short and deep.

Oakland also inked their second red-shirt selection, Mickey Cox, a 6'2" tackle from LSU, escalating the signing war between the two leagues and drawing the ire of the school's athletic director, Jim Corbett, who also served as director of the NCAA's college professional relations committee and earning his promise to put an end to the practice of signing college players with remaining eligibility. With a meeting already scheduled between Corbett and commissioner Rozelle on other matters, the NFL's top man agreed immediately to cease its pursuit of underclassmen, months before the AFL followed suit, giving temporary high ground to a group that seemingly returned to the former tactics and procedures that landed had them in federal court facing a $10 million anti-trust suit a few years earlier. Their subsequent escape in the previous matter serving as fuel, the NFL played a pivotal role when the AFL looked to expand in Atlanta Georgia. Investors there were making a strong effort to secure an AFL club until a visit was paid to the city by the NFL commissioner, who unbeknown to those in the American League, found his own set of investors and the necessary stadium commitments and pulled the rug out from underneath them in the Georgia capital. Atlanta became an NFL city with a franchise called the Falcons set to take the field in 1966. Despite interest from other NFL cities such as Philadelphia, Chicago and Los Angeles, pro football's expansion in both leagues remained focused in the South. Comedian

Danny Thomas, along with Minneapolis attorney Joe Robbie, appeared to be outsiders in the quest for American Football League expansion before being granted the league's ninth franchise in the city of Miami, Florida. Looking to add a tenth team to join the league the same year, the AFL knew sooner where it wouldn't be, New Orleans, Louisiana. Investors there had lobbied for three years for an AFL franchise but withdrew their interests in the league when the loop moved its scheduled All-Star game to Houston following a walkout by African-American players over the unjust treatment they had received in the city. Instead, New Orleans welcomed NFL expansion with open arms in 1967, as the Saints marched their way into Tulane Stadium. The AFL eventually went north into Ohio the next year, granting a team to former Cleveland Browns head coach Paul Brown, who would mentor his franchise the Bengals as well as own and manage his squad two years after the entry of Miami's Dolphins.

(2)

Raiders' officials made arguably the most important move of the off season by tendering a five-year contract extension to head coach and general manager Al Davis, who in turn continued into the third and final year of his rebuilding tenure. Despite the wealth of talent at the receiver position with Art Powell, Biletnikoff and Bill Miller returning from injury, the Boston Patriots found the price tag on flanker and return man Bo Roberson far too costly, as the Raiders required a Tom Addison or an Art Graham as compensation for the former Olympian. Dave Grayson, a current two-time All-AFL cornerback and kick returner from the Kansas City Chiefs, was brought in exchange for three-time All-Star Fred Williamson.

As Dobie Craig returned to Oakland after a yearlong exile on the Houston Oilers taxi squad, fullback Alan Miller reemerged from Boston University's School of Law. His return, coupled with the addition of Roger Hagberg, a free agent acquisition from the CFL's Winnipeg Blue Bombers, the returning Bob Jackson and Billy Cannon created a logjam at fullback. Cookie Gilchrist insisted on becoming an Oakland Raider, despite being dealt to the Broncos for fullback Billy Joe. Gilchrist, who made an annual visit to the mile-high city, as did all AFL players, responded to his swap by asking, "What's Denver?" The disgruntled former Bill first refused to sign, pointing to the example of Wahoo McDaniel, who was traded away to

New York and enjoyed a $35,000 per season salary and star status he never knew in Denver. The Broncos met Gilchrist's high salary demands, though it was revealed months later that Buffalo refused to deal their troubled star to Oakland following Al Davis' ridicule of the waiver wire incident of the past November. Instead, the mean Davis boy from Oakland was left with the welcome dilemma of utilizing the multitude of talent he already possessed, as was the case at linebacker, with 11 able bodies vying for the six available positions behind the defensive line. Former 49er and Washington Redskin Gordon Kelly was added with plans to utilize his skills up front where he would compete for a job behind Ben Davidson with rookie Richard Jackson from Southern University.

With Cotton Davidson and Tom Flores running the Oakland offense the acquisition of Dick Wood, for a draft pick from the New York Jets, came as a surprise to many in Oakland. Though Wood was later blasted by coach Ewbanks for being a "can't win" quarterback, he added depth to an Oakland position that hadn't been thin since 1963. The final ingredients added to the Raiders stew came in one huge chunk as seven free agents were signed just before training camp was to commence. Leroy Whittle, a fifth fullback, was once compared to Tony Lorick and Charlie Taylor while at Oregon State, veteran defensive end Issac (Ike) Lassiter, a Denver Bronco the past two seasons, and five rookies reporting to the El Rancho Motel early as would all new Raiders veterans and first year players. An unexpected veteran, Billy Cannon, reported early as he was added to the mix at receiver. These men, along with thirty-five others, accounted for the first wave of players to report along with 23 returning veterans who reported later to face fierce competition for their jobs.

With the training populace complete, they began their ritual of two-a-day workouts in what instantly proved to be their most spirited camp to date. Even from the first scrimmage an offensive line complete with rookie talent impressed for 14 plays, giving newly obtained passer Dick Wood the time to find Billy Cannon wide open after the former fullback beat Dave Grayson for the first touchdown of 1965's training session. The offense's fire was not unmatched by their defensive counterparts. Rookie defensive end Richard Jackson was involved in three altercations with as many offensive linemen over a twelve-play period, leading the way for his teammates as they battered each other despite coach Davis' mandate that they drill at ¾ speed. One rookie defensive end concluded his playing career after a single practice session, realizing he had no chance of making the squad behind the 6'8" Ben Davidson, looking the intimidating rogue with his full red beard and handlebar mustache. A far more intimidating foe made its return to the Raiders Santa Rosa summer home as injuries began to accumulate. First to fall victim was veteran tackle Frank Youso. With a deep-rooted blister in the ball of his foot that required surgery to remove, Youso was lost for three weeks as rookies Bob Svihus and Rich Zecher were forced to carry the load in his absence. Yet no Oakland ache could be as potentially devastating as the loss of quarterback Cotton Davidson, who re-injured his throwing shoulder in a goal line passing drill.

Along with Youso and Davidson, three more Oakland veterans, Clem Daniels, Jan Barrett and Bob Mischak, wouldn't make the first trip of the preseason to face the Chargers, a team that excelled in hobbling Raiders players at a rate of 4 or 5 per game. In their place, Bob Svihus started for Youso, while newly acquired rookie Marv Marinovich stood in for the former AFL-All Star Mischak. Gene Mingo and Fred Gillett stood in for Daniels and Barrett. While a competent replacement for Davidson emerged from the bench in Tom Flores, the Oakland offense accounted for zero first downs in the opening period against San Diego. Trailing 3-0 after a first quarter field goal, Kent McCloughan made a move that would have him elected mayor of Oakland in a landslide had he been on a ballot, stepping in front of a John Hadl pass intended for Lance Alworth and dashing 42 yards for Oakland's lone touchdown. Leading 7-3 at halftime, former New York Titan and Jet Lee Grosscup took control of Oakland's offense and finally moved it in a forward direction. Collecting 11 first downs in the second half, the Raiders were in striking distance three times, the first two resulting in missed field goals from Mike Mercer and the third a perfect 49-yard boot from Gene Mingo, who earned the job of kicking field goals while Mercer, perfect in his career in extra points, retained that duty and the punting chores on Oakland's special teams.

Taking the momentum of their 10-3 victory, the Raiders first ever exhibition decision over San Diego, to Salt Lake City to meet the new look Denver Broncos team in the first of their three neutral site exhibitions in 1965. Loading up on talent in the offensive backfield as Abner Haynes was acquired to join Cookie Gilchrist, the Denver Broncos looked poised to become an offensive powerhouse, threatening to add legitimate competition in Oakland's bid to sit atop the AFL's Western Division as they struggled to pry control away from the Chargers and the surging Kansas City Chiefs.

They didn't go into battle unarmed; returning to the lineup was Clem Daniels and Alan Miller, whose play contributed greatly to Daniels' 1963 MVP campaign and Oakland's 10-win, 4-loss glory days. While the Raiders' pass protection was ineffective against San Diego, bumps and bruises claimed only defensive victims on the roster as Dalva Allen and "Hoot" Gibson took in a professional contest for the first time in their careers from the sidelines. Oakland's healthy offense ignited first as Flores found some of his personal magic, throwing deep to Bo Roberson, who had beaten defender Nemiah Wilson for a 61-yard touchdown midway through the opening quarter. As their second touchdown was called back by an illegal procedure penalty, Gene Mingo hit on a 15-yard field goal for a 10-point lead early in the second. Denver answered on their next offensive play with a 64-yard strike as a Mickey Slaughter's pass found its intended target, flanker Bob Scarpitto who was planted by Larry Todd, being given a look in the secondary on the Oakland 12-yard line. Losing seven yards over the next three plays, Denver called on Gary Kroner to kick a 26-yard field goal, yet the score was tied after an interception by Broncos' middle linebacker Jerry Hopkins led to a 12 yard sweep by Gilchrist who bulled though a Warren Powers tackle on his way to the end zone. Kroner put the Broncos ahead for good as time expired in the opening half at 13-10 as his second field goal connected from 16 yards. The score remained stable until the midway point of the fourth period when a busted play turned to a Denver success story that could have only been dreamt up by children playing a schoolyard pickup game. Slaughter, doggedly pursued by the defensive line, made a shovel pass to Hewritt Dixon who before enduring a pummeling of his own, lateraled to Abner Haynes, who ran 61 yards to push the Bronco lead to 10 points. Another pass to Dixon, a bomb that covered 76 yards, put the contest out of Oakland's reach at 27-10. With a shade more than three minutes remaining, Grosscup cut seven points away from the insurmountable Denver lead by finding Fred Biletnikoff just inside Denver territory at the 48. Running through and over Nemiah Wilson, Biletnikoff completed the play 80-yards from the line of scrimmage in a 27-17 defeat.

Making their only appearance of the exhibition schedule at Frank Youell Field, the Raiders also made their debut on NBC television, in color and with seven rookies in their starting line up. Yet the story Raiders fans were most concerned with was the return of Fred Williamson. Having taken some tough parting shots at coach Al Davis and Art Powell, the outspoken cornerback was remarkably silent during the game while the player for whom his services were exchanged, Dave Grayson, broke the contest open, intercepting a Pete Beathard pass intended for Chris Burford and making a 34-yard return for a touchdown. The Kansas City offense accounted for a pair of field goals, while the Raiders added four field goals and an Art Powell touchdown over his former teammate for a 23-6 victory.

Before they could depart for Portland, Oregon, for their second neutral-site contest, the coaching staff was charged with slimming the roster to conform to the league-mandated limits. Sporting professional football's largest roster, Davis and his coaching staff were required to trim nine names from their lineup such as Lee Grosscup, Dobie Craig, Gordon Kelly and the fiery Richard Jackson to accompany five rookies on the waiver wire. The survivors, minus Dave Costa, who had fallen ill, made the journey to Portland's Multnomah Stadium to face the San Diego Chargers. Treated to 30 minutes of competitive ball as each team posted 10 points, Portland's football fans witnessed a complete second half reversal. Earl Faison's hammering of Dick Wood for a safety gave the lead to San Diego for good at 12-10 and began a 36-point second-half barrage, as the Chargers avenged their earlier loss, 46-17.

Clancy Osborne, unable to perform with his injured knee, was given his release before the final exhibition leaving only one Raider out of the lineup for the Broncos rematch in Sacramento, quarterback Cotton Davidson, who was added to Oakland's injured deferred list. Dick Klein's retirement and the emergence of Bob Svihus into the starting lineup gave coach Davis fits in practice having two rookies playing on the outside of his offensive line throughout the preseason and playing them against his own defensive front four (consisting of Ben Davidson, Mirich, Costa and newcomer Ike Lassiter) didn't help in alleviating his worries, but their performance against the rough-playing Broncos (one official remarked that games between the two drew twice as many penalties) finally allowed their mentor to breathe easily. Keeping Tom Flores upright to complete 7 passes in 13 attempts (with several drops) and helping Clem Daniels to put up 98 yards on the ground in the first half, where he had faltered throughout the exhibition slate averaging less than 1 yard (19 total yards on 22 carries) per attempt rolled Oakland to a 20-6 halftime lead on the strength of Bo Roberson's 105-yard return of the opening kickoff and Daniels' runs of 34, 21 and 46 yards. These feats contributed directly to Flores' success as he found Art Powell for a 33-yard touchdown strike in the first half. Assisted by two Oakland fumbles, Denver roared back in the third period as Cookie Gilchrist slammed over for the first score and safety Goose Gonsoulin's recovery and 22-yard return with the other knotted the score at 20 heading into the fourth quarter.

As the offense allowed their opponents back into the contest, the defense played their best in the final period, forcing Denver to punt from deep in their own territory enabling Gene Mingo to reclaim the lead for Oakland with his third field goal at 23-20 with 6 ½ minutes remaining. Oakland's unrelenting defenders hounded Slaughter deep in his end zone. To avoid a safety, he forced a poor pass for Gilchrist that John Robert Williamson stole and walked back five yards to climax a 30-20 defensive triumph.

Finishing the exhibition schedule with their third consecutive 3-win, 2-loss mark, the Raiders' coaching staff was required to cut their roster to the (now) 38-player limit (a move made just before the team departed for Portland) and create the final mold of the 1965 Oakland Raiders. What transpired in the days before the regular season opened was the result of a youth movement set in motion late the previous November with the entry draft and resounding recruiting success as the top five draft picks would be Raiders on opening day as they began their final season at Frank Youell Field, Kent McCloughan, Carleton Oats, Larry Todd, who had been returned to the halfback position, and linebacker Dick Hermann, a teammate of Fred Biletnikoff's at Florida State (waived at final cut then quickly reacquired as Arch Matsos spent two weeks on the injured deferred list) were joined by several new veterans including exhibition standouts Ike Lassiter and Dave Grayson. To make room several veterans were cut. Dalva Allen and Tommy Morrow, on the squad since 1962 along with receiver Bill Miller and fullbacks Bob Jackson and Keith Kinderman, who was picked up for a draft pick during camp, were waived. The only rookie let go was Marv Marinovich, who cleared waivers and was added to the taxi squad. Deeper at every position than ever before, the 1965 Oakland Raiders were professional football's youngest team on opening day against the Kansas City Chiefs, but it was a new veteran and the defense, allowing 112 yards rushing and 61 yards passing on only six completions, making all the difference for the Silver and Black. With Tom Flores hit hard on the game's third play and less than coherent over the next two series, coach Davis was left with no alternative but to replace his starter with third-string passer Dick Wood. Deemed not good enough to unseat a pair of rookies in New York during the off season, Wood completed 12 passes in 25 attempts with two going to Art Powell for touchdowns; the first for 14 yards to tie the game in the second quarter and the other from 9 yards to pull away from Kansas City 20-10 as the third quarter came to an end. Following Mingo's third field goal, Kansas City's next possession was short. Being brutalized by an oncoming Rex Mirich, Len Dawson coughed up the ball on the 17 where Ike Lassiter recovered. Moving to the 4, Wood, behind the blocking of Wayne Hawkins, Bob Svihus and Powell, ran around left end and scored, pulling away by 20 points. Later, "Hoot' Gibson brought a punt back 58 yards for a touchdown turning Oakland's opening contest into a 37-10 rout.

Winning their opening game in such convincing fashion did nothing to boost coach Davis' optimism for their week-two match up, as the eternal realist and his Raiders were again facing his former team the San Diego Chargers at Youell Field. First, to keep the Southern Californians off balance, Davis delayed the announcement of his starting quarterback until later in the week to force coach Gillman and his assistants to prepare for three Oakland passers, Wood, Flores and the returning Cotton Davidson. Flores was chosen and immediately began playing a game of catch-up after the Chargers opened with a 10-play, 72-yard touchdown drive. The remaining 54 minutes proved to be a defensive struggle with both squads exchanging field goals and Oakland adding another to trail 10-6 at halftime. Only San Diego was able to drive into enemy territory making two trips in the second half, penetrating no deeper than the 48-yard line on their own. They were given a free pass into scoring position as a Wood pass into traffic found its way into the hands of Chargers' safety Kenny Graham and was returned to the Raiders' 18. After losing seven yards on first and second down, Hadl sent Lance Alworth on a crossing pattern and connected with him on the 5 for a touchdown, sealing a 17-6 victory.

The final game of the opening home-stand pitted the Raiders against the resurgent and undefeated Houston Oilers. Sweeping the final two games of the 1964 campaign, all five preseason contests and their first two of 1965 brought the Houston win streak to nine games. A 3-½ point underdog to Oakland and their defense ranked atop the AFL after the first two weeks, the Oilers had grand designs on pushing their good fortune into double digits. Following an exchange of punts, George Blanda and his veteran squad went to work victimizing the young Raiders' defenders with a 52-yard strike to halfback Ode Burrell for an early 7-0 lead. The Oilers' advantage lasted all of 56 seconds. Dropping back, Flores fired a pass to Daniels on the Oilers' 35. With his coverage badly beaten, he traveled the remaining distance unmolested for a 69-yard score. A late field goal put Houston up by three and the heroics of Howie Williams, intercepting a Blanda pass before the half, held the Oilers at bay before the intermission. Claiming the lead 14-10 on the second half's opening possession, Flores went to the air and found Powell down the middle for 43 yards on the drive's seventh play. A pick play by Charlie Hennigan on Joe Krakowski lead to Houston's regaining the lead 17-14 with 4:06 remaining in the final period and a Gene Mingo miss from 25 yards with 1:51 remaining seemed to seal the Raiders' fate. Keeping the ball on the ground to run the clock out and walk way from Frank Youell Field victorious for the first time since 1962's tenth week, reserve quarterback Don Trull, having never gained full possession of the ball from center attempted a handoff to Charlie Tolar that hit the ground leaving the halfback to fight for possession with his legs, only to lose the battle to Arch Matsos on the Oilers 17-yard line with 1:26 to go. A 12-yard pass to Powell on second down moved the ball to the 5 and stopped the clock as he fell out of bounds. With the stoppage in play, coach Davis called an aggressive play and flooded the end zone with five receivers. Pass protection held and Powell drew his traditional double coverage, leaving fullback Alan Miller open for Flores' winning touchdown pass with 56 seconds to go. As the final seconds expired, Houston's win streak came to an end while the home team exited Youell Field with their second win of the season.

With their 21-17 victory in hand the Raiders left their home for the first time in league play for the dreaded annual swing through the Northeast. They landed first in the city in which they had posted their last victory on this tour back in 1961, Buffalo, New York to take on the Bills, professional football's last undefeated team. Although Buffalo hadn't faced a team with a single victory in 1965 the 2-1 Raiders dropped the ball, both figuratively and literally, in front of 41,246 onlookers, as another record crowd assembled to greet the Oakland club at War Memorial Stadium. Completing only 6 passes in 25 attempts on the afternoon, Flores was able move the offense 77 yards in 7 plays with the running game before resorting to trickery with a halfback option from Clem Daniels to Bo Roberson that covered 42 yards. The original Raiders' quarterback then completed 1/6 of his passes and found Alan Miller for a touchdown. Mingo, despite his struggles, tied the game at 10 before the half only to fall behind the league champions, who added a touchdown midway through the third quarter. Penalties pushed Buffalo back to their 1, forcing Jack Kemp to the air needing 18 yards for a first down. Feeling intense pressure from Dan Birdwell, the future senator and vice presidential candidate sought safe haven out of bounds and awarded Oakland a safety. Trailing 17-12, Oakland's defense stood firm, keeping the Bills out of scoring range the remainder of the afternoon but the offense was plagued by a pair of fourth quarter fumbles. Their second loss dropped them into third place in the West.

Next was a stop in the only AFL city the Oakland Raiders were still winless in, Boston, Massachusetts. Awaiting them there was a prime opportunity to change their fortunes once and for all, as the Patriots were yet to post a victory in 1965. As the press and fans alike voiced their displeasure with Babe Parilli and coach Mike Holovak, home field wouldn't be an advantage for the Boston team in week five. Facing criticism in the media for faring poorly in draft pick signings and spending little to attract free agents like the other AFL squads, owner Billy Sullivan also found himself embattled in Beantown over his club's run of futility that now dated back ten games (including five preseason) to the last week of 1964 where the Patriots let the Eastern Division crown slip away losing to The eventual league champion Bills 24-14. These three found an unlikely sympathizer in Raiders quarterback Tom Flores. Calls for his ouster came from Oakland's sports pundits following his disastrous outing against Buffalo as Cotton Davidson was expected to return from injury (he would not as the soreness in his throwing shoulder was in fact a muscle tear, forcing him to miss the entire season) and with the early success of Dick Wood. The Raiders' fifth match-up of 1965 up was billed as a "win or else" game for Flores back home.

With help from one of Art Powell's team record setting 11 receptions, the Raiders' passer first quieted his detractors with a 65-yard touchdown pass for a 7-0 lead. Gene Mingo's continued struggles, connecting just once on four tries, kept Boston in the game as Parilli directed a 14-play, 80-yard drive to bring Boston to within a field goal at 10-7. Moving 44 yards in 9 plays to open the second half Flores buried Boston deeper with his second touchdown pass to Powell, a 2-yard throw to go ahead 17-7. Firing back with passes to Cappaletti, Tony Romeo and Jim Whelan, Parilli quickly moved Boston into scoring range. On third and goal from the 2, the Patriots' passer rolled to his right and was steam rolled by a blitzing Howie Williams, and lost four yards. Cappaletti's field goal brought Boston to within a touchdown only to watch helplessly as the Oakland offense carved away at the Patriots' defense, grinding away 90 yards in 10 plays, running time away and posting a 24-10 win.

Along with speculation regarding Tom Flores' job security, Art Powell's 11-catch performance quieted a long-running rumor of the receivers' night blindness and sent the Jets coaches scrambling to come up with a different game plan to cover him after expecting a break from his supposed disability. Now, they expected the Oakland offense to come to Shea Stadium running full throttle. For the second time on the trip and the second time in as many visits with the Jets, the Raiders played in front of their largest audience as 54,890 New Yorkers came through the Shea Stadium turnstiles to see their winless club and golden boy quarterback fall behind in the second quarter as Dave Grayson picked off Joe Namath's pass for George Sauer. Blocks from Ike Lassiter and Dan Birdwell, who rocked the rookie passer, cleared the way for Grayson as Oakland took a 7-0 lead at the end of a 78-yard return. Managing only 5 completed passes in 21 attempts, Namath led his Jets back with his ground game. First with a 9-play, 67-yard drive that knotted the contest as Bill Mathis smashed over from the 1. Following a Jim Turner field goal Namath garnered 56 of his 126 passing yards, firing deep to Don Maynard, who beat dual coverage for a 17-7 lead. Starting on their own 25 with 2:16 remaining in the half, Flores went airborne. Completing 5 passes in 7 tries, a 31-yard scoring pass to Powell pulled the Raiders to within three at halftime.

Safety Howie Williams forced a fumble on the Oakland 40 that John Robert Williamson scooped up and returned 13 yards to the Jets 47. A personal foul penalty committed on the tackle moved the ball 15-yards farther to the 32. A short field led to a quick score as Clem Daniels recaptured the lead at 21-17 with an 11-yard touchdown reception. A 38-yard field goal put the visitors up by a touchdown and their defense, unable to touch Namath for most of the contest despite intense pursuit from their front four of Davidson, Lassiter, Birdwell and Carleton Oats, finally introduced the Jets quarterback to the ground as Davidson's hit forced him to limp off the field and substitute Mike Taliferro to come on. Ineffective at first, Taliferro and the Jets were given a gift as a high snap from center made it impossible for Mike Mercer to punt the ball away and the Oakland lead was erased on first down as Don Maynard took a toss from the understudy passer who was brutalized as he threw by John Robert Williamson. Two Mingo misses, the first from 28 yards with the ball centered and from 42 yards with 6 seconds left, both fell wide and short as Oakland's most successful Northeastern road swing reached its conclusion with 1 win, 1 loss and a frustrating 24-point tie.

Due to his struggles Gene Mingo openly contemplated retirement as coach Davis demoted him to kickoff duties after managing only 8 field goals in 19 attempts and returned Mike Mercer to the field goal kicking duties he held for two seasons. Another Raider wouldn't be making the trip home at all. Bo Roberson, having requested a trade as he was playing without a contract, was dealt to the Buffalo Bills for two veteran players to be named at seasons end. By trading the former Olympian, Davis finally made room for Fred Biletnikoff, who had yet to play a single down in league competition coming into the season's seventh week. Nor had Larry Todd, who was now slated as his relief. The Florida State rookie gave the home fans a reason to cheer, making a spectacular catch for 18 yards on the game's opening play and his 7 receptions drew coverage away from Art Powell, who, defended man to man, hauled in a pair of touchdown passes from Dick Wood (Flores was knocked out of the game by Larry Eisenhauer and lost for a month), opening up a 23-7 Raiders' lead midway through the fourth quarter. A pair of Patriot touchdowns made it close at 23-21 but Oakland's defensive front four had the final say, as they pursued the enemy passer forcing an errant pass that landed in the arms of linebacker Gus Otto, who iced the game with his 34-yard return for a touchdown in a 30-21 victory.

With the home stand lasting only one game, the Raiders took to the road again for their fourth and fifth visits over a six-week period. The first stop was in Kansas City to challenge a favored Chiefs team where a win would retain second place in the Western Division, a half game behind the Chargers or a loss could tie them a game and half back with their opponent in this defense-dominated match-up. Deadlocked in the fourth quarter at seven, a questionable pass interference call gave the Chiefs a first and goal on the Oakland 1 yard line. Len Dawson's sneak for a touchdown put Kansas City ahead 14-7. With 2:08 left in the contest, plenty of time remained for the Raiders to rally for a tie yet the drive was thwarted by two blatant non-calls for interference. The second of which saw both Dick Wood and Art Powell ejected for protesting the official's poor vision and Al Davis and the bench being penalized 20 yards for running onto the field to express their disbelief. Unable to advance, Oakland dropped their third game of 1965 and into a tie with a grateful Chiefs team.

In the aftermath of the loss to Kansas City, Oakland found they were not alone in their disappointment in the quality of AFL officiating. The Houston Oilers, winners of their previous contest against the Buffalo Bills the week before also spoke out against the performance of those in striped shirts, despite mandatory league fines for doing so. This new commonality with the Raiders did nothing to slow Larry Todd, who picked up 149 yards on the ground in his league debut or to quell Dick Wood and the Oakland offense from opening a 20-0 second quarter lead. Forced to the air, Blanda passed the Oilers back into the contest with a pair of touchdown strikes to Willie Frazier that were answered with a 57-yard catch and run by Clem Daniels as Oakland surged ahead 27-14. Penalties helped Houston take its last gasp in the third quarter as former Raider Bob Jackson went over from a yard away bringing Houston within six points. A pair of field goals from Mercer sealed a win for the best team George Blanda said he'd played against in 1965, 33-21.

Home for a week, the Raiders needed to establish something that had eluded them throughout the season if they were to have any hopes of catching the first-place Chargers, a win streak. Every game was now of the utmost importance with five weeks remaining on the schedule. Their first task was to defeat the Buffalo Bills. Rains transformed the grass field of Frank Youell Field into mud, complicating the passing game. Buffalo's combination of Wray Carlton and Billy Joe gave the Bills a distinct advantage on the ground. Still, Clem Daniels swept left for 41 yards for only the second touchdown the Bills had given up on the ground in 19 games for a 7-0 lead. A turnover early in the second quarter gave Buffalo possession on the Raiders 20 and in five plays the Oakland lead was erased when Billy Joe crashed over from the 1-yard line. A fierce defensive battle ensued with both squads accounting for nine first downs on the afternoon (six through the air and three on the ground for both clubs) as they held each other scoreless until the fourth period when another turnover, this time committed by the Bills on their 2-yard line, gave Wood and the offense a prime opportunity for points which they earned with a pass over the middle to Daniels. Trailing 14-7, Buffalo moved into Oakland territory but on a second and 9-play Jack Kemp was driven back to his side of the field and was dropped by Ben Davidson for a 17-yard loss. Picking up 21 yards on third and 26, coach Saban sent kicker Pete Gogolak in to attempt the field goal from 37 yards out. He connected, trimming the Raider lead to 14-10. Punting away their next possession, the Raiders left 4:49 on the clock and 62 yards of turf between the visitors and a go-ahead score. Grinding away with a 12-play drive, Buffalo left just 7 seconds for the home squad to mount a comeback as Billy Joe plowed through for his second touchdown and a 17-14 Buffalo win.

Having squandered an opportunity to move within a game of the division leaders as San Diego's loss to Kansas City dropped them back into a tie with the Chiefs in the Western Division, the ingredients for a Raiders' revival lie ahead in a home and home series with the last-place Broncos. Trading California rains that turned their practice field at Hayward High School into a swamp for the cold climate of Colorado and the obligatory snowfall put a freeze on the warm weather Oakland club that desperately needed to pick up a half game on the idle Chargers. Scoreless through the opening period, Flores returned to the starting lineup and directed an 80-yard drive in 8 plays and found Clem Daniels alone on the Broncos 8-yard line for a 34-yard touchdown. Misfortune plagued Denver as John McCormick's pass to Bob Scarpitto bounced out of the intended recipient's hands on the Bronco 20 to Warren Powers, who returned the gift 14 yards to the 6 and a personal foul penalty called against Eldon Danenhauer moved the ball half the distance to the goal line. Flores and Art Powell reconnected and ran Oakland's lead to 14-0 with 1:26 left in the second quarter. Making the most of what little time remained, McCormick zipped passes to Lionel Taylor and to Hewritt Dixon for a 60-yard jaunt that concluded on Oakland's 11-yard line where Howie Williams dragged him down. Another pass to Taylor covered 10 yards as the Raiders' lead was cut in half as time expired after a 1 yard run by Wendell Hayes. The late touchdown swung the momentum toward the Broncos, who held the ball for fifty plays in the second half; six of these resulted in a 60-yard drive that tied the score at 14 with an 11-yard slant to Lionel Taylor midway through the third quarter.

A string of 25 consecutive plays kept Denver's offense on the field yet yielded 14 Oakland points. Taylor's success, catching 11 passes for 141 yards, enticed McCormick to hit his hot-handed receiver one time too many. Rookie linebacker Gus Otto stepped in front of his throw on his 32 and raced 68 yards for the go-ahead score as Dave Costa cleared the final obstacle, McCormick, for Otto's second interception return for a touchdown. Two minutes later it was Dave Grayson's turn, stepping in front of a pass intended for Cookie Gilchrist on the Broncos 42 and waltzing uncontested into the end zone for a two-touchdown Raiders' lead. Bronco coach Mac Speedie benched McCormick immediately upon his second misfire in favor of Jacky Lee. The move produced one final Broncos' score. Ike Lassiter's pursuit of Lee caused his pass to fall incomplete on the 2-point conversion. Denver fell 28-20 as Otto and

Grayson were named the AFL's Defensive Players of the Week when they and their teammates returned home for the Thanksgiving holiday and a much-needed week off.

The weeklong amnesty applied to the players only. As they sat in front of their televisions with their hearts supporting the Buffalo Bills and their minds expecting an encore of the 34-3 shelling the league champions experienced in week five, watched with their families as the league's top teams battled to a 20-20 tie hurting Oakland more than helping as the Chargers needed to lose twice in three weeks while the Raiders could not afford a single slip. An equally pressing matter was the escalating draft war between the American and National Football Leagues. As the NFL scheduled their earliest draft ever on November 27, the American League played its traditional role of one-upmanship by planning theirs on November 20. As several conferences threatened to boycott the American League, commissioner Foss reset the draft date to November 27; the very day most pro hopefuls played their final collegiate game, as each league would battle simultaneously, drafting the same slim talent pickings. As the NFL lobbed their now yearly allegations of a secret AFL player draft, Jets' owner Sonny Werblin took the offensive, naming thirteen players the NFL had chosen as "must have" to undermine the efforts of their counterparts in the American League.

Passing twice, Oakland finally selected their first choice of the 1966 entry draft, 5' 11" defensive back from the University of Kentucky Roger Bird. Following him were Butch Allison of Missouri, a 6' 4" defensive end, tight end Tom Mitchell from Bucknell, Richard Tyson, a tackle from Tulsa, who eventually turned down a higher paying contract with the Rams to be near his parents who had relocated to the East Bay and Miami halfback Pete Banaszak completed Oakland's first five rounds. Concentrating on the inconsistent offense, Tyson signed following Tulsa's appearance in the Blue Bonnet Bowl, while Oakland's first, third and fifth selections Bird, Mitchell and Banaszak, immediately agreed to be Raiders.

After watching Rookie of the Year Joe Namath and the New York Jets being pummeled by the San Diego Chargers 38-7, Oakland welcomed the 8-point underdog Broncos to Youell Field and began working them over on the sixth play of the contest by knocking Mickey Slaughter from the game with a dislocated shoulder. Still, the Broncos scored first on a 13-yard field goal from Gary Kroner. Forcing Denver to punt, "Hoot" Gibson's 16-yard return from the Raiders' 35-yard line, got his offense started in Denver territory. Taking a 7-3 lead in four plays, Clem Daniels paved the way with a 35-yard reception, a 1-yard run and a 10-yard pass interference penalty drawn against Tom Erlandson for a first and goal from the 3. Flores pitched the ball over Art Powell's right shoulder for the score. In two minutes and four plays of their own, Denver reclaimed the lead, first passing 41 yards to Hewritt Dixon, then for 33 more to Wendell Hayes for a touchdown. The Raiders came right back with their second 2-minute retaliation. From his 40-yard line, Flores found Daniels 21 yards away on the Bronco 39-yard line. Breaking the tackle of former teammate Jim McMillin, Oakland's #36 finished the play by scoring from 60 yards and recapturing the lead for the Raiders at 14-10. Denver, like the Raiders team from 1963, refused to quit, moving quickly into scoring position with a 63-yard Jacky Lee bomb to Lionel Taylor. Unlike like that team from 1963, Denver failed, turning the ball over on downs settling for a four-point halftime deficit. To open the second half, they were buried deeper with a 33-yard field goal from Mike Mercer. Alan Miller added a touchdown run from the 1-yard line after Flores connected with Ken Herock and a 17-yard sweep by Daniels exploited Denver's porous defense. Despite allowing another Lee bomb, the defenders held firm in the short yardage game and forced another Kroner field goal as they captured their seventh victory of the season 24-13.

(3)

Even with everything at stake for the Oakland Raiders, their thirteenth contest of 1965 against the New York Jets was bittersweet as fans and alumni gathered one last time at their teams first real home at Frank Youell Field where the Raiders had been dominant the past three seasons posting 15 victories in 20 games over that span. Progress now dictated reality for the Oakland Raiders, whose home games would be played a few miles south at the new and comparatively palatial Oakland Alameda County Coliseum in 1966. With its 53,000-seat capacity, it was a model for all of professional football. The AFL's orphan team surpassed its seven elders and both of their former cross bay locales with their modern new facility. The new coliseum would stand as a monument of the prosperity enjoyed by the city of Oakland with the Raiders and to the team itself, now turning a profit after five years of financial shortfalls. This final Youell contest was the last time the Oakland Raiders or the New York Jets played a regular season game in front fewer than 20,000 fans. The

19,013 in attendance saw "Hoot" Gibson dash Jet hopes, intercepting a Joe Namath pass on the 1-yard line. As far away from a touchdown as a team could possibly be, the offense made the journey in just seven plays. Flores' 66-yard bomb to Powell dug Oakland out of its hole and Clem Daniels followed Alan Miller between Ken Rice and Bob Svihus into the end zone. Later, Flores and Powell connected again for 29 yards, wrapping up a 9-play, 80-yard drive to give Oakland a 14-0 lead. In the second half, Namath connected on some long passes of his own finding Bake Turner for a 39-yard score and the tying blow to Don Maynard from 43 yards. As Oakland's defenders blanketed the Jets outside receivers Namath began passing over the middle to Bill Mathis. Driving for the go-ahead score, the Alabama rookie went back to the outside and was picked off by All-AFL cornerback Dave Grayson on the Oakland 23, returning it 18 yards to the 41. With the help of a personal foul call, Flores maneuvered the offense that was dormant through most of the second half into field goal range. Mercer's kick was true from 24 yards out as Oakland regained the lead 17-14 with 2:28 to go. Unable to move after the kickoff, Namath and the Jets' offense turned the ball over on downs clearing the way for one last bit of Raiders' magic at Frank Youell Field as Clem Daniels swept to his right on third down. Cutting back and into the clear, Daniels outraced the defense 30 yards for the final touchdown, the last bolt of lightning to strike at the Raiders' makeshift home and a proper sendoff to the facility that would fulfill its ultimate destiny by becoming a parking lot at the city's Laney College.

Unbeknown to the Raiders' players and coaching staff, San Diego erased a 26-20 deficit with 17 fourth quarter points to capture their eighth win of the season 37-26 over the Houston Oilers. No matter who won the battle of eight win teams in Balboa Stadium, San Diego's 2 losses and 3 ties would keep them ahead of the Raiders in terms of percentage points even if the team from Oakland finished the season with a victory over the Chargers and one more for the year. San Diego had already clinched the Western Division crown and would represent the West in the AFL championship game against Buffalo. Speaking of pride throughout the week, the disappointed Raiders took the fight to San Diego by opening up a 14-0 lead, 12 minutes into the second quarter. Hungry for a score before halftime, San Diego attacked Oakland deep to advance the ball quickly and to exploit the Raiders lone defensive weakness, the big play. It worked; Hadl passed to Jim Allison for 37 yards and for 22 more to Don

Norton for a score. Down 14-7 to open the second half, the Chargers continued their aerial assault, finding Lance Alworth for 44 yards setting up Norton's second score. The abuse inflicted upon Hadl by Oakland's front four eventually took its toll on the league's leading passer. Don Breaux replaced Hadl but Sid Gillman's plan of attack remained unchanged. Concluding an 80-yard drive in 6 plays, the Chargers pulled ahead for good by unloading a 66-yard bomb to Alworth that put San Diego ahead 21-14 and iced the game by adding a field goal with 1:02 to go. The Chargers season-ending 24-14 victory over Oakland came at a heavy price as Keith Lincoln, Don Norton and tackle Ernie Wright all missed the championship game with injuries suffered in this final league contest and their shorthanded team went on to its second consecutive championship game loss to the Bills, falling 23-0, having never advanced beyond the Bills 24-yard line.

CHAPTER SEVEN
A BRIEF SABBATICAL 1966

Even the traditionally pessimistic Al Davis agreed. Players and fans alike had been predicting an Oakland Raiders title run as far back as 1963's miracle season and through three years of steady improvement, the Raiders' dynamic head coach conceded the time was now for his team to capture its first American Football League championship. He had plenty of reason to gloat. This was his team, his creation. Save only a small handful of holdovers from the team's gloomy days, the Oakland roster was stocked with talent Davis had handpicked to comprise a football monster molded in his vision of pride and poise.

As the expansion Miami Dolphins raided the Oakland roster of four names, quarterback Dick Wood, tackle Rich Zecher, running back and kicking specialist Gene Mingo and guard Ken Rice, the Raiders progression into the 1966 campaign without them was seamless, due to their rosters' depth and the emergence of rookie prospects into fine veteran talent. With this, the Oakland Raiders made only one trade this off-season, swapping middle linebacker Arch Matsos for tight end Hewritt Dixon of the Denver Broncos. A fullback in Denver before being moved to tight end, Dixon longed for a return to his former role and his blocking and running skills would complement his reliable pass catching abilities perfectly in the Raiders' offense. Bill Budness and Dan Conners would battle for Matsos' spot in training camp.

The relative stability experienced in the Raiders' lineup ended there. It was believed the open manner in which commissioner Foss conducted league business, led directly to the NFL's raiding of AFL expansion territory in Atlanta, forcing them to find another home for their ninth franchise. Fed up, the league's owners made an offer of the commissioner's post at the league's winter meetings to Al Davis. Refusing the deal initially, as he wished to remain in Oakland as head coach and general manager while Joe Foss gave guarantees to anyone who would listen of further expansion, a common draft and a playoff system between the two leagues to decide an ultimate champion by 1967. Despite his infinite qualifications as a two-term governor and Congressional Medal of Honor winner, Foss rebuffed suggestions that he make a run for the Republican nomination for the presidency in 1968 (a nomination that was eventually won by former vice president and previous presidential and California gubernatorial hopeful Richard Nixon) even as his days as commissioner counted down to none. Foss' resignation in early April gave the AFL owners what they wanted and in his place they appointed the man they needed to handle both the affairs of the league and to lead the battle against the National Football League.

On April 8, Al Davis was named the American Football League's second commissioner and in Oakland, John Rauch, the first assistant Davis hired upon taking over the Raiders' wreckage was promoted to the head coaching position. Public relations director and former *Oakland Tribune* beat writer Gordon "Scotty" Sterling whose January 4, 1960 article entitled "Oakland in line for pro grid team" and subsequent reporting, lit a small flame that became the fire of the hurried struggle to bring the AFL to the East Bay was elevated to the general managers' position. Now in control of the Raiders fifth regime, Sterling and Rauch began a search to fill their former positions and that of scouting director as Ron Wolf, who joined Davis in New York. The new commissioner, compared to a white shark circling his prey (the National Football League), eager to devour a victim, the vast majority of football observers felt was vastly overmatched. The writing was on the wall. The "war" between the leagues would soon reach its climax.

Given a resolution in the California assembly for catapulting the city of Oakland into the forefront of sports eminence and greatly stimulating the local economy, the reluctant new commissioner outlined his plan for AFL prosperity. Dispensing with the rhetoric of unity and commonality between the leagues and expressing his disinterest in a common draft as the AFL's nine teams were signing their draft picks away from the NFL's fifteen teams 65% of the time, building its teams for a stronger, more competitive future. Nor was there a championship game on the horizon between the rival leagues under Davis' regime. Mirroring the stance of the opposing commissioner, Davis' main concern was the American Football League, with his rival non-existent.

(2)

The pay imparity between veteran players and rookie prospects had widened as new talent was secured by their respective teams in both league's with salaries that often tripled those of professional football's established veteran stars. Teams in both leagues now faced a new foe, labor organization. As the Teamsters union attempted to organize players from each coalition into one union, forcing their employers to elevate their pay to a comparable level with their young counterparts, threatening to put a heavy financial strain on the pocketbooks of owners on both sides who were less than super rich. With the new AFL regime in place, these issues become quickly insignificant compared to the signing of Buffalo Bills free agent place kicker Pete Gogolak by the NFL's New York Giants, the first shot fired in the final battle between the warring leagues.

Giving only a verbal commitment to the Buffalo Bills, Gogolak had played out his option following the Bills' second consecutive championship and, in fact, was a free agent. Even so, the Giants' signing of the Bills place kicker violated an unwritten agreement between the leagues. AFL players, signed or not, belonged to the AFL and likewise for the National League. Yet the Giants' bold move opened the floodgates and AFL money came pouring through, enticing some well established and shamefully underpaid NFL veterans to finally receive the contractual equality they deserved.

The first NFL player to jump was Los Angeles Rams quarterback Roman Gabriel. Signing with the Raiders, who had drafted him first overall before the 1962 season, Gabriel quickly resigned with Los Angeles, creating another double signing snarl as Giants' owner Wellington Mara cried foul as four of his players had agreed to play out their options in New York and join either the Houston Oilers or the San Diego Chargers. To prevent further defections, the National League threatened potential jumpers with revocation of their pensions should they choose greener pastures in the American League; yet the move backfired. NFL players who were intent on staying looked to move to challenge this threat feeling their pensions were earned and irrevocable. Mara warned his Giants' players that they would be waived immediately should they come to terms with an AFL club. At the peak of the battle, Oilers owner Bud Adams publicly boasted that more than 100 players had either signed or had made contact with the AFL either directly with the teams or through the league offices, eager for a raise, a change of scenery or both. The most notable jumper was San Francisco 49ers quarterback John Brodie, who signed a 10-year $750,000 agreement with Adams' Oilers that forced commissioner Davis, who remained publicly silent save a few "no comment" quotes, to order a freeze to keep the bidding from getting too far out of hand.

The NFL's star players, such as Mike Ditka of the Chicago Bears, universally acknowledged to be the best tight end of his era, signed with Houston and running back Paul Hornung of the Green Bay Packers was rumored to become a New York Jet when his deal expired. This forced the NFL owners to the bargaining table. Rumors quickly leaked of the closed-door sessions indicating that if there were to be peace between these factions it would be on the AFL's terms. As peace was achieved AFL loyalists and enthusiasts cried sellout. The two leagues were to become one, merging in 1970 with a common draft and interleague exhibitions beginning in 1967 pitting local cross-league rivals against one another, such as the Raiders Vs. the 49ers, the New York Giants Vs. the Jets and Bills or the Los Angles Rams taking on the San Diego Chargers in preseason contests; and, finally, a championship game to take place following the 1966 campaign pitting the champions of the National Football League against the best of the AFL. The American League was born out of the NFL's stubbornness regarding future expansion and three AFL owners, Lamar Hunt, Bud Adams and Ralph Wilson, the main negotiators of the merger agreement, realized their dream of owning an NFL franchise as the league they began in the summer of 1959 would cease to be as the current nine AFL clubs and their expansion team in Cincinnati joined the National Football League (with Pete Rozelle remaining as commissioner) and its 15 squads and New Orleans expansion to form a 26-then a 28-team league in the middle 1970s with the inclusion of teams in Seattle, Washington and Tampa, Florida.

Making the transition as peaceful as possible, all NFL players were returned to their respective teams (with the exception of defensive back Willie Williams, waived by the New York Giants upon his signing with Oakland) and the AFL would pay $18 million in reparations over the next 20 years with $8 million payable to the New York Giants from the Jets (a decision that eventually drove Sonny Werblin to sell his interest in the Jets to his partners) and $6 million to the 49ers from their neighbors in Oakland for the direct invasion of their National Football League territory. Owners of both NFL teams threatened to vote against the merger if these demands were not met along with a 49ers attempt to force Oakland into allowing them use of the new coliseum for four games per season. Beginning in 1967, the San Francisco 49ers would play in the new Oakland Alameda County Coliseum as a visitor.

(3)

There was little need for Al Davis to remain at the commissioner's post he'd held for approximately 60 days. Upon tendering his resignation, the AFL appointed its second in command, Milt Woodard, to succeed the former Oakland coach as Davis himself looked into further opportunities in professional football at the executive level. Davis gave no insight of his next destination, only stating that his coaching career was over. His former Raiders team had moved forward under its new regime as coach Rauch added Stanford assistant Bill Walsh to drill the offensive backfield, former Raider Clancy Osborne was brought aboard to tutor the Raiders' young line-backing corps as Doug Haefner assumed Ron Wolf's role in the scouting department.

Announcing as camp began that it would be several weeks before an ax fell on the Oakland roster so the coaches could concentrate on educating their players in the Oakland system, some players chose to cut themselves, making the coaches job unfortunately easy and unexpectedly difficult at the same time. Joe Labruzzo, the LSU tailback being given a look at the free safety spot chose retirement after his first practice as a pro despite the efforts of his college All-Star teammate Roger Bird and former LSU great Billy Cannon to change the undrafted, yet highly touted rookie's mind. Further depleting the numbers of those in professional football's smallest training camp was the departure of veteran tight end Ken Herock. Disappointed in his future prospects as a pro as Billy Cannon entrenched himself at the tight end spot. The three-year Raider vet chose to look into a coaching career while original Raiders' draft pick and midseason free agent acquisition Pervis Atkins was given a look at tight end behind Cannon and Bucknell rookie Tom Mitchell.

Cotton Davidson reported to camp throwing without pain and sporting (as were Tom Flores and rookie Charlie Green) red "do not touch" jerseys to prevent further injuries at the hands of overzealous defenders. Defensive tackle Rex Mirich, caught under the influx of talent on the defensive line with the addition of Tom Keating (obtained with guard George Flint from Buffalo for Bo Roberson), was switched to the offensive line to protect him. Fullback Alan Miller found his Milwaukee law practice difficult to break away from, asking for one extension on his arrival at camp and then another until finally realizing he could no longer balance football and his chosen profession and retiring from the former. All of these losses combined couldn't compare to the absence of either Art Powell or Clem Daniels and both held out as camp began. Threatening to make such a nightmare a reality unless they found financial parity of their own. Each man was responsible for 12 of Oakland's 35 touchdowns in 1965 and these twin terrors demanded identical three-year contracts, with $50,000 in salary and a no-cut clause. Frustrated that his deal wasn't renegotiated during the off-season while the merger played out, Powell demanded a trade, which according to general manager Scotty Sterling found no takers. Sterling, advising both men and their attorney that there would be no negotiations until they reported to camp in Santa Rosa, both Daniels and Powell stood their ground and refused to report until new deals had been worked out.

It was the players who finally relented. Despite their reluctance to negotiate after practices and meetings, citing the distraction caused by the need to concentrate on money and conditions while trying to prepare for the upcoming season, both men arrived in Santa Rosa together then astounded coaches and teammates alike with their unrivaled pass catching brilliance. With their case strengthened, the duo quickly departed camp in an abrupt walkout prior to a failed attempt to get their teammates to join them. The pair learned quickly that the team now would not only not negotiate with them until they returned but that they had been placed on reserve, putting a hold on their options and forcing them to play in Oakland in 1967 (should they not return) and play out their options, unsigned, at a rate 10% lower than their 1965 salaries.

Without the offensive firepower of Daniels and Powell, the Raiders made a trip to Houston to open the exhibition schedule, with all preseason games taking place away from Oakland (as well as the first two weeks of the regular season as the new Oakland Coliseum neared completion) and 54 of Oakland's 56 players (Jim Otto missing the first contest of his career, held out by coach Rauch to recuperate from a minor knee injury, quarterback Charlie Green was the other) faced two formidable opponents: the Oilers and the Texas heat that was more reminiscent of Death Valley than the Rice Stadium they were accustomed to. New addition Ernie Ladd led the Oilers' defense, holding the Californians to three first-half points as the George Blanda led offense tallied a touchdown pass and 4 field goals (in 7 attempts) opening a 19-3 lead heading into the fourth quarter. In his first action under center since training camp the year prior, Cotton Davidson exposed a softened defense. A strike to Fred Biletnikoff, free 10 yards beyond the nearest Houston defender, went for a 70-yard touchdown. Later, Davidson connected on five consecutive throws leading Oakland to the Oiler 1. Free agent rookie Dave Alexander broke through for Oakland's final score, opening the John Rauch era by losing 26-17 to the recently rehired Wally Lemm led Houston Oilers.

The 11-day lull between the exhibition opener in Houston and the next contest in San Diego was, in the very least, eventful and ultimately historical. Aside from the two travel days necessary to return to Santa Rosa and to depart again for Southern California, two-a-day practices resumed and three wayward Raiders returned to their roost. Holdouts Powell and Daniels (facing an AFL cut down deadline that would force the team's hand to either trade them in an option year, making it unlikely: waive them outright and receive only $100 from their new club as compensation; place them on reserve ending their season before it could begin or carry them forcing coach Rauch to waive two other ball players who were in camp and ready to perform as Oakland Raiders to bring the roster total to the league decreed 49-man limit) reported again and quickly signed agreements. Each negotiated with general manager Scotty Sterling individually, with neither mans' meeting taking longer than 30 minutes. Both emerged with a substantial pay increase and were eager to play football after missing the first 19 days of camp.

Rejoining them with the Oakland Raiders was former head coach, general manager and AFL commissioner Al Davis. Negotiating his Raider renewal even as the final battle between the warring leagues raged, Davis came home to Oakland joining Ed McGah and Wayne Valley in the Raiders partnership. As the details of any deal were not disclosed per Raider fashion (it was later learned that Valley and McGah estimated the team's value at $185,000 and sold Davis 10% of the club at the estimated value of $18,500, an incredible bargain in light of Barron Hilton's sale of the San Diego Chargers to Gene Klein for $9,000,000 a few months earlier), it was assumed Davis invested some of the monies paid to him by the AFL when it bought out his 5-year contract after only three and a half months of official service and purchased a minor stake in the team he'd led from professional football's most inferior to the cusp of prominence.

When queried regarding the job description of a managing general partner, Wayne Valley stated flatly that Davis was brought back to complete the mission he'd begun in 1963, to bring a championship to Oakland. What was clear was that Davis wouldn't be coaching or acting as general manager. These positions were in the capable hands of the men he chose to guide Raiders football. Following their opening exhibition loss most expected an encore against the Chargers. Davidson's success in the latter portion of the Oilers game encouraged coach Rauch to name him his starter in San Diego only to have the Texas rancher injured recovering a fumble on the contest's opening play. In his second erratic performance in as many games, Flores completed only 15 passes in 34 attempts for 189 yards including a strike over the shoulder to a wide-open Fred Biletnikoff who reached the end zone untouched for a 7-0 second quarter lead.

Hounded and battered throughout the evening with prejudice by the Raiders' front four of Ben Davidson, Ike Lassiter, Dan Birdwell and first-year Oaklander Tom Keating San Diego passer John Hadl launched a pass from inside the 5-yard line to Lance Alworth, who'd singed Willie Williams near midfield for an 89-yard Chargers' score that tied the game. It was to be the only sign of life the San Diego offense exhibited under the constant onslaught of Oakland's defenders. With 5:17 left, the offense found its touch, maneuvering 83 yards in 14 plays, topped by a 13-yard pass to Powell that put the visiting Raiders ahead with only 53 seconds left earning coach Rauch his first victory, 14-7.

Five names were cut from the roster, most notably second-year linebacker Dick Hermann, lowering the Raiders' head-count to forty-eight. Forty-seven of them would take the field against the Boston Patriots in Anaheim in the first game of an AFL doubleheader (a Chiefs/Chargers clash would follow) as Cotton Davidson's sore ribs injured in Houston and re-aggravated in San Diego kept him to the sidelines against the Patriots who sought to end a seventeen-game exhibition losing streak that dated back to 1962. Flores again completed 17 passes, scattering them over 35 attempts and gaining 180 yards but, trailing 7-0, coach Rauch got his first look at rookie Charlie Green. Moving the offense 80 yards in 11 plays, the scrambling Green's daredevil passes brought Oakland to the Patriots 1-yard line and Hewritt Dixon tied the contest with a plunge.

Backed up to his end zone by a perfect coffin corner punt, Green, known as the Wittenberg Whip, directed the offense from his own 2-yard line 84 yards to the Patriots' 14. Mike Mercer put Oakland ahead with a 21-yard field goal. Jim Whelan's second scoring reception put Boston back in front at 14-10. Moving goal ward, Green was pressured by Boston's blitzing defenders and his erratic throw fell into the hands of Dick Felt, who, with a touchdown sealed Boston's first exhibition victory in four years when they bested the old New York Titans.

With only a week and a half before the regular season, the task of cutting down the roster had again been made easy for coach Rauch. Dave Costa, upset over his inactivity with the emergence of Tom Keating as a starting defensive tackle had asked for a trade. "Hoot" Gibson retired and was added immediately to the Raiders scouting department. Ken Herock made his second defection from camp upon learning coach Rauch planned to request waivers on him. Former USC Trojans guard and captain Marv Marinovich followed.

Apart from the two unheralded rookies let go to meet the league mandated roster guidelines, a nearly complete 1966 version of the Oakland Raiders traveled to Denver to meet a Broncos team playing on four days rest following a brutal clash with the expansion Miami Dolphins, that former Raiders' defensive captain Arch Matsos termed the hardest hitting game he'd ever played. As a result of this carnage Denver was forced to start a half-dozen rookies as five of their veterans (including Goose Gonsoulin, Lionel Taylor and Willie Brown) were out of action. Cotton Davidson with a healthy veteran Raiders' squad enjoyed easy pickings with Denver. Dave Grayson picked off a John McCormick pass intended for Eric Crabtree and rolled 32 yards for an Oakland score just 82 seconds into the contest. McCormick's second errant toss, a rifle shot down the middle of the field that was seized by Bill Budness on the Oakland 33 was returned 12 yards to the 45; 55 yards and 6 plays from another Raiders touchdown that Art Powell claimed on a 22-yard play. Ahead 14-0 midway through the opening period, the visitors found themselves tied 15 minutes later as the Broncos mounted a pair of scoring drives capped by a pair of Charlie Mitchell touchdown runs. Regaining possession on the 20, Oakland required only 6 plays to march 80 yards for a go ahead score including a 34-yard swing pass to Clem Daniels and a 35-yard toss to Powell that the big receiver fought down for a first and goal at the Bronco 1 yard line. Slamming over for 21-14 advantage, Daniels gave Oakland a lead they wouldn't relinquish. Trading touchdown passes in the third quarter subsequent to a 24-point Oakland onslaught. Flores 25-yard scoring pass to Dixon, complimented by Howie Williams 59-yard interception return for a touchdown and Pervis Atkins 14-yard jaunt around left end as time expired helped Oakland match their regular season scoring mark, smashing the aching Broncos 52-21.

A game against an exhausted Bronco's squad seemed to be what the doctor ordered. The 52 points tallied in Denver more than doubled the 41 acquired by the anemic Raiders over the practice slates' first three contests giving life to the struggling Silver and Black machine. A cross country trek and a Friday game cut into the rest and preparation time but it seemed to many the (now) 40 men who comprised the 1966 Oakland Raiders had caught a break, opening the regular season against the expansion Miami Dolphins in the Orange Bowl. Coach Rauch had a major concern. Even though the fledgling team was preparing to take the field in their first ever league contest, they featured a veteran line up with such AFL luminaries as Wahoo McDaniel, Dave Kocourek, Al Dotson, and Jim Warren as well as former Raiders Dick Wood, Bo Roberson, Ken Rice and Rich Zecher. Former Buffalo Bill Joe Auer returned the opening kickoff 95 yards for 6 Miami points and another Raider of the past, Gene Mingo added the extra point as the Dolphins shocked the Raiders and the football world by taking a lightning quick 7-0 lead.

Named the starting quarterback coming in despite a season on the sidelines due to injury. Cotton Davidson fared poorly against Miami completing 7 of 19 passing for 80 yards and a trio of interceptions. The Raiders rough and tumble defense posted a pair of their own. The first by Howie Williams at the Dolphin 48 and return to the 12 gave Oakland a prime opportunity to score, which parlayed into a 16-yard Mike Mercer field goal. Two plays later, Dave Grayson dashed in front of Bo Roberson on the Miami 41 and raced back 25 yards to the 14-yard line. A 12-yard toss to Powell put the offense on the 2 with a first and goal to go where new starter Jim Harvey opened a hole from his right guard position that Hewritt Dixon exploded through for a 10-7 Oakland lead.

As the second half began, Davidson's bid to work a full game ended with his third interception forcing Rauch to allow Tom Flores to run the offense, a move that paid an immediate dividend. Directing an 81-yard, 10-play march Flores completed 5 passes in 7 attempts with a pair of drops then found Powell in the corner of the end zone for his sixth completion, a 19-yard touchdown strike extending the Oakland lead to 17-7. Miami also swapped passers, using Rick Norton in relief of Wood and making the most of a Clem Daniels' fumble, covered on the Oakland 5 by Mel Branch. Norton's 2-yard pass to Rick Casares cut their deficit to three. Flores mounted one final scoring drive, a 72-yard, 9-play affair that resulted in Bucknell rookie Tom Mitchell hauling in a 16-yard touchdown pass for a 23-14 lead just prior to the 2-minute warning. Mike Mercer, looking to add to his string of 118 consecutive extra-point conversions, saw his streak ended by Wahoo McDaniel, who batted the kick down and held Oakland's margin of victory to nine points.

For the services of Dave Costa, the Buffalo Bills offered a high round draft choice to Oakland to add depth to their defensive line. Featuring AFL All-Stars such as Tom Sestak, Roland McDole and Jim Dunaway, the disgruntled former Raider stood an equally low chance of cracking the starting lineup as a Bill. Mike Mercer looked to begin anew against the Houston Oilers in the sixth and final game of the Raiders longest road trip, which would come to a close in the place in which it began. Both Oakland and Houston had scored no less than 45 points over the Denver Broncos in the past two weeks and the 31,763 on hand in Rice stadium expected a high-scoring shootout between the clubs that, three years earlier combined for 101 points at Frank Youell Field. Instead, they were treated to a high scoring yet remarkably one-sided affair with Oakland turnovers leading directly to their demise. Doug Cline pounced on a fumble in the end zone for the first Houston score in the second quarter while two more fumbles and four interceptions on the afternoon, including two would-be touchdowns, dropped Oakland to a 1-1 mark and elevated the Oilers to 2-0 with a 31-0 embarrassment of the Oakland Raiders.

Six consecutive weeks on the road, coupled with the rigors of two-a-day practices in training camp, had taken their toll. Second-year receiver Fred Biletnikoff joined rookie lineman Dick Tyson and safety Joe Krakowski on the injured deferred list, ending their immediate availability to coach Rauch; the latter pair were nursing groin injuries as a laceration under Biletnikoff's left eye left him without full vision. Biletnikoff also suffered from exhaustion and was ordered to rest by team doctors. Former New York Giant Willie Williams and longtime reserve Bill Miller were activated from the taxi squad in relief while another longtime Raider would not be joining his mates in opening the new Oakland Alameda County Coliseum against the heavily favored Chiefs. Kicker Mike Mercer was waived midweek following a veterans' walk through of the new facility. Mike Eischeid, an unproven rookie whose professional career longest field goal of 33 yards came in an exhibition game as a Chicago Bear against the college all stars, took his place.

As the players and coaches prepared for their week-three battle, the 700 new coliseum employees worked frantically to prepare the stadium as an expected 45,000 attendees would not only constitute the largest professional football crowd ever in the Bay Area, but would more than double the largest home audience in Oakland Raiders history. It was Raiders week throughout Alameda County with the mayors from each city and town in the county giving proclamation as such. Their constituents in Oakland and the surrounding areas were in for a feast. Expecting to sell 36,000 beers and soft drinks apiece, nearly 10,000 bags of peanuts, 9,000 cups of coffee and more than 40,000 hot dogs including 800 "Colossal" dogs, a huge hotdog on a french roll and loaded with sauerkraut, (an invention unique to the new Oakland Coliseum) East Bay sports fans would eat better at their home park than at any other stadium in the country!

The East Bay's vision was now a reality. On September 18 1966, the new Oakland Alameda County Coliseum was dedicated with a 17-minute ceremony highlighted by jazz vocalist Nancy Wilson's singing of the Star Spangled Banner. Raiders' rookie defensive back Roger Bird fielded Tommy Brooker's opening kickoff on the 2-yard line and moved it ahead 16 yards to the 18, officially opening America's newest multiuse sports complex. Roger Hagberg took a handoff from Cotton Davidson on the first play and plunged through the line for 11 yards and an Oakland first down. The Kansas City Chiefs were the first to make an impression on the coliseum's new 4' x 80' scoreboard with a 27-yard Brooker field goal made possible by safety Bobby Hunt's stealing a Davidson toss from the hands of tight end Billy Cannon on the Oakland 48 and return to the 2-yard line. Oakland answered, marching 66 yards in five plays including a spectacular 12-yard gain from Art Powell who snared the throw left handed near midfield, a 24-yard Clem Daniels run aided by a rough block by rookie guard Jim Harvey on Fred Williamson and the final 22 yards though the air as Daniels pulled down Davidson's throw for the first touchdown pass in the new coliseum giving its home team an early 7-3 lead.

Benefactors of a questionable pass interference call against cornerback Kent McCloughan, the Chiefs' offense landed on their enemy's 20. Calling a classic trick play called "The Flea Flicker," the entire Oakland defense fell for this chicanery then watched helplessly as Len Dawson lobbed an easy pass to fullback Curtis McClinton, who was 15 yards from the nearest defender.

Despite his inexperience as a pro, Mike Eischeid expertly rolled a pair of punts out of bounds inside the Kansas City one-yard line. These victories in the battle for field position paved the way for easy points. Burt Coan's fumble, secured by Gus Otto, gave Oakland possession on the Chiefs' 23-yard line. Eisheid's place kicking caught up with his punting, kicking true from 31 yards and tying the score with less than a minute remaining in the half. The swarming Chiefs, who their adversaries in Oakland claimed post game were playing their best football since the league began play in 1960, blocked an Eischeid punt in Oakland territory, reclaimed the lead with a 5-yard Dawson pass to Fred Arbanas. Fred Williamson blocked his second field goal attempt and current Heisman trophy winner Mike Garrett cashed in, picking up the loose pigskin and running 42 yards for a score and a 15-point lead after a faked extra point found its way to Arbanas. Another Arbanas score ended the game. The 12-yarder added seven Chiefs' points as the visitors from Kansas City left the state of the art Oakland Coliseum victorious 32-10, undefeated and tied for first place with the San Diego Chargers in the Western Division.

Outscored 63-10 over the last two weeks, the players and coaches remained optimistic in spite of their offensive inconsistencies and special teams' failures. Promising local boosters that his squad would refrain from any conservative style of play to break themselves out of their current funk that rendered them listless in the gaze of the American Football League's top teams; Rauch faced further complications as the San Diego Chargers, perennial AFL Western Division champions, were next to visit the Raiders new home. Favored by an identical 6-½ point margin as was the Kansas City squad seven days preceding, the Chargers needed a victory in Oakland to keep pace with the undefeated Chiefs, who scored a 42-24 victory over the Patriots in Boston. Maintaining the commonality with their division rivals in Kansas City, the Chargers opened with a field goal. The Oakland kicking game was tested on the next series and as the 37,183 (down more than 13,000 from opening week) held their breath as Mike Eischeid connected from 49 yards out for the tie and the longest Raiders' field goal since George Fleming hit for the team record 54 yards in 1961's fourth week. Despite these heroics, the kicking game added the word *comical* to accompany the term *painful* to its description when long snapper Dan Birdwell sent the ball high over Eischeid's head and through the end zone for a safety. Undetected by the local meteorologists, the dark cloud that loomed over Oakland's special teams brought forth a shower of boos from the home crowd as San Diego added to their 5-3 lead taking a leisurely 10 plays to stroll 45 yards into the end zone with a 1 yard jaunt by quarterback John Hadl.

The resolute Raiders, seemingly eager for their first home victory of the season, opened the second half firing, running only 6 plays in an 80-yard scoring excursion and gaining yardage in huge chunks as Roger Hagberg took a Davison toss 41 yards and an interference penalty against safety Bud Whitehead put Oakland on the enemy's 1-yard line with a first and goal. Clem Daniels, taking the handoff, found the Raiders payoff by pounding his way into the end zone as he and his associates came within two points at 12-10. Yet in four plays Oakland's luck again turned sour. Quarterback John Hadl fired a 19-yard touchdown pass pushing the Charger lead back to nine points and to 12 after Dick Van Raaphorst's field goal was made possible by Speedy Duncan's third interception off Davidson on the Oakland 30. Tom Flores was again brought in late to spell Davidson and, despite an equally low completion percentage (Flores' completing 6 of 17 to Davidson's 5 of 14) the original Raiders' passer brought his team back with an 8-yard touchdown pass to Biletnikoff (whose vision still hadn't returned fully in his left eye) for the second-year end's first career touchdown reception. Eischeid added a 33-yard kick to come within two again at 22-20. Moving quickly, covering 68 yards in three plays, San Diego sealed a win 29-20 with an 8-yard Gene Foster run.

(4)

The week-five bye week came as a welcome pause for the Oakland club, bringing a much-needed recess from the rigors of eight weeks of football with six consecutive games on the road. Although afforded the luxury of sleeping in their own beds over the last two weeks the early hardship had clearly taken its toll on the Raiders' rank and file. A strain of the influenza virus affected many players (including cornerback Kent McCloughan, illness notwithstanding held the Chargers' All-Star receiver Lance Alworth to a pair of receptions, shutting him out of the end zone) possibly curtailing a finger-pointing epidemic caused by their recent heartache. Even as the American Football League leader in both receptions and yardage, Art Powell took to the offensive blaming conservative, predictable play calling for Oakland's recent failures while the local press joined the league of critics demanding coach Rauch to consider a change at quarterback. Many saw the return of the former Baylor star Cotton Davidson to the starting line up as hurried. With his ineffective performance, opposed to Tom Flores', who moved the offense well when given the opportunity was looked upon as the cause of the team's troubles by the media and the fans alike. In week-six all were made happy. The visiting Miami Dolphins departed the Oakland Coliseum in the same winless condition in which they entered as Flores, being named AFL Offensive Player of the Week, completed 14 passes in 24 attempts for 261 yards and a trio of touchdowns as the Oakland pirate ship sailed to an easy triumph in front of the 30,787 on hand to witness the Raiders finally capture their first victory in their new home, 21-10.

Their second victory over the winless Dolphins was a morale boost to the Oakland Raiders as the hardest part of their schedule lay directly ahead of them. The meetings with Miami cut into the Raiders' Eastern Division schedule, eliminating their annual visit to Buffalo's War Memorial Stadium. Unfortunately, the AFL schedule makers added a stop in Kansas City en route to New York and Boston, where a Chiefs teams posting a 4-1 mark was dubbed a 14-point favorite to pummel their guests from Oakland. There was logic to the odds makers thinking. Oakland had only beaten a team that hadn't beaten anyone and in their three contests with established clubs including these same Kansas City Chiefs, the Raiders fared poorly, posting a trio of losses. With Flores at the helm, Oakland's offense ran like a bull in a china shop, destroying the Chiefs' defense at will while Tom Keating, sidelined the previous week with a swollen knee, made 15 tackles and a pair of fumble recoveries, justifying coach Rauch's optimism that his club was finally on track following the second victory over the Dolphins.

Trailing 3-0 following a Mike Mercer field goal (the former Raider had signed with Buffalo, was given a nice raise and was loaned to the Chiefs two weeks prior), Flores retaliated, first with a 75-yard bomb to Billy Cannon for the lead at 7-3 and three insurance strikes to Hewritt Dixon (who'd gained 5 yards on 3 carries with no receptions coming into Kansas City) from 76 yards for his first score, a one yard run following Keating's first fumble recovery and a 10-yard reception with two seconds remaining in the opening half vaulting Oakland ahead 28-6 at the break, allowing them to coast to an easy 34-13 decision over the favored Chiefs.

Surging toward the top of the Western Division, the Raiders faced a major obstacle in the New York Jets. Atop the Eastern Division with a record of 4-1-1 Weeb Eubanks team featured pro football's golden boy passer in Joe Namath, protected by an offensive line that had allowed zero sacks to date, complemented by a defensive front four considered by many to be the best in the American Football League; The Jets were eager to get back on the right track following a 24-0 humbling at the hands of the Houston Oilers, who'd posted their second shutout victory of the season (in what amounted to a 3-win, 11-loss campaign). Again the underdog, the Oakland club, despite the league's top rated defense (ranked just ahead of the Jets) and the league's hottest passer in Flores saw their enemy quarterback Namath, find glory by taking a two-yard bootleg in for a New York score for an early 7-0 lead. Punting from deep in Jets' territory, Curly Johnson's kick angled off the side of his foot and traveled only 21 yards opposite the line of scrimmage giving Oakland a first and 10 on Jets 35. A 4-yard gain by Clem Daniels (in his best performance of the season, picking up 104 yards on the ground) gave the Oakland offense a second and six on the Jets 31. Flores fired to Powell for the tying score halfway through the second quarter. Aided by four Oakland penalties (two major) and a 26-yard reception by Bill Mathis on the Oakland one-yard line, New York had a first and goal. Runs by Mathis and Matt Snell but came up empty until Namath called his own number on third down and busted through on a quarterback sneak for his second score of the afternoon to lead 14-7.

Trailing late in the third quarter, Mike Eischeid's third punt of the period was muffed by Sammy Weir following a fair catch signal. Jim Otto's recovery on the New York 27-yard line gave Oakland the spark they needed. An 18-yard Clem Daniels scamper behind Harry Schuh gave the Raiders a first and goal on the 9. On second and goal from the 8, Flores displayed his prowess as a ball carrier dropping two steps then bolting up the middle without the slightest defensive protest as the entire Jets squad watched helpless and baffled by this deceit. The score was tied again, 14-14, but the deadlock was short-lived. Dave Grayson's vicious hit on George Sauer Jr. jarred the ball loose (Grayson's second forced fumble of the contest) near midfield was returned to the New York 29 by Gus Otto. Three plays netted four yards and Eischeid was forced to break the stalemate with a 32-yard kick. Namath had an answer for Oakland's surge, passing to Matt Snell for 21 yards, to Don Maynard for 12 and to Mathis for 18 more then handing off to Snell, who broke several tackles en route to a 14-yard touchdown run and a 21-17 Jets' lead. Cooling off with only 16 completions in 33 attempts, "the Ice Man" Flores showed another brand of cool, starting at his own 17-yard line with 5:01 remaining. Beginning with a pair of handoffs to Daniels, followed passes to Hewritt Dixon for 6 and 12 yards then a bomb to Art Powell to the New York 24-yard line with time running out. A quick strike to Dixon delivered Oakland to the two. Calling his own number again, Flores plunged into the end zone. The officials ruled the play short of a score despite half of Flores' body and the ball being over the goal line. This officiating blunder served to help the Raiders instead of hurt as precious time ran off the clock. Dixon took a handoff and plunged in for the winning score with only two seconds remaining giving "Broadway Joe" and his Jets no chance to retaliate as Oakland sealed their third consecutive victory, 24-21.

Escaping with a three-game winning streak intact, only one game remained until the Raiders returned to their new coliseum and the comforts of home for the first time in a month. Set for a visit with the Boston Patriots, those in the (football) know looked ahead to an offensive clash between Art Powell and Boston fullback Jim Nance while the players themselves spoke of each club's defensive might. Each was looking to take control of their respective divisions midway through the season with Oakland trailing Kansas City by a single game and San Diego by a half while Boston, with help, could control the Eastern Division with a win.

The Patriots utilized their main weapon, Nance, so much that quarterback Babe Parilli attempted just 11 passes on the afternoon, completing only 4 for 67 yards. The pair of interceptions garnered by Oakland's defenders did them little good as Nance pounded the ball 38 times for 208 of Boston's 289 rushing yards. His first of two touchdowns, a 2-yard plunge that capped a 73-yard, 9-play drive to open the game was complemented by a 92-yard, 4-play affair that ended with a 24-yard strike to Gino Cappaletti for a 14-0 lead as the opening period drew to a close. Davidson, sent in for Tom Flores, who was knocked unconscious by defensive linemen Larry Eisenhauer and Jim Hunt while attempting his sixth pass, struck with a short pass to Daniels along the right sideline that the halfback took through two broken tackles for a 51-yard touchdown run that coach Rauch termed "the greatest run I've ever seen." In return, Nance ripped through the Raiders defense for huge gains giving the Patriots a first and goal on the 7-yard line. Cappaletti added a field goal for a 10-point halftime lead that grew from Oakland's misfortune in the third quarter as a turnover put Boston in business on the Raiders' 22. Six plays later, Nance slammed over from the 1, burying the Raiders 24-7 with 16 minutes remaining. Collecting huge chunks of yardage of their own, the Oakland offense marched 71 yards in 5 plays the last of which Clem Daniels turned into his second touchdown behind the blocking of guard Palmer Pyle and Jim Otto en route to the end zone. Jim Nance's sole blemish was a fumble recovered by Dan Conners on the Patriots 24. Oakland cut the Boston lead to three points with Daniels third touchdown. Trailing 24-21 with 2 1/2 minutes to go, the Raiders' bid for a last minute miracle in consecutive weeks ended as Chuck Shonta intercepted a Davidson pass. Boston ran out the clock, catapulting their way into first place in the AFL's Eastern Division and halting Oakland's three-game winning streak 24-21, sending them to a 4-4 record and keeping them a game and a half game out of second place in the West and two full games out of the division lead as both Kansas City and San Diego were victorious in week nine.

Back home, the Raiders were named 6-point favorites over the Oilers at The Coliseum. Following their 31-0 smashing of Oakland in the second week of the season, the Oilers had posted only one victory in the past seven games, a 24-0 shutout of the New York Jets which proved to be their last win of the season. The soon to be 3-11 Houston team had lost seven starting players since their domination of Oakland and coach Lemm made the decision to sit the aging and recently inconsistent George Blanda (throwing 20 interceptions on the season and 8 in the past two weeks). The Houston roster was in such poor shape that they seemed lucky to not be wheeled into Oakland on a stretcher!

Their hosts, on the other hand, were the picture of health. Tom Flores despite his sore chin and chipped tooth, souvenirs from the visit to Boston, remained at the helm of Oakland's offense and Willie Williams resumed his duties as kick returner. Flores, who completed only 10 passes in the rain in 26 attempts gained 78 of his 269 passing yards on a third down pass to Biletnikoff that fired Oakland ahead 7-0, 91 seconds into the contest. Houston quarterback Don Trull, getting the nod to start as injuries claimed second-string passer Jacky Lee moved the Oilers 52 yards in 7 plays running the ball the final 23 yards for a tie (his fourth rushing touchdown and only the Oilers sixth of the season on the ground), the elusive passer brought his club close enough for a 44-yard George Blanda field goal and for another touchdown to put Houston ahead by 10 points. Instead of a 17-7 lead early in the second quarter, Gus Otto smothered an Ode Burrell fumble in the end zone for an Oakland touchback. Going to work from the 20 the shortfall was erased in 10 plays by a 6-yard run from Daniels. A 46-yard bomb to Powell fielded at the enemy 6 turned into a half-dozen Oakland points as their star receiver spun and waltzed in for another touchdown. Eischeid added a field goal and Daniels made his second trip across the goal line, a 4-yard jaunt to put the Raiders ahead 31-10 as the final quarter began. Hoyle Granger's 69-yard run gave Houston a final breath before being suffocated by Daniels, who completed his second consecutive three-touchdown performance, sending Houston to a 38-23 defeat.

The Houston game was only a one-week layover at home for the Raiders who departed for their final two road games of 1966 and their fourth and fifth such contests in another long six-week span. Unhappy with his 11 receptions over the past five weeks, Art Powell was demanding a trade back to New York where he could serve as a target for Joe Namath while the three remaining original Raiders Flores, Wayne Hawkins and Jim Otto, were saddened to learn midweek that former head coach Eddie Erdelatz had succumbed to stomach cancer at the age of 53. Erdelatz had long ago seen something great in all of them. Despite his unceremonious exit early in 1961, each praised his former coach, crediting his influence in establishing their successful professional careers.

Even with these distractions, the Raiders of Oakland arrived in San Diego to take on the Chargers with each club's future hinging on the outcome of this tenth contest of 1966. With a mark of 5-3-1 San Diego led the 5-4 Raiders by a half game. The winner would hold second place in the Western Division by themselves while the loser would watch their hopes of catching the top-ranked Kansas City Chiefs (unbeaten since Oakland's week seven visit) disappear. Trailing 10-7 at the opening period's conclusion Flores completed a 74-yard, 9-play drive with a 1-yard toss to Powell as Oakland's self-proclaimed decoy notched his second score of the afternoon and he and his teammates never looked back. Ahead 14-10, the Oakland offense padded its lead by adding touchdowns from Dixon and Daniels. Running away from the Chargers 28-10 at halftime, Dick Van Raaphorst's field goal cut the San Diego deficit to 15 with a 39-yard boot. His second attempt, broken up by the chin of Gus Otto halted the Chargers and 4 plays and 78 yards later the competitive phase of the ball game came to an end as Dixon slammed through a pair of Chargers defenders launching Oakland ahead 35-13. The relentless Raiders secured second place in the AFL's Western Division in week 11, by slamming San Diego 41-19.

The final road contest lay ahead and a 2-7 team such as the Denver Broncos was viewed as a welcome relief as Oakland needed to remain undefeated while first-place Kansas City needed to lose three times in four outings for the Raiders to capture the Western Division crown outright, or two Chief losses and an unblemished Raiders' mark would force a playoff for the division title. Interim head coach Ray Malavasi, taking over for Mac Speedie in week three had remolded this Denver squad with 18 rookies who were coming off a 17-10 victory over Boston and were fully rested following a bye. Battered by five sacks and absorbing punishment following every pass attempt and some running plays, Flores stated post game that he couldn't remember spending so much time on the ground. His 6 completions for 141 yards were big numbers in comparison to Max Choboian who completed 9 of 30 for 93 yards with a pair of interceptions. The first-year quarterback was beaten back by Raiders defenders with losses on sacks totaling more than 60 yards. A third of Flores 6 completions were for scores, an 18-yard strike to Powell (his lone reception of the afternoon) in the second quarter and a two-yard toss to Larry Todd (elevated to the starting role as Fred Biletnikoff was lost for the season to knee surgery) as time expired in the half. Mike Eischeid added a 12-yard field goal with 1:19 remaining in the game as Oakland kept its hopes alive, winning by two touchdowns, 17-3.

The road had been kind. Capturing five victories to only two defeats away from their new palace, these knights in silver would now don the home blacks for the final three contests at the Oakland Alameda County Coliseum where they were unbeaten in their last two appearances. Still featuring the league's top-rated defense and the Associated Press' Defensive Player of the Week in second year cornerback Kent McCloughan, whose inspired play (a pair of interceptions and a blocked field goal) was credited to his becoming a new father. McCloughan and his cohorts needed to remain as impervious to the opposition as they were just four days before in Denver. Serving as ungracious Thanksgiving guests, the defending two-time American Football League champion and Eastern Division leading Buffalo Bills, out west for the holiday festivities were rudely laughing off Oakland's top defensive rating, reminding everyone that the toughest, most consistent defensive unit in the AFL made its home in Buffalo.

Yet it was the Bills defenders' to first show weakness, allowing an 80-yard march in just 6 plays. Oakland went ahead 7-0 with a 16-yard pass from Flores to tight end Billy Cannon. With an 80-yard drive of their own the Bills and Jack Kemp victimized both McCloughan and Dave Grayson, finding Bobby Burnett along the sidelines for a 26-yard score and a 7-7 tie. Quickly, Flores was firing again. Strikes to Art Powell, Tom Mitchell, Roger Hagberg and Larry Todd brought the Raiders to the Buffalo 1 yard line. Unable to find the end zone at point-blank range, coach Rauch sent his kicking unit on and Mike Eischeid connected with an 8-yard field goal. Buffalo matched Oakland with less than three minutes to go in the half.

The Raider offense looked ready to explode. A Flores bomb to Todd on the Bills 10-yard line found its way from the receiver's chest to the turf and a sure six points were lost. His next pass discovered grass but only after a long journey. Intercepted by Butch Byrd on the Bills 33 and returned 27 yards to the Oakland 40, Byrd fumbled back to Roger Hagberg. The Bills maintained possession after an official ruled him down. Despite the disagreement of the Raiders, the 36,781 on hand and a national television audience who had the luxury of slow motion instant replay saw the referee to be in error, yet the play stood as called, paving the way for the Bills to take the lead for the first and final time with an 8-play drive finished with an 11-yard Wray Carlton run. The Oakland team came out in the second half flat on both sides of the ball, seeming lifeless on offense and allowing a pair of Buffalo touchdown runs. A pair of Oakland players, speaking on the condition of anonymity, complained post game that their teammates quit during the second half as a result of locker room bickering. With the Raiders' 31-10 Thanksgiving Day failure, Kansas City locked up the Western Division crown with a 32-24 victory over the Jets in New York.

Post game, an irritated coach Rauch took to the same platform as his anonymous pair, to debunk their charges of their Oakland teammates quitting. Claiming that only Tom Flores was the target of halftime criticism for failing to find open receivers instead of the mass finger-pointing epidemic that was fed to the media, the Oakland headman finally expressed confidence in Flores publicly and made a point to praise his opponent from Buffalo, predicting their third straight league title and to their representing the American Football League against the National Football League in the first AFL/NFL championship in January.

To achieve a mark of 9-5, the second best in team history, and to lock up their second consecutive second place finish, Oakland players and coaches returned to their practice facility to plan and rehearse for the impending visit of "Broadway" Joe Namath and his New York Jets brethren. Rains left small ponds across the coliseum field midweek forcing the grounds crew to double its numbers to aid in the draining of this new swampland. The slowed footing caused by the remaining mud did little to slow the passing game of either squad, especially New York's, as Namath attempted 42 throws but completed only 19 under the intense pressure being applied by both the Raiders front four and its line backing corps.

Namath donated 5 interceptions to his enemies cause, the first by Roger Bird. Named NBC Television's Rookie Player of the Year, Bird pilfered a Namath toss on the second quarter's opening play. Already down 3-0 following a 9-yard Jim Turner field goal, Oakland took over from its 41-yard line. Packing the ball for 25 yards and taking a Flores pass 24 more, Clem Daniels got the offense in close. Hewritt Dixon hauled in a 5-yard toss on the drives seventh play and Oakland went up 7-3. Just as quickly, the lead was lost again. A scrambling Namath found rookie running back Emerson Boozer open in front of a charging Warren Powers on the Oakland 48. Evading the tackles from a half-dozen defenders, Boozer completed his jaunt 70 yards from the line of scrimmage putting the Jets ahead 10-7. Then the mud provided the Raiders with a home field advantage. With Jets' cornerback Billy Baird face down in The Coliseum slush Art Powell stood alone in the end zone awaiting an easy 32-yard pass from Flores that swung momentum back to Oakland at 14-10.

Interception trouble plagued both quarterbacks. Firing to the Jets' 3-yard line Flores saw safety Jim Hudson thieve his throw. Namath's 30-yard toss to George Sauer and a 26-yard run from Boozer brought New York to Oakland's side of the field but the imposing Raiders' defense halted their advancing visitors, forcing a 36-yard field goal from Turner to maintain the slimmest of leads at 14-13. Third down magic was in full effect on New York's next drive. Mike Eicheid's third missed field goal of the day gave the Jets possession on their 21. Gaining 14 yards on third and 8 and 44 yards on a third and 28 situation with a rifle shot to Bill Mathis, Namath found Sauer open on the drive's final third down, completing the 79-yard journey with a 4-yard scoring pass. Down by six as the third period drew to a close, Flores answered his flashy counterpart's heroics with his own brand of whirlwind flamboyance, hitting Billy Cannon for 43 yards and Art Powell for 31 more and a score. The 1-point Oakland lead grew when Ben Davidson draped himself on Namath and the former Alabama star's attempt at throwing the ball away backfired when the pass squirted only a few yards ahead and into the hands of middle linebacker Dan Conners for his second steal of the afternoon, securing AFL Defensive Player of the Week honors while returning the gift 23 yards for Oakland's second touchdown in 43 seconds! Seemingly safe with an 8-point lead with less than a minute to go, coach Rauch sent his punting unit on to bury the Jets deep in their own territory so Namath and the offense could watch desperately as time ran out on them and his Raiders wrapped up their eighth victory of the season. Fate had other ideas. The muddied ball carried off the side of Mike Eicheid's foot and his punt covered just 12 yards. From the 47, a pitch to Boozer was all the Jets required to find the end zone, as the rookie

All Star went around the end and outraced a shocked Raiders' defense to bring his squad within two. A quick pass to Sauer tied the contest as the Jets snatched a 28-point tie from the brink of sure defeat.

Aside from Conners' Player of the Week laurel, the somber Oakland locker room had another reason to raise its head. Quarterback Tom Flores, warming the bench at the seasons outset, had directed the team to a 6-2-1 mark at the offensive helm since spelling Cotton Davidson. He had completed 134 passes in 278 attempts for 2,402 yards and sat a mere 95 yards behind Cotton Davidson's team mark of 2,497 yards set in 1964 and equaled Davidson's touchdown mark of 21 established that same year. Both records fell in the Raiders' final contest of 1966 against the hapless Denver Broncos. Denver, 4-8 on the year, again faced Oakland coming off a win and deemed themselves a hot team posting two consecutive victories and taking three of their last four, having faltered against Oakland alone in the last month of play.

Flores first captured the touchdown record with a 46-yard bomb to Powell over cornerback Willie Brown. Taking possession on their 22, Max Choboian's screen pass to Abner Hayes fooled no one as Ike Lassiter dropped the original Minneapolis draft pick for an 11-yard loss. On second down and 21 Gus Otto hounded the Bronco passer in his end zone, and a screen to get out of immediate trouble proved costly as Dan Birdwell stole the pass on the five and fell forward on the three. Making the most of a prime opportunity, Clem Daniels bulled over right tackle for the score. After a Denver field goal, Flores led the offense on a long, slow walk scattering 75 yards over 15 plays with Hewritt Dixon taking a pass the final 2 yards, leaving 9 seconds in the opening half for Denver to retaliate. With the competitive phase of the ball game ended at halftime, Flores' 45-yard fourth quarter bomb to Art Powell served only to pad his record-setting marks, which stood at 24 touchdowns and 2,638 yards gained through the air, as Oakland locked up a 28-10 victory that did nothing to quell the frustration of two consecutive 8-5-1 performances and a pair of second-place finishes.

CHAPTER EIGHT
THE ANGRIES 1967

With a lopsided 31-7 victory over the two-time reigning American Football League champion Buffalo Bills, the Kansas City Chiefs took their crown as the league's elite team and, as champions, departed for Los Angeles to face the Green Bay Packers in the first ever AFL-NFL Championship game. Ticket sales for this first "Super Bowl" were sluggish in the host city and the lack of a sellout required both the NBC and CBS television networks to black out the game in the Los Angeles market, yet across the country interest in this clash was at a fever pitch.

As pro football experts debated over which team would emerge as professional football's world champions, three championships in the past five seasons made the odds makers decision an easy one as coach Lombardi's Green Bay Packers were installed as 12 ½-point favorites over the seven-year-old team from Kansas City. Trailing only 14-10 at halftime, the Chiefs' defense (without the services of Fred Williamson, who was knocked out by halfback Donny Anderson after being inadvertently kicked in the head on the famous Packers' sweep) forced Green Bay quarterback Bart Starr to the air in the second half. Starr fired his second touchdown pass of the day to Max McGee and brought the offense close enough for Elijah Pitts to score twice more on the ground to capture professional football's first legitimate world championship since 1959, 35-10.

No matter what the scoreboard read or the media's post game proclamations regarding the dominance and superiority of the National Football League, the Kansas City Chiefs would only concede that they'd lost one game. Claiming Green Bay's secondary was inferior to those in Oakland or Buffalo, the Kansas City squad referred to the Packers as imperfect and expressed their desire for a rematch claiming inter-league parity was at hand. Publicly unimpressed, the Chiefs exuded confidence that given a second opportunity, they would stand tall over a soundly beaten Green Bay team.

(2)

Stocking his All-Star squad with his own players, coach Rauch led a Western Division All Star squad into a rain-swallowed Oakland Alameda County Coliseum to face their Eastern Division counterparts. Down 23-2 with four minutes remaining in the third quarter, Eastern Division coach Mike Holovak and his defense mounted a comeback. Jets defensive end Verlon Biggs intercepted a pass that he returned 47 yards for a touchdown which turned the momentum. Ed Cooke's recovery of a Clem Daniels fumble on the West's 23-yard line led to a Wray Carlton score. Bob Scarpitto's punt hit his own deep blocker E.J Holub to give the East possession on the 23 once again. Rookie of the Year Bobby Burnett then tied the contest on first down. As Dave Grayson slid helplessly away in the water and muck that constituted the Oakland Coliseum's playing field, All Star game MVP Babe Parilli hit Oilers' receiver Charley Frazier for a 17-yard score that wrung the Western All-Stars out 30-23, ending the East's string of futility in the postseason's meaningless conclusion.

With the pageantry complete, Rauch, along with general manager Scotty Sterling, began trimming the fat from the Oakland roster and replacing it with new Raider muscle. Willie Brown, thought by the Oakland scouting department as professional football's best cover corner, was obtained along with quarterback Mickey Slaughter from Denver for a draft pick and forgotten offensive and former defensive lineman Rex Mirich. Nearly all of Oakland's roster moves in 1967 resembled the larceny of coach Davis' rookie season with one notable exception: the draft-day deal that acquired the AFL's most sought after reserve quarterback, Daryle Lamonica, speedy receiver Glen Bass and a pair of draft choices for a disgruntled Art Powell, the dismayed Tom Flores, who looked forward to finishing his career in Oakland, and a second round draft selection.

Lost in the fervor resulting from this blockbuster swap was an interesting yet successful entry draft for the Oakland Raiders. With the seventeenth choice (the equivalent of their third round selection when they picked first as the league's worst franchise), the Raiders obtained guard Eugene Upshaw from Texas A&I. He was thought to be heading east to the Atlanta Falcons until their third overall choice was dealt away to the San Francisco 49ers for a trio of veterans. At #17, Oakland grabbed Upshaw who graded out ahead of most of Oakland's current offensive lineman (with the exception of Harry Schuh) before NFL teams in Philadelphia and Cleveland could obtain him.

Rights to other notables were secured over the 17 rounds of the first common draft. Players such as second round choice Bill Fairband, All-American linebacker from the University of Colorado. Coach Rauch guaranteed that both his top picks would be Oakland Raiders on opening day. Round four pick, receiver James Roy Jackson of Oklahoma, and Colorado running back Estes Banks taken in the eighth round, provided Oakland with the fastest pair of rookies the club ever had. Jackson posted a 9.4 time in the 100-meter dash and Banks was close behind at 9.5; either could provide the Raider offense with a speed threat that they'd recently lacked. Richard Sligh, a 7' defensive tackle from North Carolina, joined the squad along with Duane Benson, a Hamline linebacker who earned the praise of his coach Dick Mulkern as "the finest leader in Hamline's history" and Hamline's "finest player in the past decade" and Wayne State tackle Bob Kruse.

The new era of peace and commonality brought an end to red-shirt drafting and with it the final bit of player bidding. While not securing the funds of players drafted just the year before, Rod Sherman from the University of Southern California chose to stay on the West Coast instead of heading east to become a Baltimore Colt. Awaiting them was a new veteran in Daryle Lamonica. Just two or three years older than his newly drafted teammates at age 25, Lamonica had spent four seasons serving as Jack Kemp's understudy in Buffalo and was eager for an opportunity to prove his worth in a starting role. The trade that obtained him left major question marks in the Raiders' offense. With Flores dealt away following his best season at any level, Lamonica faced competition from several different passers. Mickey Slaughter's retirement made the picture no clearer as draftee Rick Egloff, last year's starter, Cotton Davidson, incumbent reserve Charlie Green and aging veteran George Blanda, who was obtained off the waiver wire remained.

Making the competition at quarterback more clouded and possibly more crowded was a ridiculous breach of contract lawsuit filed against the Raiders, the Los Angeles Rams and both the American and National Football Leagues by quarterback Roman Gabriel, the first to agree with an American Football League club to play out his option in the National League and reap great financial rewards by jumping to the AFL once his option had been played out. Gabriel quickly re-signed in Los Angeles for half the money guaranteed him in Oakland. Speaking through his wife during the double signing fiasco, the only word from Gabriel was that he was a Ram and intended to remain so. Through his attorney Edward L. Masry (later immortalized by actor Albert Finney in the film *Erin Brockovich*) Gabriel was singing another tune, claiming he was owed an additional $200,000 that he was promised if he became a Raider despite the fact he had no intention of playing outside Los Angeles.

Reversing field, Masry soon stated that Gabriel stood a good chance of becoming an Oakland Raider. With commissioner Rozelle saying Gabriel was under contract with the Rams for 1967, the legally astute former AFL commissioner Al Davis fired a torpedo through the Rams' star's already sunken claim by informing Gabriel and his counsel that Oakland would gladly fulfill its end of the agreement if Gabriel merely showed up to camp and joined his new Raiders teammates. Without Davis' knowledge, Masry met with Rams' officials and resolved Gabriel's grievance. The Raiders' former #1 choice would never don their uniform.

The new Continental Football League and its San Jose entry, the Apaches, provided a great opportunity for Oakland's young offensive backfield coach Bill Walsh, by naming him their head coach and general manager. Within a week, coach Rauch had found his successor in former Colorado and Michigan assistant John Polonchek. Having also served as a scout for the AFL, the New York Jets and the Raiders, Polonchek had another pressing issue besides the situation at quarterback. Trading away Art Powell to Buffalo left Oakland without one of the AFL's most prolific pass catchers, leaving them with a speed burner in Glen Bass, an oft-injured and virtually unproven Fred Biletnikoff, a talented rookie in Rod Sherman, former CFL player Mack Burton, Larry Todd, Bill Miller, a victim of Oakland's depth on the outside, Oklahoma rookie James Roy Jackson with Pervis Atkins joining their ranks from the backfield.

As training camp neared Scotty Sterling dealt second-year linebacker Ray Schmautz, defensive tackle Richard Jackson and sophomore guard Dick Tyson to the Broncos for center Jerry Sturm and receiver Lionel Taylor. Jim Otto's death grip on the center position forced Oakland coaches to give Sturm a shot at either tackle post. Taylor, in spite of the

Broncos' failures ranked with Don Maynard, Lance Alworth and Powell as one of the league's elite receivers, alleviating fears that the Raiders had suddenly become deficient on the outside.

Another position solidified itself before the grind of two-a-day practices commenced under the scorching Santa Rosa sun. Having played out his option in 1966, Billy Cannon re-signed just days before he was eligible to test the free agent market and sell his services to the highest bidder. Behind him Ken Herock returned to compete with Tom Mitchell for the reserve post. Even with the new brawn in his lineup, coach Rauch was cynical, predicting another slow start as his new offensive weaponry needed time to become acclimated with their system. The second year head coach issued a stern warning; holdouts or walkouts would be dealt with more firmly than they had been in the past. As camp began there was only one absentee, halfback Clem Daniels. Saying he only wanted to be paid what he was worth, Daniels remained in Oakland, working at his new liquor store until the eve of the first preseason game against San Diego. His teammates prepared to play in 1967 without him. Larry Todd expressed his desire in the press to return to his college position and in Daniels' absence his wish was granted. Pete Banaszak distinguished himself during drills and earned a starting role until Daniels was ready to play.

With a solid front seven, the Oakland secondary displayed great promise early on with new acquisition Dainard Paulson (obtained in a trade for Joe Krakowski who retired before reporting to New York) intercepting a Lamonica pass while Willie Brown either stole or defended anything thrown to his side of the field. One thing was apparent early on. The already fierce Oakland defense would be more ferocious than ever. The reports that came back to Oakland fans from training camp in Santa Rosa was that the entire Raiders' roster was hungry. Weeks before the San Diego Chargers came to visit, the entire roster had grown tired of teeing off on each other and were eager to vent their wrath on an opponent who, no matter their depth, skill or strategy, was doomed to become the helpless prey of an Oakland club that was ready to take what they wanted, when they wanted.

Finally the time came and exiting were the questions of how well the offense could run. With Lamonica at the helm, the Raiders' offense came out roaring! Scoring on their first three possessions, Oakland raced to a 10-0 lead at the end of the opening quarter and a 17-13 margin at the half as the miscues common in the early exhibition season gave San Diego a shortened field and the opportunity to avoid a blowout. With Charlie Green taking reps in the third period, the offense stalled. The defense pinned San Diego down until the final period when the Chargers captured the lead at 20-17 on a 5-yard touchdown run and a Dave Conway field goal set Oakland back another three. Finding himself 80 yards from the end zone with three minutes to go in the contest, Lamonica used his arm and moved the offense with passes to Billy Cannon and Hewritt Dixon. When no one was open he scrambled for 10 yards to the Chargers' 25 with 1:03 to go. Going for the win, Lamonica threw high to a triple-covered Fred Biletnikoff on the goal line. The pass fell incomplete, yet a pass interference call on San Diego rookie Bob Howard gave the Raiders a first and goal from the 1. Roger Hagberg was thrown for a 3-yard loss pushing the offense back from their desired destination and ran precious seconds off the clock. The detour was only temporary. Calling the same play Cotton Davidson used in San Diego in 1963's eighth week that gave the Raiders their first victory over the Chargers, Lamonica found a neglected Hagberg on the 1. Handling Lamonica's toss, the fullback turned and walked into the end zone to tie the game and Mike Eischied's routine extra point earned a 24-23 victory.

Lamonica remained unassuming. Brushing off his first-half mastery and late-game heroics, the Raiders' new field general reminded the local media that while a victory it was only an exhibition game. He wasn't the only Oakland player to distinguish himself. Rookie free agent safety John Guillory's snatch and grab from Jacque Mackinnon, who'd just made a spectacular one-handed catch secured a turnover and Warren Powers crushing hit on Lance Alworth forced another. On the offensive side, Billy Cannon averaged more than 25 yards per reception while Hewritt Dixon's 121 combined yards were just a few of the highlights of an exemplary team effort. Coach Rauch was as temperate as his new quarterback. Stressing his squad still had quite a way to go in regards to their conditioning and overall execution, the Raiders' head man went back to work, drilling and preparing for an appearance by the Houston Oilers.

With one player released (Canadian leaguer Gary Schwertfeger) and one traded to complete a prior obligation (George Flint to Houston) for the moment the roster appeared stable by preseason standards, yet the lineup underwent several changes for Houston. Distinguishing themselves in practice, both Glen Bass and Lionel Taylor would make the start as receivers while Clem Daniels returned to his starting halfback role as Larry Todd sat out with an ankle sprain. Billy Cannon unseated Tom

Mitchell at tight end while, on defense, Bill Laskey was named the left side linebacker while Dainard Paulson, co-holder of the AFL single season interception record (12 in 1964), earned a berth as starting safety. Yet the Raider most eyes would be affixed upon was Lamonica. Coming off a 14 for 28 performance, for 224 yards and a pair of touchdowns against the Chargers most Raiders fans had but one question in mind after his heroics against San Diego, "what's next?"

Instead of a dramatic comeback, the 23,647 on hand at The Coliseum witnessed their team dominate their visitors. The Oakland defense allowed Houston passers 110 yards of offense through the air, but only a net of 68 yards as the ever scrambling Don Trull was sacked 4 times, losing 42 yards. Houston's 105 yards on the ground did them little good. Trailing 17-0 in the final minute of the third quarter, Don Trull's 15-yard pass to Hoyle Granger provided the lone Oilers' highlight as his other passing efforts found themselves in the hands of Gus Otto (and Willie Brown's twice in the second quarter) on the 5-yard line. Otto's 10-yard return gave Oakland possession on the 15 for one final march. Firing strikes to Rod Sherman and Pervis Atkins, Lamonica launched his final bomb of the contest to Estes Banks. Alone on the Oilers' 10-yard line, Banks walked into the end zone untouched as Oakland won easily 24-7.

The American Football League's crusade to attract more fans in territories where there were no local teams was again in full force this preseason. Embarking on a two non-AFL city tour, coach Rauch had the unenviable task of team cut downs made easy for him for the second consecutive summer. A re-aggravated Achilles tendon injury prompted receiver Mack Burton's decision to leave camp despite a good early showing in drills. Cotton Davidson was waived injured with a knotted chest muscle that impaired his ability to throw. A pair was cut; speedy fourth round selection James Roy Jackson was let go along with free agent tackle Len Sears. The most shocking event was the defection of offensive lineman Jerry Sturm. Immediately problematic upon his trade from Denver, Sturm threatened to not report unless he was given a guaranteed no-cut contract in Oakland. The co-owner of a Denver area bar with Broncos teammate and former Raider Jim McMillin, Sturm appeared content to retire to his business venture before reporting to Santa Rosa intent on playing out his option. A rift developed between the 10-year veteran and offensive line coach Ollie Spencer, who pulled Sturm just before Daryle Lamonica completed his game-winning toss to Roger Hagberg against San Diego. Unhappy with the prospect of being a reserve, the disgruntled former Bronco was unable to coexist peacefully with his Oakland mentor and was fined $150 after a confrontation. His defection made the fine uncollectable.

Traveling to Portland, Oregon they were excited to take on an opponent the caliber of the Kansas City Chiefs to gauge their progress. However these Raiders were run out of the Rose City again, never being competitive against the league champions. Fielding a punt on his own 28-yard line, diminutive rookie wide receiver "Super Gnat" Noland Smith shocked the Raiders and electrified the sweltering Oregonians by rumbling 72 yards for a touchdown just four minutes into the contest. The remaining 56 minutes were equally cruel to Oakland, whose lone scoring threat came from a 69-yard Rod Sherman punt return that was snuffed in one play. The first legitimate pass rush Lamonica had faced as an Oakland Raider forced the previously brilliant new quarterback to fumble on the Kansas City 21-yard line. Only a shaky performance from kicker Jan Stenerud (hitting twice in five attempts) saved them from their worst shutout defeat, as the Chiefs stole the momentum of two straight wins with a 48-0 humiliation.

Reminiscent of the black and gold racehorse that died at the starting gate in 1961, with their inability to even slow the Kansas City avalanche, the league champions looked to be shoe-ins for a return trip to the championship stage. Fortunately this outing wouldn't be held against Oakland in their quest to reign supreme in the American Football League. Sidetracked as it seemed, a trimmed line up prepared for their next exhibition in North Platte, Nebraska against the Denver Broncos. Charlie Green was waived and rejoined Bill Walsh in San Jose, along with former Raiders' teammates Greg Kent, James Roy Jackson and Len Sears. The Wittenberg alumnus would compete with former Raider Chon Gallegos for a starting role in the Continental Football League.

Traditionally the AFL's wallflowers, coach Rauch had a new nickname for the Broncos, "Champions of the National Football League." Having handed consecutive defeats to a poor sport Detroit Lions team (team captain Alex Karras refused to shake the hand of Broncos' defensive captain Dave Costa, vowing to walk back to Detroit should his Lions team lose) and the Minnesota Vikings, coach Lou Saban's squad wouldn't be taken lightly. This game had meaning. Looking to bounce back after such a resounding defeat it seemed that Oakland was headed for an encore of their Portland embarrassment as Denver raced out to a 14-0 first quarter lead. Both passing attacks faltered in North Platte, with

Lamonica completing 10 throws in 30 attempts and the newly acquired Steve Tensi hit 9 times for Denver in 27 tries. Oakland ran the ball with great success and Clem Daniels' 77 first-half yards contributed to a 17-point second quarter resurgence to give the Raiders the lead at halftime by a George Blanda field goal. The struggles of both offenses did little to excite the 6,600 Nebraskans on hand celebrating their state's centennial at North Platte High School until the middle of the final quarter when Tensi completed an 80-yard march in 12 plays with a quarterback sneak.

Leaving behind a 21-17 defeat and a tiny crowd reminiscent of the far lower than capacity turnouts in the Raiders' season at Candlestick Park, the Oakland team found a different world awaiting them when they returned home to The Coliseum. 53,254 were in paid attendance on Sunday, September 3, 1967 as the San Francisco 49ers made the trek cross-bay for a long awaited match-up that Bay Area football enthusiasts had dreamt of since Oakland was granted a franchise in January 1960. This exhibition game had been hyped months in advance, beginning with the Treasure Island (in the San Francisco Bay) coin toss that decided the game's location. Owners on both sides agreed that the victor would reap great financial benefits of being the "better" Bay Area team with the Raiders' ownership stating as much as $350,000 in new ticket revenue was at stake in the Labor Day match up.

Each team had earned the highest praises of the other early in the exhibition schedule as Raiders players and coaches made a trip to their first haunt at Kezar Stadium to watch the 49ers stomp the Cleveland Browns 42-14 while some San Francisco players spent a warm evening in The Coliseum owners' box with Al Davis, Wayne Valley and Ed McGah to watch the Raiders handle the Houston Oilers. Taking the blame for his team's current offensive struggles, Lamonica called this clash a duel between himself and San Francisco quarterback John Brodie while the local media dubbed it a Bay Area civil war. Frank Albert, the former Stanford and 49ers star, compared it to the annual Bay Area sports tradition between his alma mater and the University of California calling this contest "an old man's big game."

With Lionel Taylor joining a trio of reserves, Carlton Oats, Palmer Pyle and Larry Todd, on Oakland's injured list, former Buffalo standout Bill Miller, twice the recipient of passes in his three years in Oakland, was elevated to the starting role at split end while his opposite, rookie Rod Sherman, was given the nod at flanker. All that was left was for the game to be played and through the opening 45 minutes the 10-point underdog home squad found itself on the short side of a field goal battle. Trailing 6-3, Oakland squandered scoring opportunities and witnessed a fistfight which saw Harry Schuh and 49er Roland Lakes being ejected. The game was finally blown open as the deadly Brodie to Dave Parks combination stuck on the seventeenth play of an 81-yard drive with a 6-yard touchdown pass on fourth down as San Francisco pulled away 13 –3. Even with 291 yards in total offense, the Oakland attackers were virtually lifeless for 59 minutes until Dan Archer recovered a muffed punt on the San Francisco 41. Making what he called post-game his last reception as an Oakland Raider, Fred Biletnikoff got away from Kermit Alexander (who also mishandled the punt) and took a pass from George Blanda on a crossing route for a score on first down. The remaining 32 seconds weren't enough to attempt a comeback and Oakland dropped its third consecutive exhibition game, 13-10.

The premonition of his demise proved untrue. Fred Biletnikoff's name was not among the final eight trimmed to comprise the final mold of the 1967 Oakland Raiders but the third year receiver had been demoted. Listed behind Bill Miller and Rod Sherman at receiver, Warren Wells joined Biletnikoff as a reserve despite not seeing action as an Oakland Raider in the practice season. With his only pro experience coming as a Detroit Lion in 1964, a two-year stint in the service made him a virtual unknown in Oakland having joined the team two days prior to the exhibition finale. Roster room was made for Wells by waiving Glen Bass and Lionel Taylor, who became susceptible to injury as a Raider after a dent free career in Denver. Both found employment as Houston Oilers.

Converted receiver Pervis Atkins also found free agency via the waiver wire, as did second-year tight end Tom Mitchell, who was edged out for the backup role behind Billy Cannon by Ken Herock. Midweek, Miami Dolphins tight end Dave Kocourek was added for speed for a draft pick. The most surprising release was that of safety Dainard Paulson. A starter in the exhibition slate's final game against San Francisco Paulson found himself victimized by the depth in Oakland's secondary. Coach Rauch rounded out the final roster shuffle with the release of rookie draft choice Rick Egloff and the newly acquired Nate Johns.

Ready or not, the newest edition of the Oakland Raiders was set to begin their eighth campaign against a resurgent Denver Broncos team that many believed was on the verge of making an Al Davis style leap to prominence. Winners of four straight, Denver opened the 1967 season the week prior with a 26-21 win over the Patriots in Denver. As the media lauded the work Lou Saban had done with his Bronco squad, John Rauch was praising his defenders. With Tom Keating not ready to take the field because of injury, the Raiders utilized a 3-4 defensive set with Dan Birdwell lining up over center and being supported by the four linebackers while Ike Lassiter and Ben Davidson rushed from the outside. With one of the most dominant defensive performances ever witnessed, the Oakland Raiders sent whatever progress the Broncos had made into remission.

For the first time in 77 games, a Broncos' team had been held scoreless and while negative points are an impossibility, negative yards are not. After a 19-yard completion to Oakland native Wendall Hayes, Steve Tensi was dumped 7 times for –70 yards and finished the afternoon with 53 fewer yards overall than he began with. Denver's meager 48 yards on the ground resulted in an AFL record –5 yards in total offense. To complement this defensive feast, Oakland's struggling offense provided a spectacular output that each of the 25,423 in attendance could easily mistake for a fourth of July fireworks show. A pair of touchdowns by Hewritt Dixon and encores from Daryle Lamonica, Clem Daniels, Rod Sherman, Warren Wells and Warren Powers lit up the Broncos up for 51 points.

Coming off one of the most completely dominant performances in professional football history, the Oakland Raiders were now expected to show the Boston Patriots the same type of anti hospitality that was bestowed upon the Broncos. The memories of the previous October's 38-carry, 208-yard rushing performance by fullback Jim Nance at Fenway Park was still fresh in the minds of Oakland's coaches and defensive players, who had seven days to devise and execute a plan to stop him. Winless in two games, the Boston Patriots were a dangerous, wounded animal with an aggressive, veteran defense and a crafty quarterback running their offense. The Patriots were capable of toppling even the mightiest of football giants and accomplish this task using any number of tactics.

Traveling by air, the Oakland offense struck quickly, marching goalward with a pair of 22-yard Lamonica passes to Rod Sherman and Billy Cannon. A 32-yard strike to Biletnikoff put Oakland ahead early on. The Patriots answered immediately, charging downfield with a quartet of Parilli throws, three to Artie Graham, whose 19-yard reception after a brilliant fake handoff to Nance knotted the score at 7. This first penetration of the Oakland goal line in 1967 was Boston's last of the afternoon. Dumped eight times for losses, Patriot quarterback's managed 256 yards through the air as the 26,289 Raiders fans witnessed a desperate Boston team attempt to rescue a lost cause. Pressure from Bill Laskey caused Parilli to throw to

Gus Otto instead of his intended receiver at his 17-yard line. Dixon put Oakland ahead taking a pass behind the line of scrimmage, breaking three tackles and following Gene Upshaw (who cleared out Boston defensive back Don Webb inside the 5) to regain the lead.

The next Boston threat also met with disaster. Combining to halt Larry Garron's 49-yard catch and run, Dan Conners and Roger Bird jarred the ball loose and Conners recovered on the Oakland 20. A 63-yard bomb from Lamonica to Cannon gave the Raiders a first and goal on the Boston 3. Wayne Hawkins' block on Jim Hunt made way for Clem Daniels to score easily for a 21-7 halftime lead. Administering another vicious hit, Gus Otto forced Parilli to lose the handle on his 16 and watch helplessly as Dan Conners smothered his second fumble recovery. Bill Miller got in on the scoring act with a juggling end-zone catch and a Lamonica scramble finished the Patriots, sending them to their third straight defeat, 35-7.

With their early dominance these men in silver and black were slow to gain the respect of their peers. After being rendered a non-factor, Boston fullback Jim Nance conceded the Oakland Raiders had become a good football team, but quickly added they were still not up to par with the Kansas City Chiefs. With the bump-and-run tactics employed by cornerbacks Kent McCloughan and Willie Brown, the savage handling of opposing ball carriers by the safeties and the line-backing corps and the relentless harassment of opposing quarterbacks by an aggressive front four, the defense found itself ranked atop the American Football League. Complemented by a high-octane offense run by Lamonica, contributed to two consecutive victories by a combined score of 86-7. Seemingly the only thing able to stop these Raiders was the schedule maker's. A bye week forced the football world to wait an additional seven days to test Jim Nance's theories when the Raiders returned to action to meet the league champions at The Coliseum.

Suffering only from the minor dings associated with athletics, the Oakland club was completely healthy for what coach Rauch termed a "supreme test" against a championship club that was reported to be better than they were the year before and light years ahead of them in Portland seven weeks prior. Both squads were undefeated in league play and with San Diego also unbeaten the importance of this game was undeniable. The third largest crowd to witness a football game in the East Bay jammed the Oakland Coliseum to witness the Western Division power struggle. For the third game in a row, the home squad never trailed. After a scoreless first quarter Clem Daniels took a 1-yard pass from Lamonica to open the second period for the first Oakland score that was quickly followed by a Blanda field goal to open a 10-0 lead. A 20-yard pass from Len Dawson to running back Gene Thomas cut the Chiefs' deficit to three with less than two minutes to go in the half. Fierce defensive play created opportunities for the offense; Ike Lassiter's pursuit of Dawson resulted in a forced fumble on the Oakland 25. Grabbing the ball in midair, the ever-opportunistic Dan Conners raced 48 yards to the Kansas City 27. Blanda added another field goal. Amassing zero yards of offense in the third quarter, Kansas City fell nine points back with a third Oakland field goal. Having done an outstanding job of containing Noland Smith for most of the day, "Super Gnat" displayed the same deadly skill as a kick returner he did in the Portland blowout and broke loose for 48 yards. His spark jump started the Kansas City offense which eight plays later, found the end zone with some flash as Mike Garrett, passing on a half back option launched an ugly wobbling duck into the corner of the end zone that was fielded by Otis Taylor to pull the Chiefs to within two at 16-14. Running nine plays in less than four minutes, Oakland was in the end zone again. From the Kansas City 29, Lamonica threw a screen pass to Billy Cannon over a pursuing Bobby Bell. Freed by a block from Wayne Hawkins, cornerback Emmitt Thomas was sent to the turf with a forceful shot from Biletnikoff as Cannon scored unmolested to extend the lead again to nine points. Another Kansas City touchdown wasn't enough as the Raiders' offense kept their opponents off the field and time ran out on the Chiefs who slipped a game back in the three-way race for Western Division supremacy, 23-21.

With a 3-0 record and the best start in franchise history the unbelievers still constituted the majority as 1967 saw the return of Oakland's three-game, eastern sojourn that had dogged them over their first six years. Stumbling to just three wins and a pair of ties over the span, success on the Eastern Seaboard had been fleeting at best. The New York Jets, Oakland's first road opponent in 1967, made further success difficult, Pitting the league's top defense against its top offense. The Jets were the Eastern Division's only winning team at the early point in the campaign with a 2-1 mark. Quarterback Joe Namath made things more interesting with his midweek accusations of dirty play from defensive end Ben Davidson, referring to him as "cheap shot" and Dan Birdwell as "dirty" for his use of a legal head slap as a part of his charge up-field that once rendered an opposing tight end unconscious! General manager Scotty Sterling quickly defended his players, especially Davidson. Unlike Birdwell, Davidson's spirited play had drawn complaints from the opposition in the past, however game films had always shown his play to be legal. The aggressive play of Oakland's defenders inspired the New York press to brand them with another tag, "the 11 Angry Men."

With the debate raging over the aggressive play of this angry eleven being unethical or illegal, in reality it was no more so than the Jets' defense copying their style as they pursued and punished Daryle Lamonica with their front four and blitzing linebackers. The intense pressure, combined with Lamonica's still strengthening grasp of the Raiders' offense aided the New York secondary in stealing four passes. Despite posting 102 of Oakland's 109 points over the first three games, the Jets' interception total raised concern about Lamonica's ability to run the Raiders' intricate offense, which sputtered and coughed to a 17-0 halftime deficit. Saved by his running game, Namath was in fact outperformed by Lamonica in the opening half as Broadway Joe completed only 2 passes in 12 attempts with a pair of Willie Brown interceptions. Lamonica cracked the Jets defense in the second half with touchdown strikes to Warren Wells and Bill Miller but Emerson Boozer and Bill Mathis provided the difference in the AFL's fifth week accounting for three rushing touchdowns. Adding a second Jim Turner field goal, New York sent the Raiders to their first defeat, 27-14 and into a tie with Kansas City for second place in the West, trailing the Chargers by a half game as they posted an inopportune 31-point tie with the Boston Patriots.

A seemingly perfect foil to their recent misfortune awaited at Buffalo's War Memorial Stadium. The Bills, missing 15 of their 40 players over the first five games of the regular season, limped home with a 2-win, 3-loss record and a far cry from the team that had dashed Oakland's division championship hopes the previous Thanksgiving Day. In most instances the home team would welcome a capacity crowd yet, in this instance, the vast majority in attendance badly wanted to undo the draft day deal that sent Daryle Lamonica west for Tom Flores (who had earned the starting job at quarterback before handing it back to Jack Kemp because of injuries to his eye and knee) and Art Powell. Battling his emotions upon his return to his former home, Lamonica also found himself wrestling with a pair of ugly rumors midweek, one suggesting he was failing to grasp the complexities of Oakland's offense, forcing Clem Daniels to call plays in the huddle and another alluding that his being traded was brought on by his disinterest in game preparations and that he was given a written test by coach Joe Collier on the Bills' offense that he reportedly failed the night before Buffalo's 31-7 loss to the Chiefs in the AFL Championship game.

Welcomed back with a standing ovation by the Bills' home crowd, Lamonica was treated poorly by his former mates. Fielding intense pressure and trailing 7-0 late in the first half, Lamonica followed a 35-yard Roger Bird punt return with a 41-yard touchdown strike to Fred Biletnikoff, who'd reclaimed his starting role at flanker. Oakland climbed ahead 10-7 after a field goal. As the clock wore down toward halftime an imminent sack on Jack Kemp by Tom Keating and Ike Lassiter aided a poor decision to throw the ball away to save yardage. His throw sailed into the hands of Dan Conners, whose knack for the turnover resulted in a gift interception that he cashed in 32 yards away for a touchdown and Oakland took a 17-7 lead into the break.

Misfortune also lent a hand to the home team. A Lamonica pass deflected by Roland McDole fell to Jim Dunaway who rambled to the 3-yard line. Former Charger Keith Lincoln punched it in to cut the Raiders lead to three at 17-14. A pass to Art Powell, who'd been battling tight coverage from Willie Brown throughout the contest, sailed high over the former Raider's head and was intercepted by safety Howie Williams. Given the opportunity to put the game away, Lamonica found Billy Cannon for a three-yard touchdown on the drive's sixth play and a 24-14 Raider lead. As the defense relaxed for the first time in 1967, Kemp moved the Bills offense 67 yards in five plays and hit Powell to make the loss appear more respectable. A botched extra point attempt made the final Buffalo tally count for only six points as the three-time defending Eastern Division champions fell 24-20.

A second consecutive four-interception performance by Lamonica was again overshadowed, as his defense created enough havoc that the opposition only appeared competitive. Even in defeat Oakland's defenders were dominant as only 9 of Joe Namath's 28 pass attempts were completed. Lamonica's struggles over the past two games, aided opposing offenses in adding six touchdowns since the Raiders departed for the Northeast bringing the yearly total to ten (five though the air and five on the ground) and equaling the number of passes intercepted by the Oakland defense. Only one quarterback had completed half of his throws against the Raiders angry eleven, Boston's Babe Parilli. Sharing the backfield with the still unbelieving Jim Nance gave additional motivation for Oakland's defenders who came to Boston's Fenway Park and held Nance to 54 yards on the ground, rendering him a non-factor again, even with a 1-yard touchdown blast. Parilli fared no better. Connecting on 10 passes in 33 tries, Boston's offense garnered only 152 total yards for the day and their two trips to the end zone were enabled by Oakland miscues as both drives covered less than 30 yards. To aid the struggling Lamonica, coach Rauch sought to add balance to the Oakland attack. Using Roger Hagberg (in relief of an injured Hewritt Dixon) and Clem Daniels, who, together, picked up 110 yards and a Hagberg score. Setting the pace 20-0 at halftime by adding an 8-yard scoring reception by Bill Miller and a pair of Blanda field goals the ground game softened the Patriots' defense enough that Oakland again took to the air. Lamonica fired scoring strikes to Hagberg, Billy Cannon and Warren Wells, whose second score, a 48-yard bomb from George Blanda late in the game, sealed a devastating 48-14 win over Boston.

Upon their return to Oakland, the Raiders were greeted by a record crowd of 53,474 for their meeting with the undefeated San Diego Chargers. Featuring pro football's most explosive arsenal and dominating defense, this seventh contest was widely thought of as a precursor to the second AFL/NFL championship game with the winner taking on the National League champions in Miami's Orange Bowl Stadium. Led by veterans John Hadl and Lance Alworth; the Chargers' offense compiled 314 yards of total offense against Oakland's uncharitable defenders, twice the weekly average of ground yielded and scoring 10 first-half points. An offensive miscue cost the Raiders an early touchdown as Joe Beauchamp intercepted a Lamonica pass on the Chargers' 4. Instead of seven, Oakland happily settled for two points when Dan Birdwell shrugged off a block and planted a defenseless Dickie Post in the end zone for a safety. A 40-yard pass to Clem Daniels late in the first quarter and a 3-yard scramble by Daryle Lamonica a quarter later granted them a 16-10 halftime edge. After intermission all bets were off.

Having never trailed in the contest, the Oakland Raiders used the second half of this contest as a demonstration of what was to be expected from them throughout the remainder of the season. Putting distance between them and the Chargers on a day when Clem Daniels surpassed Charger Paul Lowe as the AFL's all-time rushing leader, Lamonica matched his 1-yard blast also adding seven points from the 1. For his efforts in making the first quarter interception, Joe Beauchamp was scorched by Fred Biletnikoff for a 70-yard touchdown before the relief took over and added the final two nails to San Diego's coffin in the form of a 14-yard George Blanda pass that found Warren Wells in the end zone and a 7-yard run from Hewritt Dixon, who was working his way back to the starting lineup. As time ran down to none, the Oakland Raiders for the first time, made claim to sole possession of first place in the American Football League's Western Division, posting their second 51-point outing of the year and humbling their in-state rival and former tormentors by 41 points.

As soon as they seemingly became comfortable at home following a 3-game, 17-day road swing bags were packed again for a quick trip to the Rockies. Losers of six straight going back to Oakland's first 51-point onslaught, the Denver Broncos had their hopes derailed that coach Lou Saban could turn their franchise into a winner. Featuring the Offensive Player of the Week in Clem Daniels and Dave Grayson becoming the second Raider in as many weeks (following Dan Connors against Boston) to be named AFL Defensive Player of the Week by the Associated Press for his 3-interception performance, the Raiders were performing in high gear on both sides of the ball. Denver's losing string would reach its seventh game as the near freezing Denver weather could only slow the Oakland offense but not stop them as a pair of short passes (covering 2 and 7 yards) from Lamonica to Bill Miller helped to open up an 18-0 lead in the second quarter.

Snow midweek helped to make the field at Bear Stadium a slippery mess and as it caused Kent McClouhan to slip, Al Denson took a Steve Tensi pass 69 yards for a touchdown. Even with this break Denver didn't have possession on the Raiders' side of the field until the final play of the third quarter when a fumbled punt was recovered on the Oakland 34-yard line, leading to another touchdown. Bob Humphreys matched George Blanda's 100th AFL field goal yet Denver's 17 points couldn't match Oakland's 21 as the Raiders sailed to their fourth win in a row.

Even through a poor outing in Denver, the Oakland Raiders left Bears Stadium with the franchise's longest win streak still intact and with the Miami Dolphins visiting The Coliseum, there was no plausible reason to think it would stop. Featuring Purdue rookie Bob Griese at quarterback, George Wilson's Dolphins were winless since the opening game and had now lost seven games in succession. While optimistic for a positive result, the Dolphins' ownership took another stance in regard to their upcoming opponent and in his praise Joe Robbie was the first to openly predict the Oakland Raiders would represent the American Football League in the second AFL/NFL championship game.

Robbie's prognostication was less than fearless. The balance coach Rauch sought had earned his offense the league's top ranking. Tallying 267 points over eight outings Oakland had also mastered the art of ball control posting an average of 68.5 offensive plays per game. Fullback Hewritt Dixon and halfback Clem Daniels comprised a formidable 1-2 punch, combining for more than 1,400 yards of total offense between them as Daniels served as the ground force amassing 540 yards while Dixon contributed 423 yards to the air corps. Even with this offensive might Lamonica's first season starting under center was being overshadowed by the defense. Having long featured the youngest set of linebackers in pro football, Oakland's group had developed superbly and behind captain Dan Conners, who'd matured into one of professional football's best defensive signal callers, and was as fierce as Oakland's front four. The prowess of the Raiders' front seven, hurt their secondary statistically as Oakland's corners and safeties trailed both Kansas City and San Diego in the number of enemy passes thieved, yet what those statistics didn't tell was the number of passes falling harmlessly to the ground or the league best in points allowed, averaging only 14.5 per game.

With their assertions that they wouldn't overlook Miami it seemed, early on, that the Raiders had done precisely that. Falling behind 10-7 at halftime, it took less than two minutes of the second half for them to recapture the lead, beginning with Rod Sherman's 49-yard kick off return to the Miami 47. An 8-yard draw by Dixon and a 38-yard Lamonica to Miller connection gave Oakland a first and goal inside the 1. Clem Daniels' thrust into the end zone provided Oakland with a 14-10 lead, yet a freak accident later in the period made the score his last. While in pass protection, teammate Bob Svihus fell across Daniels' leg breaking the fibula, a pencil-thin bone. The injury ended his season. Billy Cannon tallied his second and third touchdown receptions in a 31-17 victory yet his heroics were quickly forgotten as the reality of the fate suffered by Oakland's greatest offensive weapon sank in.

This would be a test of Oakland's depth. Before his injury Daniels had run his AFL record career rushing yardage mark to 5,101 yards and added 3,291 yards of offense catching passes and reached the end zone on 54 occasions. Out of action since breaking a bone in his foot in training camp, Larry Todd was forced into a back-up role although he still walked with an occasional limp. Sporting a professional résumé that read nine career rushes, Pete Banaszak was thrust into the starting role. Not on pace with his superstar predecessor, Banaszak began to carve his own mark as a Raider on three days' rest in a Thanksgiving Day game against the Chiefs in Kansas City. Unlike the Indians who met the pilgrims after they landed on Plymouth Rock and taught these new residents how to survive in the new world, the Chiefs were the perfect Thanksgiving feast for the invading Raiders, who totaled 469 yards of offense. Banaszak's first career touchdown, and his 6.3 yards per carry average, was only a small part of Kansas City's woes as Len Dawson saw two of his passes intercepted and returned for touchdowns in a 44-22 rout.

The three-day break between the Miami and Kansas City games afforded Oakland a 10-day rest before returning to the road to face the San Diego Chargers for their most crucial game of the season. Unbeaten since their 51-10 embarrassment in Oakland, the Chargers remained only a half game back of the division leading Raiders and needed to remain so if they were to have any hopes of setting the pace in the Western Division and fending off a powerful Raiders team for their sixth division title in eight years. The Chargers came out gunning. Launching a bomb to receiver Gary Garrison for 60 yards and a pair of pass interference calls on Conners and McCloughan put San Diego on the Raiders 1 yard line with a first and goal. Hadl's sneak tied the game at seven 8½ minutes into the opening quarter. Oakland answered twice, first with a Blanda field goal and then with a 64-yard Lamonica to Cannon strike that launched the Raiders ahead 17-7 at the end of the period. The Chargers weren't out of ammunition, as another Hadl bomb found Lance Alworth for a 57-yard touchdown that cut their deficit to three. They would never come any closer. A 29-yard scoring grab by Bill Miller and a 2-yard run by Larry Todd, who was recovered enough to share the halfback role with Banaszak, extended Oakland's lead to 31-14 before the Chargers last gasp gave them a 29-yard Garrison touchdown reception just before halftime. Adding ten points in the second half, Oakland cruised to a 41-21 victory over a Chargers team, who post-game, joined Joe Robbie in proclaiming Oakland as the inevitable league champions.

With three games remaining in league play, the realization of Oakland's dreams of their first division championship was only two games away. Needing two wins, a pair of San Diego losses or a combination of each was all that was required over the final weeks and Oakland made half the journey before they took the field as the Chargers were shocked on the road by the Miami Dolphins, who administered a 41-24 beating to San Diego. Needing to keep pace with the Jets in the East, Houston and their defense, the current league leaders in points allowed, held current AFL Player of the Week Daryle Lamonica and the Oakland offense scoreless in the first half taking a 7-0 lead on a 28-yard Pete Beathard pass to Hoyle Granger. Able to chip away at their deficit with a pair of field goals from Blanda, a third kick put them ahead four minutes into the final period. Hopes of a Houston comeback were short-lived. Attempting to connect with Granger, Beathard watched helplessly as Dan Conners raced between him and his fullback on the 35. A pair of Dixon runs, first for eight yards followed by a 27-yard jaunt for a touchdown sealed the win and Oakland's first division championship.

Victorious 19-7 as AFL Offensive Player of the Week George Blanda closed out the scoring with his fourth field goal, the Raiders were assured a third consecutive home game as home field advantage in 1967 AFL Championship game belonged to the Western Division champions. With postseason play guaranteed it seemed like a natural time to relent. At 11-1 and the obvious favorite to capture the American Football League championship, these Raiders found a perfect source of inspiration in the form of Joe Namath and the New York Jets. Memories of 1967's only shortcoming and the pre-game accusations of the Jets' quarterback were still fresh in the minds of both the Oakland players and the fans that packed the Oakland Alameda County Coliseum. To them this was no meaningless football game. New York, tied atop the East with Houston, could not afford a loss to the Raiders or in San Diego the next week where they were winless through seven seasons. Not having won in Oakland since becoming the Jets, the New York team would make history by defeating the Chargers in San Diego in the final week but first they would need to survive their thirteenth contest in Oakland.

On his way to making professional football history as the first quarterback to pass for 4,000 yards (at 4,007) Namath would complete this feat, enduring the pain of a fractured jaw through the final seven quarters of 1967 courtesy of a violent shot from Ike Lassiter. In all 17 penalties were assessed (nine against Oakland) and fights broke out throughout the afternoon. Displaying the heart of a warrior, Namath led his Jets' team throwing 28 yards to Don Maynard to go ahead 7-0. Lamonica brought the Raiders from behind, finding Warren Wells for an 18-yard score and the lead at 10-7. Namath later picked up a fumble on the Oakland 3 and carried it in for a 14-10 edge at halftime. The effort of New York's "hippie" (as he was referred to by the Oakland press), while valiant, were overshadowed by Lamonica's, who took the lead for good with a four-yard toss to Banaszak. Soon to be dubbed "The Mad Bomber" Lamonica fired 47 yards to Cannon for a score and a 72-yard shot to Banaszak set up a 6-yard run around the right end for another. Down 31-14, Namath had no choice but to take to the air. He found George Sauer for a 24-yard touchdown and later lobbed Don Maynard his second score of the afternoon from 5 yards out. This war was settled 38-29 in favor of the Raiders who avenged their sole loss and left them just one game away from history.

Five years removed from the American Football League's worst record at 1-13, the Oakland Raiders stood poised to re-establish the league's best mark with a complete reversal of fortune at 13-1. The laurels of a 12-1 mark were heavy in Oakland. Starting at the top, coach John Rauch was named American Football League Coach of the Year while his quarterback rebounded from his early struggles with the complex Raider offense as Daryle Lamonica was chosen as the league's Most Valuable Player. Kent McCloughan, Tom Keating and Ben Davidson joined Jim Otto, Billy Cannon and Lamonica as AFL All-Stars while a half-dozen of their teammates Harry Schuh, Wayne Hawkins, Hewritt Dixon, Dan Conners, Willie Brown and Roger Bird, joined them on the Western squad in the AFL's All-Star game in Jacksonville, Florida. Five Raiders, Otto, Schuh, McCloughan, Conners and Keating (the only player to be given the nod from all nine American Football League head coaches), were named to the All-AFL coaches' list.

For the Raiders' organization and their fans alike the success of the 1967 season was a dream come true. Yet early in their Christmas Eve league finale against the injury riddled Buffalo Bills, the Oakland team appeared to be sleep walking early on. An early turnover allowed the Bills to strike first with a 30-yard field goal from Mike Mercer and a fierce rush from Jim Dunaway and Howard Kindig, with the latter ripping the ball from Lamonica's grasp on the Oakland 11. The ball taking the ultimate Buffalo roll, headed toward and into the end zone where Tom Sestak recovered for a touchdown and a 10-0 lead. Regaining possession on their 20 after a touchback, Lamonica directed a 7-play, 80-yard drive that resulted in a 28-yard improvisation to Billy Cannon for Lamonica's thirtieth and final touchdown of the season that saw him complete 220 passes in 425 attempts for 3,228 yards. Plunging through the line to run the clock and send Buffalo to the locker room at halftime ahead at 10-7, fullback Wray Carlton was met by Dan Conners. Instead of making a tackle Conners wrestled the ball from Carlton and romped 21 yards for the go-ahead score and a 14-10 Raiders' lead.

Mercer's second field goal cut the Raiders' lead to one to open the second half and as they had when Lamonica struggled early in the season, the defense took over when he was rested for the postseason. George Blanda was able to enjoy an eight-point cushion as Carleton Oats matched the Bills, grabbing a Jack Kemp fumble on the 11-yard line and scoring on the return. Another memorable highlight saw Gus Otto, Ike Lassiter and Dan Birdwell chase Kemp back and touching him down for a 31-

yard loss. On second down and 41, a quick pass to Paul Costa proved costly as the tight end broke Warren Powers tackle and raced 63 yards for a touchdown. Kemp's two-yard run tied the score at 21 on the conversion but his misfortune led to Buffalo's demise. His second interception (both by Powers) gave Oakland possession in Bills territory at the 47. As 2:13 remained the Raiders earned the AFL's best ever, regular season record at 13-1 as Hewritt Dixon slammed over from the 1 and Oakland finished the campaign with a 28-21 victory.

Demonstrating that great teams find a way to achieve victory even when handicapped by lackluster production, the Oakland Raiders in 1967 had become arguably the best team ever fielded by the American Football League in their eight years and its one-time orphan now had a date with destiny. Like lambs to the slaughter the Houston Oilers, with help from Oakland's 38-29 mauling of the Jets two weeks prior, arrived at the Oakland Alameda County Coliseum for a New Year's Eve showdown for the American Football League Championship and the opportunity to represent the AFL in Miami's Orange Bowl Stadium against the National Football League champions in the second AFL/NFL championship game. As league champions in the AFL's first two seasons and runner up in its third, the Houston Oilers had a long history of unkind treatment of the Oakland Raiders. Beginning with the 37-22 home beating in 1960's opening week, to the ungracious treatment of the Raiders to open the 1961 campaign in Houston, setting an AFL record with a 55-0 slaughter that began the end for Eddie Erdelatz and the 31-0 thrashing administered the season before in Houston eight days before Oakland could open its new coliseum. Yet times had changed dramatically. Now Oakland had the better team, a remarkably better team that many in the AFL felt Wally Lemm's Oilers' club had no business competing against. Their trip out West was earned and just 21 days before this championship match-up, the Oilers in defeat gave Oakland their toughest fight of the season. Another low-scoring clash was expected with Oakland's 11 angry men expected to yield nothing to Houston's very little.

In the week leading up to Oakland's first title game coach Rauch scoffed at the odds-makers appointing his Raiders a 10-½ point favorite. Post-game he praised his squad for one of the most dominating performances in AFL championship history calling the win "a complete victory." Runs for 69 yards by Hewritt Dixon, a 1-yard scramble by Lamonica, a 10-yard toss to Dave Kocourek and George Blanda's third field goal just 44 seconds into the final quarter had turned what was supposed to be a battle into an Oakland rout as the Raiders opened up a 30-0 lead. With Houston's only sign of life resulting in a 4-play 78-yard drive that ended with a 5-yard Willie Frazier touchdown from Beathard, Oakland added another field goal and a 12-yard Lamonica scoring pass to Bill Miller to complete the Houston humiliation. Dispatching the runner-up Oilers with a 40-7 defeat, the Oakland Raiders, as champions of the American Football League, packed for Miami to meet the Green Bay Packers.

CHAPTER NINE
BOMBING SWITZERLAND
1968

Amassing 14 victories over 15 outings in 1967 and racking up an astounding 508 points since the beginning of league play couldn't keep the American Football League champions from being installed as 10-½ point underdogs against the champions of the National Football League. Winners of four NFL championships in six seasons and posting a victory over the Kansas City Chiefs in the inaugural inter-league championship the year before, the Green Bay Packers were an experienced and potentially overpowering opponent for a young California club gearing up for their biggest game in Miami. They wouldn't be alone. Three Bay Area travel agencies announced tour packages, which were snatched up by approximately 4,000 Raiders fans eager to trek the 3,144 miles to join their team in Orange Bowl Stadium. They would meet nearly 10% of the 800 residents of Crivitz, Wisconsin, all lifelong Packer fans, who headed south to root for the Raiders, as their favorite son Pete Banaszak's team had remained unbeaten since he assumed the starting halfback role in the absence of Clem Daniels.

Despite the groundswell of support and stellar on-field results a monumental foe lay ahead. Vince Lombardi's Packers were as close to perfect in terms of their overall execution as any football team would ever come. With a club stocked with players like Bart Starr, hailed as "the complete quarterback" throwing to a battery of receivers such as Boyd

Dowler, Carroll Dale and Max McGee. He was joined in the backfield by veteran halfback Donnie Anderson and rookie fullback Travis Williams, running behind an offensive line led by Forest Gregg and Jerry Kramer; on defense Green Bay could be equally intimidating. Led by middle linebacker Ray Nitschke, Packers defenders' held their opponents to 10 points or fewer five times in 1967, posting a pair of shutouts. With an All-Pro line-up featuring defensive backs Herb Adderly, Bob Jeter and Willie Wood, linebacker Dave Robinson and defensive lineman Willie Davis, the Raiders opponent's in this world championship game were not only the best the National Football League had to offer but arguably the greatest professional football team of all time.

No new wrinkles were added to the Oakland attack, as execution needed to be as near perfect as the opponent they faced if coach Rauch's squad were to defeat the mighty Packers, who would take the field this one last time for coach Lombardi. On January 14, 1968 they were not. The hard-charging defensive line was equal to the task of the Packers protective wall, disrupting Green Bay's attack and holding the National League champions to a pair of Don Chandler field goals as they took a 6-0 lead 17 minutes into the ball game. As Oakland's 11 angry men hounded Starr, Daryle Lamonica enjoyed outstanding protection from his lineman but was often off target as the Raiders' offense sputtered early. On first down from the Packer 38, Starr faked a handoff to Travis Williams. Fooling both Kent McCloughan and Howie Williams who came up play the run, Boyd Dowler was alone on the Oakland 40 and Starr made the Raiders pay with a 62-yard touchdown strike. Down 13-0, Oakland went to their ground game. Handing the ball to Dixon and Banaszak opened up the passing game and with a 23-yard Lamonica pass over linebacker Dave Robinson to Bill Miller, they were on the board. Trailing by six points, opportunities to tie the ball game were blown as George Blanda kicked short on a 47 yard field goal try and a back-breaking botched fair catch by Roger Bird came with 23 seconds remaining in the half. Dick Capp's recovery on the Oakland 45 led to Chandler's third field goal of the half as Oakland found themselves trailing by nine at intermission.

Through the air in the second half, Starr sliced the Raiders' secondary to ribbons with a 34-yard pass to McGee, followed by an 11-yard strike to Dale and a 12-yard swing pass to Anderson for a first and goal on the 2-yard line. Powering through the line and over Bill Laskey, Anderson put Green Bay ahead 23-7. Don Chandler's fourth field goal set Oakland back another three points as the Raiders offense, in a hurry-up mode early in the fourth quarter, became defenders as Lamonica's pass for Biletnikoff was picked off by Herb Adderly on the Green Bay 40. Blocks by Henry Jordan on Wayne Hawkins and Ron Kostelnick on Gene Upshaw provided the perfect escort for Adderly, whose touchdown buried Oakland in a 33-7 Packer avalanche. The Raiders found the end zone once more with a 23-yard Lamonica to Miller encore to pull within 19 points. Though the defense continually hounded and harassed Starr, no further opportunities arose. Time expired and Green Bay had secured its second consecutive world championship, 33-14.

(2)

As 11 players remained in Florida to take part in the AFL All-Star game in Jacksonville an equal number returned to Oakland and were greeted with a heroes' welcome at the airport, while the remainder of the roster scattered across the country, returning to their off-season homes. Yet before any could arrive anywhere it was learned that one in eight on the squad were no longer Oakland Raiders. With the 1968 college entry draft scheduled two weeks after the championship game, the AFL had little choice other than to schedule the expansion draft at the earliest possible date to give Paul Brown a chance to stock his new Cincinnati club with veteran talent while giving the remainder of the league (save Miami, who were exempt from this process) as much time as possible to reassess their needs in light of these sudden departures.

As veterans were secured by the Bengals from across the league, Brown's team tapped into Oakland's youth movement as five men, all having just completed their rookie campaigns, were chosen to play in Southern Ohio. Among them was Dan Archer, one of those welcomed by appreciative fans at the Oakland airport, 7' defensive tackle Richard Sligh, halfback Estes Banks, his taxi squad counterpart Nate Johns and Rod Sherman, 1967's starting flanker, left unprotected after Fred Biletnikoff regained the top spot.

The loss of Sherman was a focal point in the upcoming draft. Wanting a speedy receiver but forced to wait and see what remained when Oakland picked twenty-fifth overall and nearly last in every round, the hopes of obtaining a Haven Moses from San Diego State, an Earl McCullouch of Southern California, a Dennis Homan from the Alabama Crimson Tide or a Jim Biernes from Purdue were slim. Barely missing the opportunity to select McCullouch, who was taken twenty-fourth by the Detroit Lions, only the Boilermaker Biernes remained. With him on the board the Raiders went in a different and somewhat surprising direction by choosing quarterback Eldridge Dickey from Tennessee State. Leading the TSU Tigers to a 7-3 record and a Midwestern Conference championship, Dickey was a gifted runner, posting times of 9.6 seconds in the 100-yard dash and 4.5 seconds in the 40 wearing full football gear. The 6' 2" 198-lb. Dickey, the first African-American quarterback ever selected in the first round of the pro football draft, also possessed superb pass catching abilities and the physical toughness to handle the punt and kick return duties at TSU. He was expected to continue in Oakland.

Called both "a $200,000 bonus baby" and "the best quarterback I ever had" by Alabama head coach Paul "Bear" Bryant, Kenny "The Snake" Stabler lasted until the end of the second round. Perhaps many cash conscious teams were leery of the high price tag put on him by his coach, his being selected in the second round of Major League Baseball's draft by the Houston Astros or his being left handed contributed to his falling so low. However when it became the Raiders turn to choose a second time they wouldn't pass the opportunity to get him. For Stabler, the opportunity to play for a team he admired made his choice between baseball and football an easy one. The Houston Astros had wasted a second round selection as Stabler quickly chose to play football in Oakland.

To protect these new passers as well as the incumbents Maryland State University two-way tackle Art Shell was selected third. Standing 6'5" and weighing 270 lbs., Shell was considered the best pro prospect from the school since Emerson Boozer became a New York Jet. Before transferring to Utah, halfback Charlie Smith was a Junior College All-American at Bakersfield J.C. and would return to his native Oakland where he starred at Castlemont High via a fourth round pick and 6'10" 280-lb. John Naponic became the second two-way tackle to join the club, coming in round five.

Every AFL team donated their sixth round selections to Cincinnati but in the seventh Oakland had two picks and found another gem in the form of defensive back George Atkinson. A speedster in his own right, Atkinson could cover 100 yards in 9.7 seconds. Weighing only 185 lbs. despite his 6'2" frame, Atkinson was a punishing tackler at Atlanta's tiny Morris Brown College and was given an All-American Honorable Mention laurel, as was ninth round choice tight end John Eason from Florida A&M. Eason wasn't the only tight end selected. Colgate Red Raider Marv

Hubbard was taken with Oakland's first pick of round 11 and would be converted to fullback while the second choice, Ralph "Chip" Oliver, was a kamikaze linebacker from USC who looked to fit nicely into Oakland's punishing defensive unit.

(3)

Apart from another stellar draft the Oakland Raiders settled into a relatively quiet off-season. The only real changes would occur in the front office. Scotty Sterling, the former publicist, would resign from the general manager's post he'd held with the team since April 1966 when Al Davis left to become AFL commissioner. Unsure of his future at the time of his departure, Sterling found work in the National Basketball Association while his duties would be absorbed by Bob Bestor the public relations director given the new title of business manager and Del Courtney, the promotions director turned director of administration. Filling Bestor's role in public relations was former quarterback Lee Grosscup, who had spent the two years since his football retirement as sports director at KCPX TV, in Salt Lake City.

Evolved and newly intact, the Raiders' directorship began stocking for the upcoming season. Building on an intact championship club in 1968, outside of an outstanding rookie crop added more fodder than force. Brought aboard from the Miami Dolphins for a conditional draft choice was veteran defensive end Ed Cooke. Ultimately his retirement prior to camp cost the Raiders nothing while leaving the reserve status on the well-stocked defensive line clouded with the addition of Bill Keating from Denver, who stood to see significant playing time in the exhibition slate as his older brother Tom faced an easy summer recuperating from an Achilles tendon injury suffered in the AFL Championship game that required off-season surgery. Other Broncos journeyed west to audition for duties on the Raiders' offensive line as guard Ernie Park was dealt west for the multi skilled, taxi squad player Rick Egloff. Veteran center and tackle Dave Behrman also came in to compete for a reserve role.

With the lone exception of Kenny Stabler, who was recovering from a knee operation that would keep him out of action as a Raider in 1968, a full complement of rookies and new veterans reported to Santa Rosa to begin drills. Following them a week after was nearly a full complement of returning veterans, save the mending Tom Keating and Bill Fairband.

These men, like Stabler, wouldn't see action in the coming year and George Blanda, whose-off season conditioning kept him in excellent physical shape was rewarded by coach Rauch with an extra few days of vacation. Fortunate enough to miss the screening of the horror film that was shot in Miami as the Raiders malfunctioned against the Green Bay Packers, Blanda was not only greeted by Lamonica, Cotton Davidson, who was seeking a return to action from the press box, Charlie Green, taking another shot at the AFL after a successful stint in the Continental League, but a new kicking coach. Louis "Bugsy" Engleburg, was hired by coach Rauch after taking two injured kickers (a punter and a place kicker) both under doctors' orders to refrain from football and turning them into league leaders. Engleburg would work with not only Blanda on his place kicking, but with punter Mike Eischied, guard Gene Upshaw and Gus Otto should Blanda be unable to perform, as well as mentoring rookie John Eason should Eischied be unable to punt.

With their eyes set on a second consecutive AFL championship prize, the Raiders found their exhibition schedule clouded. Labor issues in the National Football League brought forth a promise from Vince Lombardi, remaining in Green Bay as Packers' general manager to not field a team against the college All-Stars that was not in top condition and announced his intention to ask the game's sponsors to invite the Raiders to take their place. Instead of facing the college All-Stars on August 2, the Raiders played host to their originally assigned opponent, the Baltimore Colts, a day later at The Coliseum. Featuring arguably professional football's greatest quarterback, Johnny Unitas, and what in 1967 was the National Football League's stingiest defense allowing a mere 21 touchdowns in 14 games and thieving 32 enemy passes, the Colts were another club with more experience than the one that ran up a 13-1 regular season record en route to an American Football League title.

The success enjoyed the season prior gave many players whose deals had expired added confidence in asking managing general partner Al Davis for more money in exchange for their services. For the most part negotiations went smoothly. The reigning AFL champions, in camp preparing for the historic opening preseason game where an experiment would be held regarding how the point after touchdowns were awarded, received a scare as one of their most popular and destructive defenders walked out of camp in a dispute and threatened to retire. Though being spelled ably by Carleton Oats, Tom Keating's absence meant the Raiders could ill afford to lose Ben Davidson but were forced to plan their future without him and traded a 1969 draft selection to the Houston Oilers for 6'7" defensive end George Allen, a second year man who spent the last half of the 1967 campaign on the Houston taxi squad.

Wanting to rejoin his teammates, Davidson set aside his dissatisfaction with team management in time to face Baltimore. Aside from Oats' elevation to the starting lineup 10 of Oakland's 11 angry men remained from their championship run. On offense the changes were also singular as Warren Wells moved ahead of Bill Miller to assume the starting split end role. A sell-out crowd at The Coliseum saw the NFL's Most Valuable Player, Johnny Unitas, complete 10 passes in 17 attempts, bringing the Colts in close for a pair of Baltimore touchdown runs from Tom Matte and Jerry Hill. Trailing 14-0, the AFL's top player, Daryle Lamonica, connected on six throws of his own in eleven tries. His squad failed to reach the end zone and settled for a 9-yard field goal from George Blanda and an 11-point halftime deficit.

With most of both teams' first units done for the evening, their respective coaches began to evaluate their newer talent. A returning Raiders quarterback was given the opportunity to prove himself. Exchanging a place in the press box for a role under center, Cotton Davidson led a 12-play, 76-yard drive that culminated in a 19-yard touchdown pass to Wells, cutting six away from the Colts' 11-point lead. The conversion, an experimental idea conceived by NFL commissioner Pete Rozelle took the option of place kicking away and required a team to either pass or run for a single extra point. Lenny Lyles, not about to be beaten again as he had on Wells' touchdown, batted Davidson's throw to The Coliseum turf to keep Oakland down by five points. Dormant, the Baltimore attack failed to add to their lead but the Oakland offense only managed another field goal and dropped their opening exhibition game 14-12.

Injuries would take a bite from the Raiders' roster. Daryle Lamonica bruised his knee and Kent McCloughan was ailing from a groin pull post-game. Midweek the offensive line lost Wayne Hawkins as a practice mishap sidelined him for the coming game against San Diego. Lamonica recovered quickly, outracing fellow quarterbacks in drills while Jim Harvey assumed Hawkins spot in the starting lineup until the nine-year vet was able to return and safety Dave Grayson in the meantime moved over to McCloughan's corner spot. These moves, along with nine players, including quarterback Charlie Green, returning Raiders' lineman Rich Zecher, who had bounced to Buffalo, and the expansion Bengals franchise after being taken by Miami two years earlier in the expansion draft and converted to defense, and Tom Keating's younger brother Bill were cut, along with a half dozen rookies; notably converted fullback Marv Hubbard and receiver Larry Plantz from Colorado. Yet these scares, shifts and losses were greeted by some heartening news as the league's all-time leading rusher, Clem Daniels, would make his return to action and to the starting lineup against San Diego.

Aside from giving his veterans another tune-up, coach Rauch would get a good look at several of his new rookies. Among them, Art Shell, Charlie Smith, Chip Oliver, John Eason and George Atkinson; and against the Chargers each would have an impact. Trailing 7-3 early in the contest Atkinson took kicker Tom Dempsey's kickoff 2 yards deep in the end zone and raced 57 yards into San Diego territory. A scrambling Lamonica then found Billy Cannon for 25 yards. Following a Hewritt Dixon run, Wells broke open for a 14-yard touchdown and a 10-7 lead with 6:03 gone in the first quarter. The offense was back in the end zone two minutes later when Lamonica found Biletnikoff with a 30-yard pass.

After turning the game into a runaway early on, Oakland's coaches went to their reserves. Roger Hagberg and Charlie Smith carried the bulk of the load on an 8-play, 71-yard drive that resulted in a Hagberg fumble on the Chargers' 1-yard line that Smith recovered for six points. From his end zone, San Diego punter Dennis Partee sent a kick off the uprights that went out of bounds three yards from the goal line. On first and goal fullback Preston Ridlehuber scored and the Chargers went away losers, 31-7.

It was 14 days between Oakland's second and third preseason games. Two full weeks for Clem Daniels to give assurances of his legs' complete rehabilitation and confess to acquiring rust due to inactivity. The roster numbers thinned as John Guillory was waived after an outstanding season playing for the San Jose Apaches, as was former Utah tackle Greg Kent, the 1965 red shirt who saw limited action as a rookie in 1966. As these two departed another new face was brought aboard via a trade as a draft choice was dealt to Miami in exchange for receiver John Roderick. A 9.3 sprinter at Southern Methodist, Roderick had been sidelined for the majority of his two professional seasons, seeing action in only six games due to both illness and injury.

With a pair of streaks in hand, two preseason games without a touchdown scored against them through the air and 12 (regular, post and pre-season) consecutive games undefeated against American Football League competition. Eldridge Dickey took the opening kickoff in

Kansas City for a spectacular 46-yard return, giving Oakland optimum field position but a miscue on first down cost them dearly as a Roger Hagberg fumble was recovered by linebacker Jim Lynch on the Oakland 44. Following an offside call on the defense, Len Dawson punctured the previously impervious Oakland air guard with a 39-yard bomb to Otis Taylor, who had worked himself away from McCloughan. Almost immediately, disaster struck again. Trying to hit Hagberg with a pass, Lamonica's aerial was deflected by linebacker Chuck Hurston into the hands of Willie Lanier at midfield and was returned to the Raiders 25. On the Chiefs second successful play from scrimmage, Dawson victimized the secondary again by putting a pass over Willie Brown to Frank Pitts for a 14-0 Kansas City lead just 4:04 into the opening period.

In their third possession the Oakland offense got rolling, traveling 80 yards over 7 plays. A Lamonica strike to Wells covered 45 yards and good work by Billy Cannon to free himself from Caesar Belser on the Chiefs 10 provided a clear path to the end zone with a 17-yard touchdown reception. In spite of this success, misfortune continued to plague the offense. As the second quarter began Jim Lynch secured his second takeaway, stealing a Lamonica pass intended for Eldridge Dickey and returned it 37 yards to the Oakland 28. A touchdown by Mike Garrett handed Oakland back its 14-point deficit. After his hot start, Dawson relearned that playing with a fiery Raiders defense was an excellent way to get burned as Dave Grayson stole a pass intended for Pitts. In close, courtesy of a 36-yard pass interference penalty called against cornerback Emmitt Thomas, Lamonica spotted Dickey uncovered on a crossing route and delivered a 12-yard touchdown. Setting the pace 21-14 at halftime, the Chiefs opened the second half with a 76-yard return from "Super Gnat" Noland Smith that led to a Jan Stenerud field goal. Wendell Hayes later capped a 52-yard, 8-play drive with a 1-yard touchdown blast as the Chiefs pulled away. Charlie Smith would add a meaningless tally late in the game as Oakland fell to Kansas City 31-21.

Unlike the year before, the Raiders' next meeting had only been hyped for weeks in advance. The next destination aside from their Santa Rosa training facility was to their original home at San Francisco's Kezar Stadium. By their admission the pressure was on. Having come up short in two exhibition games versus the rival league and the mistake-riddled shortcoming in Miami against the Packers in the championship game, the AFL champions were one of two American League squads (the Boston Patriots being the other) that were winless against the NFL. Midweek, the 1968 edition of the Oakland Raiders was becoming clearer as several players were cut loose. Among them were veterans Ken Herock and John Robert Williamson while rookies such as John Eason and Chip Oliver were added to the Oakland taxi squad.

Returning to action was veteran guard Wayne Hawkins, healed sufficiently to resume his duties as starting right guard and Hewritt Dixon, who midweek received the praises of managing general partner Al Davis as "the best fullback in the game," was ready to test his foot after suffering a heel bruise. Clem Daniels made claims of a "relaxed confidence," a term echoed by some his teammates, but the men in silver and black found a pessimist in the form of head coach John Rauch. Stressing the importance of this local rivalry, the Oakland coach stressed "There's a lot of pride involved, no matter how well the teams do during the regular season, the outcome of this game will be the talk of the entire Bay Area for a whole year."

In front of the first Kezar Stadium sellout since the 49ers lost 31-27 to Detroit for the NFL's Western Division championship in 1957, the Oakland team evened the score with their cross-bay adversary. Down 6-0 at the end of the first quarter following a 50-yard George Mira pass to John David Crow, it took only 47 seconds of the second period for the lead to be erased with a 36-yard strike from Lamonica to Dixon before the duo chimed in with a 7-yard encore 2:51 later. Oakland's "Mad Bomber" connected with Dave Kocourek for the conversion to go ahead 13-6.

The 49ers seized a prime opportunity to tie the game when Jim Johnson stole a pass intended for Larry Todd on the Oakland 24. On the drives' fourth play San Francisco found the end zone with a 1-yard Dwight Lee run. Another conversion try failed, as Mira's toss to Crow fell incomplete. Running the halfback option, Daniels found Fred Biletnikoff open and completed a gorgeous pass for six points and Dixon added the extra point on the ground. Billy Cannon joined in the scoring act four minutes later, hauling in a 53-yard bomb to lead 26-12. Kermit Alexander's 56-yard punt return for a 49ers touchdown theoretically gave the 49ers a chance at a victory but it would be their last gasp. The Raiders left Kezar with a 26-19 victory in their fourth exhibition and removed all doubt as to which Bay Area city had the better football team.

"Raiders win the big one," trumpeted *The Oakland Tribune* the following morning yet any jubilation felt by finally toppling an NFL opponent quickly dissipated as the team learned the fate of linebacker Bill Laskey. Having been carted off the field early in the second quarter,

Laskey was flown to Los Angeles for surgery to repair his snapped Achilles tendon and was lost through all of 1968. As Duane Benson inherited the starting role, Chip Oliver was recalled from the taxi squad to add depth. Bill Fairband was finally able to begin practicing with the team and hoped to be able to take the field by midseason. With one exhibition game remaining the 1968 Raiders' squad appeared nearly set, as they were one man over the league mandated 40-player roster limit a week and a half before the regular season began.

As placekicking was returned as an option for a touchdown conversion with run and pass conversion again equaling two points, the Oakland club was off to the scene of some recent pre-season disasters, Portland, Oregon's Multnomah Stadium. The Raiders fortunes' had been anything but good in the city, being outscored a combined 94-17 by the Chargers and Chiefs over the past two summers. The third time around was the charm. Looking sharp in this final tune-up before league play was to commence, Lamonica completed 8 passes in 15 attempts for 3 touchdowns, including a 71-yard strike that Billy Cannon caught over safety Pete Jaquess on the Denver 42 before racing off for a 21-0 lead. With Steve Tensi missing from the Bronco lineup for at least half a season veteran John McCormick was at the helm of Denver's offense and averted a shut out with a 28-yard scoring pass to Eric Crabtree. Denver appeared intent on remaining at the bottom of the AFL West as Larry Kaminski centered a snap high over his punters head and out of the end zone as time ran down in the second quarter, giving Oakland a 23-7 victory to wrap up the exhibition schedule.

With the roster nearly set before the Portland excursion there was but one cut prior to opening day in War Memorial Stadium, that of one Mr. Clemon Daniels. Having rehabilitated his broken leg and returned to the starting lineup, the American Football League's most prolific runner vowed he would play again and eventually signed with the San Francisco 49ers.

(4)

Bob Svihus and Ike Lassiter, both suffering injuries against Denver would face the Bills when the Raiders opened the season in Buffalo, while rookie tight end John Eason's torn calf muscle would keep him on the sidelines to begin the 1968 campaign. Following the lead of Ben Davidson, who'd signed a new contract in the days leading to the Oregon trip, Daryle

Lamonica returned to his former stomping grounds far wealthier for his MVP performance and league championship after agreeing to a new three-year deal rumored to be worth $200,000. These veterans led their squad, including George Atkinson, who would be named AFL Defensive Player of the Week for starting a barrage with an 86-yard punt return for a touchdown. Directing traffic as he had before, Roger Bird led the rookie 52 yards on his second return that ended nine yards shy of the end zone. Down 14-0 after Banaszak scored on first down, the Bills slowed Oakland's electrifying rookie but were forced to deal with their explosive offense which exploited them for touchdowns on the ground by Hewritt Dixon that covered 17 yards and a Lamonica strike to Wells as their guests built a 31-0 lead at halftime.

In a performance reminiscent of 1967's opening week, Oakland's defense matched the firepower of their offensive counterparts, flattening Buffalo quarterback Dan Darraugh eight times for loses totaling 94 yards with 16 of his 20 passing attempts falling harmlessly incomplete. Two passes to Bob Cappadonna aided a Bills' scoring drive. With a good effort, Cappadonna tore away from a Bird tackle to give Buffalo six points, Oakland's sole defensive blemish as Duane Benson stopped the 2-point conversion attempt. In relief of Banaszak, who left the game midway through the third period with a muscle strain in his leg, Larry Todd made an impact with runs of 11 and 31 yards for the final two Raiders' tallies. Before most of the shocked Bills fans could exit War Memorial Stadium, Buffalo owner Ralph Wilson informed Joe Collier that his services as head coach were no longer necessary.

In the American Football League no cross-country road trip was brief. Following the 48-6 desecration of Buffalo the Oakland club based themselves in Niagara Falls as they had in years past and began preparing for a trip south to face the Miami Dolphins. Waived, claimed by Cincinnati and waived again only to be reclaimed by Oakland, Warren Powers not only returned to the roster but to the starting line up. Joining him would be USC rookie linebacker Chip Oliver, who played well in Buffalo in place of a hobbling Gus Otto.

To atone for a disappointing 10 for 30 performance that was forgotten in the end zone parade the Raiders held in Buffalo, Lamonica answered with his best day as a professional, connecting 15 times in 24 tries with four first half touchdowns, including two bombs (a 73-yarder to Wells and the other for 49 yards to Banaszak) as Oakland lit the Dolphins up for a 21-0 lead just barely into the second quarter and a 33-14 score at halftime. Lightning also struck on the ground as Banaszak scored from 49 yards after a Dave Grayson interception. Another interception on the Miami 27 was returned for a score by Willie Brown. The host team was run out its own stadium for the second straight week by the Raiders, who romped to their second win 47-21.

"I've never seen such a variety of skillful athletes on one AFL club," said a Dolphins beat writer following the second week shelling, but the high praise did nothing to ease the concerns of coach Rauch, who was already beginning to hear the predictions of an AFL title repeat. Recalling the opening week win over Miami in 1966 and follow up 31-0 embarrassment in Houston, the Raiders organization chose a different approach than it had previously and decided to stay in Texas to get used to the oppressive humidity that had contributed to their malfunction against the lackluster Oilers two years prior.

Weather concerns were frivolous. Their third contest would be a first for them, playing indoors in what Texans called "the 8th wonder of the world," the air-conditioned Houston Astrodome. The only real concerns were the fast footing on the carpeted field aiding an offense John Rauch said was identical to his own and the fatigue of his squad, who was facing their sixth consecutive game away from the Oakland Alameda County Coliseum. Falling flat in the first half, Oakland's shaky offensive performance early on did little to slow the overall production of Hewritt Dixon, whose 26 carries garnered 187 yards of Astroturf. While stellar, Dixon's performance was far from perfect. He fumbled twice, the first at the end of a 23-yard jaunt on the 31 that Houston took 69 yards the other direction in nine plays to take a 7-0 lead. The other halted an Oakland drive on the Oilers' 17. On second down, Dave Grayson stole his first of two passes of the day and erased the Raiders first deficit of 1968 with a 27-yard return for a score. Missing on his first nine passing attempts in a 7 of 22 performance, Lamonica was leveled by linebacker Olen Underwood for a safety. Taking the lead at halftime with a 34-yard field goal by George Blanda after Duane Benson recovered a Bob Davis (under center as coach Lemm benched Trull after his tenth consecutive incompletion) fumble. Through his struggles, Lamonica found Wells on a post pattern and the lead grew to 17-9. The following Oilers' drive stalled on the Raiders' 29, Don Trull's passing attempt on a faked field goal attempt (handicapped by Dan Conners' wrenching his head), was complete to John Wittenborn, who was promptly buried for a 7-yard loss. A 9-yard scoring grab by Billy Cannon set the host Oilers back 24-9 but they would find success keeping the ball on the ground. Hoyle Granger spearheaded a drive and scored on a 1-yard blast. Poised for an encore. Granger was met hard by Warren Powers and fumbled. Grayson recovered and his third takeaway of the day ended Houston's chances. With no visits to Boston or New York scheduled in 1968 with the addition of the Cincinnati Bengals, the Oakland club completed their three-game eastern road swing with an undefeated record following a 24-15 win.

The road had been kind to Oakland in the standings but it had been hard on their bodies. Larry Todd was lost due to a pair of fractured bones in his wrist. The knee injury suffered by Wayne Hawkins in the preseason still lingered and had worsened over time, keeping him out of the line up. Adding to the injury woes was Kent McCloughan suffering from sore ribs, Gus Otto had a broken nose, a hip pointer caused discomfort for Ike Lassiter, second-year guard Gene Upshaw endured a sore back and stiff neck while Warren Wells re-aggravated a thigh injury that kept him from the starting lineup but not from taking the field or making an impact when the Boston Patriots visited The Coliseum.

A noontime rubdown and an ice pack eased the pain in his leg caused by a baseball-sized knot buried in his muscle tissue enough for the split end to come on in the second quarter and erase a 7-0 deficit with a 9-yard touchdown reception and electrify the home crowd with a 41-yard end around early in the third. Wells' heroics sparked a 34-point onslaught in the second half that saw Hewritt Dixon, Fred Biletnikoff and Dave Kocourek make visits to the end zone in a game that mercifully subsided with the expiration of the game clock with the scoreboard reading Oakland 41, Boston 10.

At 4-0 and resetting the team standard for beginning a season, the Oakland Raiders were alone in first place. Kansas City sat a half game back at 4-1 while San Diego lagged by a full game at 3-1. One slip however could drop Oakland all the way back to third place and the visiting Chargers were eager to provide the banana peels.

A midweek clean bill of health proved to be a mirage for Billy Cannon, who had reportedly returned to peak condition, but was slowed by a calf muscle pull and an ankle sprain while coach Rauch was forced to return safety Roger Bird and fullback Preston Ridlehuber from the taxi squad as injured waivers were asked for both Wayne Hawkins and Warren Powers.

The Chargers were a formidable opponent even if the Raiders were at full strength and San Diego ranked first in defense, having not allowed a single touchdown through the air. John Hadl was firing to Lance Alworth as a primary target while Gary Garrison was proving to be a dangerous weapon in his own right, providing a wicked Chargers 1-2 punch, and after fourteen consecutive victories in league play the Oakland club were ripe for the picking. Falling behind 10-0 in the first quarter George Atkinson, after fumbling twice fielding kicks, got his team on the scoreboard and into the game with an 82-yard punt return. But it wasn't until after San Diego added another touchdown, a 38-yard Alworth (who made 9 grabs for 182 yards) reception that the home crowd was given a reason to cheer. Down 17-7 with less than a minute remaining in the half Lamonica and the offense rattled off 8 plays in just 38 seconds and the Chargers' impenetrable air defense watched Warren Wells take in a 7-yard pass to cut the San Diego lead to 17-14 at the intermission. Managing only 45 yards of offense on the ground the entire day, the league's top offense (averaging 427.3 yards of total offense per game) never threatened in the second half. San Diego added a pair of field goals and sailed to a 23-14 upset.

Due to tiebreakers the Raiders had dropped back to third place in the Western Division. Though Kansas City, leading by a half game, was experiencing a rash of injuries that could aid the Oakland cause in regaining the division's top spot. Injured waivers were requested for receiver Otis Taylor, who suffered from a severely pulled groin muscle. Mike Garrett made his way on crutches because of what was described as ankle soreness while an x-ray of Gloster Richardson's ankle promised to keep him from action when the Raiders visited Kansas City's Municipal Stadium.

Garrett had recovered enough to take the field, but without his top receivers, coach Stram utilized a rare formation called the "straight T" (with three backfield runners and a pair of tight ends) made famous by coach Clark Shaughnessy's "Wow Boys" (Frankie Albert, Hugh Gallarneau, Pete Kmetovic and Norm Standlee) on Stanford's 1941 Rose Bowl club. Executing the retread formation to near perfection, Kansas City picked up 294 yards on the ground and opened up a 24-0 lead after 40 minutes of play and pushed Oakland deeper into third place with a 24-10 triumph.

In the midst of the first losing string endured by the Oakland club since dropping three in a row early in 1966, these shortcomings against teams in the thick of the Western Division race did nothing to dim the confidence of the entire Raiders' organization. San Diego and Kansas City were to meet twice and a split would bring Oakland a game closer to them both and with the Raiders' appearing once more on each club's schedule, neither could breathe easy as the defending AFL champions were still in contention for a repeat. The race for the Western Division title promised to be a dogfight.

Returning home to meet an expansion team was the obvious path of least resistance toward the top for Oakland. Bengals' coach Paul Brown had a new wrinkle. Starting Tennessee rookie Dewey Warren at quarterback in place of John Stofa gave a team that faced only three passes the week before (Dawson completed 2 for 16 yards) a handicap as they were the first to see the former Volunteer as a pro. Cincinnati also fielded a veteran squad featuring former Raider Rod Sherman, who led the Bengals in receiving, as well as tight end Ken Herock and Estes Banks, who served as a backup to rookie Paul Robinson who was elevating the blood pressure of opposing coaches charged with devising methods of stopping him. Another rookie, tight end Bob Trumpy would be named to the All-Star squad at season's end and was joined in Cincinnati by former Chiefs' veterans Sherrill Headrick and Chris Burford.

Unhappy with the talent obtained from the allocation draft, coach Brown went on the offensive and changed the way the nine other AFL teams dealt with injured players. Injury waivers were no longer a safe alternative to add healthy bodies to a team's roster. Making claims for wounded athletes such as Larry Todd and Denver's Steve Tensi required evasive action by teams to withdraw waiver requests to avoid losing these men. Posting victories twice in their first three games prior to starting their current four-game skid, Brown was pleased with his club's progress but against Oakland they were outgunned in every way imaginable. Post-game coach Rauch seemed almost disinterested in discussing the game in which his defense allowed 87 of Cincinnati's 95 rushing yards on a single Paul Robinson touchdown jaunt. Of interest to Oakland's headman (aside from the cold chicken he munched as the press conference began) was the score of the afternoon's Chiefs/Chargers match-up. The news of Kansas City's 27-20 victory temporarily added a frown to Rauch's face that until then looked as if he'd been through a dull formality rather than a dominating 31-10 victory.

San Diego's shortcoming amplified the importance of the next contest against the Chiefs who were coming to The Coliseum the following Sunday. Another injury suffered by Kent McCloughan added to the woes of a team halfway through the season that had experienced a 25% turnaround of the previous years championship squad. Otis Taylor and Gloster Richardson had returned to the Chiefs lineup, marking the return of Kansas City's passing game and its use of the I formation. Longer practices were held midweek to drill for the most important game of the year, as Oakland, surprised by the straight T two weeks prior, would now be prepared for anything.

For one quarter the rematch with the Chiefs looked to be a competitive football game as Richardson hauled in a 29-yard pass from Len Dawson to tie the game at seven. From the commencement of the second quarter Kansas City was bombed by a 31-point barrage that was silenced 3:44 into the third period. With the Oakland natives enjoying a laugh at the expense the visitors from Missouri, their joyful mood turned serious as Chiefs linebacker Jim Lynch fell shoulder pad first into Daryle Lamonica's knee. As Lamonica lay writhing in agony on The Coliseum turf the merriment enjoyed by the Raiders and the 53,357 in attendance effectively ended. With assistance, Lamonica rose to his feet and hobbled to the sidelines to cheers which were virtually the last of the afternoon as the somber crowd watched the Chiefs add a pair of touchdowns (including the second Dawson to Richardson scoring connection, covering 92 yards). Oakland held on and won easily 38-21 and earned a three-way tie for the top spot in the Western Division.

The injury to Lamonica's knee amounted to no more than a charley horse as test results revealed no tissue or cartilage damage that would require surgery. Back spasms later in the week kept the current AFL Player of the Week (off his 18 of 32 outing compiling 352 yards and a pair of touchdowns in just 2 ½ quarters of play) out of action. Joining him as the result of a groin injury was halfback Pete Banaszak. Along with the largest crowd in Colorado sports history each man watched his understudy (Blanda for Lamonica and Charlie Smith for Banaszak) dismantle the Denver Broncos. Opening up a 12-7 lead by the end of the opening period, Blanda accounted for 10 of Oakland's points with a 17-yard pass to Warren Wells and a 42-yard field goal. Aided by excellent blocking, Smith broke the Broncos with a 64-yard touchdown run. Blanda finished his own bid for Player of the Week honors by pitching a pair of touchdown passes to Fred Biletnikoff and a 94-yard strike to Wells that re-established the team mark for longest play from scrimmage. In the aftermath of a 43-7 embarrassment, Broncos' coach Lou Saban apologized to Denver fans for his team's "horrible performance." As the Broncos tried to understand how a four-game winning streak could come to such a rude ending, Oakland had a dilemma of its own ahead in The Coliseum, how to stop Joe Namath and the New York Jets?

Already having its share of crucial games over the first nine games of 1968, number 10 would be no different. Equal to Oakland with a mark of 7 wins to a pair of losses, New York enjoyed a three and a half game lead over Houston in the East with five games to go and were looking forward to home field advantage against the winners of the Western Division's dead heat. Still mending, Lamonica was listed as doubtful while Blanda, having rested plenty on the bench, had returned to the championship form that kept the Oilers atop the Eastern Division from the leagues inception to the final game of 1963, the previous week. The identity of which Raiders' quarterback would be under center at The Coliseum was withheld until the last possible moment to give the Jets' coaching staff a dual load as they prepared for each Oakland passer.

Having beaten every Western Division team they'd faced to date in 1968, the Raiders were eight-point favorites to dash New York's hopes of a sweep at The Coliseum. In what proved to be the best game of the year, Lamonica with his back pain eased, erased a 6-0 Jets' lead with a 9-yard pass to Wells late in the first quarter and padded the lead with a screen to Billy Cannon that covered 48 yards 1:30 into the second quarter. Driving late in the half the Jets cut into the lead with just 5 seconds to go as Joe Namath scored on a keeper from 1-yard out. Babe Parilli's incomplete pass on the conversion held the score at 14-12. Given possession on the Oakland 30, the Jets had a short field and needed just four plays in the second half to recapture the lead with a 4-yard run by Bill Mathis. Answering quickly, Charlie Smith added his second touchdown in as many weeks. Hewritt Dixon's 2-point conversion pushed Oakland ahead by a field goal, 22-19.

Driving deep in New York territory while looking to put the game out of reach, disaster struck Oakland on the Jets 3-yard line as Gerry Philbin recovered a Charlie Smith fumble. Namath and Don Maynard victimized rookie George Atkinson for two receptions and 97 yards of real estate (in a 10-catch, 228-yard outing for Maynard) as New York surged ahead by four at 26-22. Down by a touchdown after Jim Turner's third field goal on the afternoon, Fred Biletnikoff tied the game at 29 with a 22-yard reception to conclude an 8-play, 88-yard march. With 1:05 to go Jim Turner added his fourth field goal, kicking true from 26 yards to seal a New York victory, or so the majority of Americans watching the game thought.

Taking the kickoff nearly 5 yards deep in the end zone, Charlie Smith managed to only make it to his 18-yard line before being stopped. Picking up 20 more on first down, no one outside of the capacity crowd on hand in Oakland or listening to a radio broadcast were aware that the nineteenth and final penalty (for 238 total yards) of the afternoon had been called on New York for face masking bringing Oakland 15 yards farther up field. By the time the referees could call the infraction a history making decision had been made, to cut away from the final 50 seconds and begin airing a made for television children's special called "Heidi." As the young Swiss Miss (portrayed by actress Jennifer Edwards) began yodeling to the Alps, calls flooded the NBC switchboard causing an overload and a blown fuse as frantic Jets fans wanting to watch their team down the defending league champions and position themselves as the AFL's elite squad, were blissfully unaware that Daryle Lamonica had found Smith open on the next play and the former "Castlemont Comet" outraced Mike D'Amato for the go-ahead touchdown. Fielding Mike Eischied's kickoff on a bounce, Earl Christie ran into teammate Mark Smolinski and fumbled. It was recovered by fullback Preston Ridlehuber in the end zone, and the Raiders had scored their second touchdown in just eight seconds! The final minute would be aired on the late news that evening on the east coast but those who went to bed early were shocked by the headline in the *New York Times* that read "New York 32 Oakland 29 Heidi 14!"

Trailing the idle Kansas City Chiefs by a half game gave Oakland a prime opportunity to move into a tie for first place in the Western Division and with the expansion Cincinnati Bengals waiting in sold-out Nippert Field, the Raiders' claim to the top spot lay on the other side of another 60-minute formality. Crossing midfield once in each half, Paul Brown's squad never reached the 20-yard line while the Raiders' defense held the AFL's leading rusher, Paul Robinson, to 73 yards on 15 carries. New starter Charlie Smith gained 118 yards on the ground and reached the end zone twice. Lamonica completed 24 of 32 for 368 yards as the offense accounted for a league record 33 first downs as the home crowd watched the visitors take an easy 34-0 victory.

As the Raiders had suffered from injuries throughout the year, their comparative bumps and bruises could not compete with those endured by the Buffalo Bills. At 1-10-1 on the season, Buffalo came into The Coliseum starting their fifth string quarterback Ed Rutowski. A former AFL All Star, Rutowski earned such distinction as a flanker before being converted to quarterback by interim coach Harvey Johnson. Rutowski would be making his first start under center. Joining the ranks of Buffalo's first four passers were tackle Dick Hudson, tight end Paul Costa, guard Billy Shaw and fullback Ben Gregory. Others, such as Gary McDermott, who would start in the backfield, managed to remain just healthy enough to make the Thanksgiving Day start in Oakland as 24-point underdogs.

With the Bills' current debility, there was no reason they should have been as competitive as they were when the Raiders ran them out of War Memorial Stadium 48-6. But luck and a short turnaround would have far more to say in the outcome of this game than any injury report or betting line. Tied at a field goal apiece at halftime, George Blanda kicked true for a second time and rookie George Atkinson stepped in front of a Rutowski pass on the Bills' 33 and raced into the end zone for a 13-3 lead 44 minutes into the contest. Overall both offenses faired poorly. Buffalo managed to sustain the only long march of the afternoon running 10 plays to cover 81 yards leading to rookie Max Anderson's 5-yard touchdown run. Down by a field goal, Rutowski had upstaged his former teammate Lamonica and may have had the lead had it not been for personal heroics from Atkinson (again named Defensive Player of the Week) who intercepted a second pass intended for Haven Moses and later forced a fumble on the 1-yard line that bounced to Warren Powers. With less than a minute remaining the Bills were left with an opportunity to tie on a 43-yard field goal try from Bruce Alford. Straight but low, the kick sailed a foot below the crossbar. Oakland had its tenth win of the year at 13-10 in what could have easily been their third loss.

It was a lesson in humility according to coach Rauch. Still with a victory, Oakland kept pace with Kansas City who drew the attention from the football world in their thirteenth game as they traveled to San Diego to face the Chargers. Still at a three-way heat to reach the top of the Western Division the outcome of this game would decide much in the race for the division crown. Should San Diego win they could potentially force a three-way tie in the division and a playoff scenario that gave them a week off while the Chiefs and Raiders battled for the right to face them on their home turf for the division crown. A Chiefs win could put them ahead in the division by a game, should the Raiders falter against Denver, sending coach Stram's squad to Shea Stadium to face the Eastern Division champion New York Jets for the AFL Championship and the right to represent the American Football League in the AFL/NFL championship game now officially renamed "The Super Bowl."

Recipients of no aid from Southern California as the Chargers offered no resistance to Kansas City who conquered them 40-3, the American Football League's upstate representative opened up a 7-0 lead on their visitors on the game's third play from scrimmage with a perfectly executed 65-yard Charlie Smith run to the weak side. As they feared, Denver wouldn't step aside for Oakland as San Diego had done for the Chiefs. Instead a scrambling Marlin Briscoe created opportunities with his feet and launched a 44-yard pass to Al Denson to erase Oakland's lead. A Charles Greer interception put Denver on the Raiders 30. A pitch out to Floyd Little gained 20 before Briscoe hit the second year halfback on a slant pattern that gave Denver a 14-7 advantage just 5:03 into the opening period.

Bobby Howfield connected on a pair of field goals. Blanda answered the first with a 26-yard kick. The offense became a factor in the contest mounting an eight-play drive that saw Billy Cannon make a pair of catches that accounted for 50 yards. Warren Wells had a first and goal at the 1 after a 20-yard reception that Hewritt Dixon, the league's second leading rusher cashed in to bring Oakland to within three. A 20-yard kick from Blanda tied the contest at 20 with six seconds to go in the half.

His third field goal put Oakland ahead for good. Wells, whose 10 receptions accounted for 162 yards of offense, set Denver 10 back with a 6-yard score. Still, the resilient Broncos wouldn't quit. Under intense pressure throughout the game, Briscoe was on the run when he found Denson for their second scoring connection. The 26-yard pass showed Denver was very much alive though trailing 30-27 with 10:03 remaining. Blanda's fourth field goal made a tie improbable, as a touchdown and an easy extra point would propel coach Saban's troops to an upset. Dave Grayson's second interception off Tensi and 54-yard return ended Denver's hopes as Oakland fended off defeat for a second straight week, winning 33-27.

The resistance shown by the Denver Broncos failed to reappear in Kansas City. There the visiting underdogs resembled the Chargers team which crumbled against the Chiefs as they fell 30-7, assuring coach Stram's club no worse than a tie in the division race and a playoff tie breaker in Oakland. The Raiders received no sympathy in San Diego. Eliminated by their breakdown seven days earlier, the Chargers made no bones about their desires for Oakland and their bid to repeat as league champion. "I want to beat the Raiders just because I don't like them," stated safety Kenny Graham. While coach Sid Gillman brushed off his squads last outing and expressed his confidence in a Charger rebound claiming, "We're a better team than the Chiefs and we're going to win.

For the first 30 minutes Gillman seemed prophetic. Charlie Smith's fumble on the game's opening play was recovered by Joe Beauchamp on the Oakland 26 and led to a 13-yard field goal. Reserve Oakland linebacker and former Bronco Jerry Hopkins' recovery of a fumbled punt proved to be a wasted opportunity but Dan Conners was quick to land on the ball when Gene Foster lost control on the San Diego 21. George Blanda tied the game with a 28-yard kick. The battle took to the air in the second quarter as John Hadl launched a 62-yard bomb to Gary Garrison for a 10-3 lead. Linebacker

Jeff Staggs halted one Raiders' drive with an interception but with time running out in the half Lamonica engineered a sputtering 11-play, 80-yard drive that saw Biletnikoff take a 13-yard slant pass for a score. A hurried San Diego march gave them a 13-10 lead at intermission as Dennis Partee ended the half by hitting from 34 yards out.

When a hamstring injury sent safety Warren Powers to the bench in the first half, his replacement, third year man Roger Bird gave further testament to Oakland's depth with an interception on the Chargers' 22 and waltz to the end zone. Three minutes later Lamonica launched a bomb to Wells. Covering 55 yards of Balboa Stadium turf, Oakland lunged ahead 24-13 just 6:39 into the second half. Partee's third and fourth field goals brought the Chargers to within five but Dave Grayson's tenth interception of the year lead to a 40-yard scoring pass from Lamonica to Smith. The following kickoff was equally disastrous. Duane Benson's punishing hit on return man Speedy Duncan jarred the ball free. Mike Eischied recovered. Blanda connected from 18 yards out as the Raiders tried to pull away at 34-19.

Not without miracles of their own, the Chargers found themselves within a touchdown as first-time Raider Nemiah Wilson mishandled a punt that was recovered in the end zone by reserve receiver Ken Dyer. Lance Alworth made a spectacular diving reception for a 2-point conversion. Ahead 34-27, Lamonica worked the clock. Running four minutes off, the defense forced a field goal attempt that missed. After draining more precious time with a 7-play drive, Eischied punted away and San Diego took over on their 29. Throwing to Willie Frazier at midfield, Hadl had another all-important first down. Two misfires brought up third down and a screen pass to Russ Smith netted negative yardage when Conners buried him for a 2-yard loss. Scrambling for an apparent first down to the Raider 39, Hadl's heroics were for naught as a leg-whipping penalty on Frazier brought up fourth down and 17. Forced to go for a first down, Hadl's attempt for Alworth was batted down by Conners whose stellar second half play ensured Oakland would stave off defeat for the third consecutive week.

(5)

For the Raiders and Chiefs, the Western Division championship and the right to compete for the AFL championship had come down to one, winner-take-all match up at the Oakland Coliseum. Kansas City, on the road, was given the nod as 2-½ point favorites to make a visit to Shea Stadium to meet the Jets and their MVP quarterback after meeting the Raiders who had performed near miracles in four of their last five outings.

Many football experts throughout the week leading up to the Western Division's first tie breaker were quick to point out Kansas City's superior personnel, perhaps the best in all of pro football, and season-long dominance. Pre-game assumptions and prognostications mean nothing when the gun fires and a football is put in play and, in one of Oakland's finest on field performances, Daryle Lamonica found Fred Biletnikoff (twice) and week fourteen Offensive Player of the Week Warren Wells, for scores in the first quarter. A pair of field goals from Jan Stenerud was all the offense Kansas City could muster on the afternoon. Additional scoring tosses to Wells and Biletnikoff and a pair of field goals from Blanda sent a shell-shocked Chiefs team home for the winter while the Raiders captured their second consecutive Western Division title with a 41-6 conquest.

Joe Namath got his wish. Prior to the Western Division tiebreaker the American Football League's newly crowned Most Valuable Player expressed his desire for a rematch with Oakland, as his Jets team had remained undefeated since the already legendary Heidi game. They were eager to avenge the loss. Surrounded by circulating rumors that their coach would not be leading them beyond the current season, nine AFL All-Stars (Jim Otto for the ninth consecutive year, rookie George Atkinson behind a pair of punt returns for touchdowns, fellow defensive back Willie Brown, defensive lineman Dan Birdwell, the opportunistic Dan Conners, Ben Davidson, the league's (now) third ranked rusher Hewritt Dixon, second year guard Gene Upshaw, and Warren Wells with 12 total touchdowns) and eleven second team All Stars (including Lamonica and Dave Grayson with his league-leading 10 interceptions) made the trek to New York with their American Football League championship on the line.

The night before the Jets and Raiders took the field to decide which squad was the American Football League's best, John Rauch educated the media on what to expect in the following afternoon's title match: "The team that gets the early upper hand will hold it and win." To his displeasure the Jets offense opened up a 10-0 lead in the first quarter, but to defeat a champion a team must execute, which Johnny Sample failed to do as Lamonica fired a 29-yard scoring pass to Biletnikoff that got Oakland into the game at 10-7. An exchange of field goals brought the halftime tally to 13-10 in favor of the Jets but from their

6 Oakland marched into New York territory with passes to Biletnikoff for 30 yards and to Wells for 40 more. Finally the offense ran out of gas at the 1 and settled for a field goal to tie the game.

A long Jets drive ensued, covering 14 plays and 80 yards. Namath converted three critical third down plays before making a 20-yard connection with Pete Lammons to reclaim the lead. Not to be outdone, Oakland's "Mad Bomber" came back firing. Hitting Biletnikoff for a 57-yard strike, Johnny Sample, beaten again, recovered and made a touchdown-saving tackle as the Raiders settled for Blanda's third field goal. Repeatedly picked on by Namath in both Raiders/Jets meetings, Atkinson repaid Namath in kind with an interception on the New York 38 that he returned to the 5. Banaszak finally claimed the lead for Oakland, blasting through to take a 23-20 lead that was short lived as Namath found Maynard for a 6-yard score after they connected for 52 yards improvising on a broken play. Down 27-23, the Raiders had just more than half a quarter to defend their crown. Oakland was moving into Jets territory where the New York defense had the offense in a do-or-die fourth and 10 situation on the 26. Try a 33-yard field goal into the wind and trail by a point and risk having Namath run the clock out or try for a first down and make the Jets beat them, was the dilemma that faced coach Rauch. Going for the jugular, Oakland went for it with a pass to Hewritt Dixon. Played perfectly by the home defenders, Dixon was dropped for a 4-yard loss and the Jets' offense took over.

The Oakland defense gave the ball back to their offense with three minutes to go. A pass to Biletnikoff netted 25 yards and a first down on the Jets' 40. Moving to the 13 as Wells gained 15 yards and a penalty was assessed for piling on, the Raiders seemed ready to make a kill shot. With both of his outside receivers and tight end covered, Lamonica went to his fourth option and threw a screen pass to Charlie Smith. The ball sailed out of his hand early and behind Smith. Thinking the pass was incomplete; the rookie halfback didn't react when New York defenders gave chase to the live ball. Ralph Baker recovered and Joe Namath and the Jets offense ran out the clock to capture their first American Football League championship, 27-23.

Ever graceful in defeat, Rauch and his squad owned up to their mistakes after the heart breaking loss, refusing to blame wind or field conditions for their shortcomings. However there was a lingering uncertainty for he Oakland Raiders as they headed into the off-season; will John Rauch be with them in the 1969 season and beyond? When quizzed on the rumor post-game he simply responded, "I have no comment on that at all."

CHAPTER TEN
THE RED FOX 1969

After three seasons as head coach of the Oakland Raiders, earning a combined 35-10-1 record, an AFL championship and a Coach of the Year laurel for 1967, John Rauch finally commented on his future with the club by resigning his post and immediately accepting a four-year contract to lead the Buffalo Bills. Saying only that his departure was to pursue another opportunity, Rauch's publicly amicable exodus left Oakland facing a major shift just two weeks prior to the college draft. Defensive backfield coach Charlie Sumner also left the staff to pursue other opportunities while kicking coach Bugsy Engleberg followed Rauch to Buffalo.

None of the questions surrounding the coaching staff were answered immediately. Instead, Al Davis and the staff's remaining assistants (having all agreed to stay) focused on finding the best collegiate talent to stock their roster. Winners of a 3-team tie-breaking lottery, they would pick ahead of both the Kansas City Chiefs and the Dallas Cowboys in the opening round with the three 12-2 clubs rotating picks throughout the remaining 16.

Before they could begin stocking for their future from a talent-thin class of rookies, American Football League MVP Joe Namath set the football world on its ear. As 18-point underdogs, Namath and his Jets teammates' were expected to fare far worse against the NFL champions than their AFL counterparts in Oakland and Kansas City had done in seasons past. His opponent in professional football's world championship game was the Baltimore Colts. 13-1 in the regular season, Don Shula's squad avenged their records' only blemish, a 30-20 week-six loss in Cleveland by hammering the Browns 34-0 to earn the title of National Football League champions.

Troubles with legendary quarterback Johnny Unitas' throwing arm led to the ascension of Earl Morrall to the starting role with a virtually seamless transition. Yet Morrall was no Unitas, a fact that Namath highlighted in the week leading up to the third Super Bowl. Boasting that there were at least five AFL quarterbacks better than Morrall, including his back-up, Babe Parilli, the remark, brushed off by Morrall, had Shula steaming. It was quickly forgotten in light of the Jet quarterback's handling of a heckler at a Miami Touchdown Club banquet honoring him as "The Outstanding Football Player of 1968." Told to "sit down" by a voice coming from the back of the room as Namath was to receive his award, Broadway Joe dismissed the outburst as "Coming from a Colts fan." Informed of his impending doom on Super Bowl Sunday, Namath silenced his detractor once and for all stating, "We're going to win on Sunday, I guarantee it."

Splashed on the front page of newspapers nationwide, his remark would be relived for decades to come. Fortunately for Namath and the AFL, he and his Jets teammates delivered, in a workhorse performance from Matt Snell, who carried the ball 30 times for 121 yards. Snell was given the perfect complement by his defense, which dominated Baltimore by holding them to their side of the field for three quarters and intercepting a trio of passes while the offense built a 16-0 lead. After experiencing interception troubles of his own in relief, Johnny Unitas guided the Colts on their lone trip to the end zone against New York's reserves. The shutout was all Baltimore would avoid as the Jets and the American Football League would win their first world championship, 16-7.

(2)

Looking to build championship squads beyond the 1969 season, the Oakland football club made 15 draft selections. The first chosen was Syracuse defensive tackle Art Thoms. At 6'5" 260 lbs., Thoms was reminiscent of Walt Sweeney, the Syracuse guard Al Davis signed as an assistant in San Diego that blossomed into an AFL All–Star. In round two came Stanford guard George Buehler. A veteran of every position on the offensive line except center, early reports had Beuhler being tried at tackle before being placed at guard. Taken third was Lloyd Edwards, a

San Diego State fullback who would be converted to tight end as a pro to back up Billy Cannon while vagabond New Mexico State defensive lineman Ruby Jackson was chosen in the fourth round. After his high school graduation, Jackson drifted around the country finding work as a lifeguard and later as a mortician. Finally gravitating west, Jackson was a teammate of first overall pick O.J. Simpson (whose high asking price created a contract impasse with the Buffalo Bills) at San Francisco City College before finishing his eligibility in New Mexico.

Among those chosen on the second day were Drew Buie, a fleet-footed receiver taken in round nine from Catawba College, a liberal arts school in North Carolina. Focusing on the linebacker position in the eleventh and thirteenth rounds. Harold Rice was chosen from Tennessee A& I and Dave Husted would come to Oakland from Indiana's Wabash College. Another speed burner was added to the receiving corps as Harold Busby, posting a time of 9.4 seconds in the 100-yard dash, came via a fourteenth round selection from UCLA.

The majority of professional football franchises operated without the luxury of an owner capable of conducting a successful draft. As a result of Al Davis' decision to wait until the draft's completion to begin his search, the field of prospective new coaches had narrowed. The Boston Patriots hired Clive Rush from Weeb Ewbanks' staff in New York to take over their operation while Baltimore Colts defensive backfield coach Chuck Noll (having also served with Al Davis as a Chargers assistant under Sid Gillman) was named head coach of the Pittsburgh Steelers. Other candidates such as Harland Svare, a former New York Giant, Cotton Davidson and Al Davis himself were ruled out of the running to become Oakland's new head man. Instead of looking around for a new coach to lead the franchise, Davis looked within and found his man in one of his four remaining assistants; 32-year-old linebacker's coach John Madden.

An All-Conference tackle at Cal Poly San Louis Obispo, Madden was a twenty-first round draft choice of the Philadelphia Eagles in 1958 but a serious knee injury ended his career in his rookie season. Dedicating himself to coaching, the native of nearby Daly City (located just south of San Francisco) became an assistant at Hancock Junior College in Santa Maria, California for two years before being elevated to the position of head coach for two more. Returning to Cal Poly to coach the alumni vs. the varsity squad, Madden earned the nickname "The Red Fox" as an opposite of varsity coach Roy Hughes, who would answer the home crowd by tipping his hat when they chanted "turn around, silver fox."

Nickname in tow, Madden would serve as defensive coordinator for coach Don Coryell at San Diego State before being contacted by the Raiders, who had him in mind to succeed Clancy Osborne in 1967.

Lauded by Davis as "a dedicated football man with a brilliant mind who is destined to become an outstanding head coach," Madden in his first press conference handled the media like an old pro. Saying that his new contract was valid for more than one year Oakland's new headman outlined his plan to hire assistants and complete the coaching staff. Having already spoken to a trio of successful coaches in the day between his hiring and the media session, coach Madden refused to elaborate on their identities because they were on staff with other teams. He also stressed the importance of their compatibility as Raiders coaches spent a great deal of time together game planning. It was these sessions, according to Madden, which acclimated him with the complexities of his new offense that was far beyond anything that he had directed in the past.

According to escalating rumor, the role of managing general partner Al Davis extended from the front office and onto the field of play. When queried on this matter Madden explained, "I feel everyone works together. On the field of play I'm the general. The decisions will be mine," he said before reminding the media that in the huddle the quarterback calls his own plays. No one was happier with the ascension of Madden than the players who formed the Oakland roster. Ben Davidson nearly echoed Al Davis' sentiment; describing Madden as "an outstanding coach first and foremost," while guard Wayne Hawkins expressed his optimism that his happiness with his new coach was reciprocated.

At 32, Madden became professional football's youngest head coach. Taking over his own team three years sooner than he had planned, he would lose a pair of veterans to similar ambitions. Warren Powers ended a productive career that saw him lead the team in interceptions in 1966 and yardage on interception returns a year later. After performing well in 1968 in relief of Roger Bird the 28-year-old safety decided to return to the University of Nebraska to assist Bob Devaney in mentoring the Cornhuskers' defense. Bill Miller also ended his playing days and made a return to his former haunt in Buffalo to replace receivers coach John Mazur on John Rauch's new staff.

Time and surgery had healed Oakland's wounded. Tom Keating and Bill Laskey were expected to return after missing the 1968 campaign. Fred Biletnikoff, Dan Birdwell and Hewritt Dixon's knees were surgically repaired in the off-season, as was Roger Bird's shoulder. Joining the ranks of the recuperated was 270-lb. defensive tackle Ray Jacobs. A former second team All-AFL selection, Jacobs had his own injury woes in Miami before being shipped to Oakland for a draft choice.

Another selection was spent to secure the rights to offensive lineman Tony DiMidio. A veteran of the New York Giants' taxi squad, Dimidio found his way onto the field in Kansas City as a Chiefs' reserve before finding his way back to New York and onto the Jets' practice team during their championship run.

A sense of urgency befell Raider coaches. George Blanda, entering his twentieth season at age 42, raised concerns about the depth of the quarterback position should Lamonica be unavailable for a substantial amount of time and his own durability, having announced his intention to retire at season's end. Eldridge Dickey was returned to quarterback while Ken Stabler's knee had healed sufficiently for him to make a start for the Spokane Shockers of the Continental League where he fared poorly, completing just 17 passes in 41 attempts with a trio of interceptions in 1968.

To help solve crises such as these and to lead the franchise into 1969 and beyond, the coaching staff and front office would grow and expand. Former Raiders guard Marv Marinovich was brought aboard as a strength and conditioning coach while a man he used to protect, Dick Wood, was hired as the teams' first receivers coach. Sid Hall would be the second consecutive San Diego State defensive coordinator to be named linebackers coach in Oakland while former Bills' defensive coordinator and defensive back Richie McCabe was appointed to oversee the defensive backfield. Evolution in the front office saw the dismissal of former quarterback and publicist Lee Grosscup and the hiring of a new executive, Al LoCasale, who had spent the past two years in Cincinnati helping Paul Brown to launch the Bengals franchise after a seven-year run in the Chargers' organization.

(3)

A new playoff system would be in place for the 1969 postseason, pitting each American Football League division winner against the opposing division's runner-up, with the victors meeting for the league championship. Beyond that, struggles to implement the AFL/NFL merger were casting doubts on how professional football would be structured beyond the next postseason. Owners from both leagues were divided almost completely on how to complete the agreement. Many favored retention of separate AFL and NFL identities, complete with their current divisions and 16-10 team ratio. This scenario was believed by some in the NFL to give the clubs the best option in terms of equally shared TV revenues.

"We purchased complete realignment under the terms of the merger," said Al Davis. Rumored to have the votes of three AFL franchises (Buffalo, Boston and Kansas City) as a condition of the merger agreement that required the Oakland Raiders to pay the San Francisco 49ers $6 million for territorial rights, Davis hinted at this at the winter meetings in the California desert, "What we, the Raiders want to establish in Palm Springs is that we can have realignment if we desire it." Over the next five days many alternatives were discussed with the 16-10 NFL advantage being strongly rejected by the American League.

No solution was reached in those meetings but progress had been made. Rumors that three NFL teams, the National Football League champion Baltimore Colts, the Dallas Cowboys and ironically, the Minnesota Vikings had volunteered to join the ranks of the American Football League began to circulate. With more clear ideas about how to effectively handle the merger changeover, the winter meetings concluded with the remaining issues tabled until the May inter-league meetings in New York. To be resolved would be the new divisional alignments. Many favored a four-division system with six or seven teams each to accommodate the 26 professional teams. Others would advocate a six-division arrangement with four to five teams apiece.

The Vikings and Cowboys were quick to voice their disproval of a switch to the American League. The New Orleans Saints and the Atlanta Falcons were seen by some in the NFL as the best candidates to switch, as these clubs were not current division winners or drawing as well at the gate as the teams in Dallas and Minnesota. Davis would outline the AFL's final merger plan. In a wire service interview, he detailed the AFL's ideas on how to effectively implement the merger as it was originally agreed to. First, most American Football League teams would retain their present, traditional rivalries. The home and home series between division rivals would remain intact, as each division would have no more than five teams. Each league would enjoy a profitable television package and would face opponents in inter-league match-ups in the regular season as well as in exhibitions.

The American League would win this final merger battle with its sole casualty being, as expected, its identity. As originally agreed, the AFL would cease to be at the end of the 1969 season and its teams would then compete in the National Football League's new American Football Conference, consisting of 13 teams. The Cleveland Browns and Pittsburgh Steelers would join the American Conference in 1970 forming its Central Division with the Houston Oilers and Cincinnati Bengals, while the AFC's Western Division would take the original form of the AFL West featuring the Kansas City, Denver, San Diego and Oakland clubs. The third and final NFL team would switch; as the Baltimore Colts would complete the five-team AFC Eastern Division, joining incumbents Miami, Buffalo, Boston and New York.

The reshuffling of the new National Football Conference was slightly more complicated. In place of the Baltimore Colts, the New Orleans Saints, who, with the three remaining NFL Coastal Division teams in San Francisco, Atlanta and Los Angeles, would form the new NFC West. The NFL's Central Division would remain intact with Green Bay, Chicago, Detroit and Minnesota while Dallas, Philadelphia, Washington, St. Louis and the New York Giants would compose the NFC East while their former Century and Capitol divisions would become obsolete at the end of the coming season. Aside from the home and home series each team would face with its division rivals, they would complete their 14-game slate with at least two-intra-conference games (for the five-team eastern divisions) and a trio of inter-conference match-ups.

Formatted for 1970 and beyond, preparations for the immediate future began with summer's ritual of training camp. As most of the new rookies (save Thoms and Beuhler) headed into camp ahead of the veterans, they were joined by some new, yet familiar faces in Oakland. Offensive lineman Dan Archer, lost to Cincinnati in the expansion draft, was released by the Bengals and rejoined his original club. Joining him was Bengals and Raiders teammate Rod Sherman, who was reacquired in exchange for guard Bob Kruse. As new blood was infused some chose to leave of their own accord. Four rookies, Drew Buie, Ruby Jackson, Harold Rice and Junior Davis, made early exits from the Raiders' Santa Rosa training facility only to return prior to the first official work out with the incumbent veterans.

Fred Biletnikoff's attempt to renegotiate his contract resulted in a four-day hold out that ended abruptly when he was informed that no discussions would take place until he reported to camp. Seldom used John

Roderick retired and 1967's second-round selection, Bill Fairband was waived early on. As the squad settled into the grind of camp the rookies were given a chance to shine. Just two weeks after reporting to Santa Rosa many first-year men were joined by a few non-starting veterans for a rookies' game against the Dallas Cowboys at the Oakland Alameda County Coliseum. To counter the threat of Heisman trophy winning quarterback Roger Staubach and the fast-moving Tennessee rookie Richmond Flowers to catch his passes, coach Madden started Ken Stabler under center with Eldridge Dickey set to take command of the Oakland offense in the second half. Featuring Drew Buie and John Eason as receivers, Gene Thomas at tight end, Marv Hubbard and Ken Newfield in the offensive backfield while veteran Ernie Park and second year man Art Shell handled the role of tackle, Dan Archer and Tony DiMidio flanked center Tom Freeman. Defensively Macon Roemer and Harold Rice formed the outside of the defensive line while Ruby Jackson and Al Dotson stuffed the middle. Del Gehrett, Dave Ogas and Dave Husted formed the line-backing corps while Nemiah Wilson, Jackie Allen, Don Ford and Charlie Warner formed the defensive backfield.

This one-time edition of the Oakland Raiders was nothing short of spectacular. Allowing just 7 completions in 26 passing attempts for three Cowboys quarterbacks (Staubach connected twice in 14 tries), the rookie defense was equal to its offense. Post-game Ken Stabler stated, "We could do anything we wanted to. After the first few plays I knew we could throw anything at them and it would work." The 32,045 who departed the history unfolding on their television sets as astronauts Neil Armstrong, Buzz Aldrin and Michael Collins made their return voyage from the moon for The Coliseum, saw a combined five touchdown passes thrown at the Cowboys (three to John Eason) as the visitors from Dallas were run out of the Oakland Alameda County Coliseum, 33-0.

This startling success was unsettling for rookie guard George Buehler. Still unsigned, the former Stanford Indian remained at his home in Southern California instead of reporting to Chicago to face the New York Jets in the college all-star game. He had missed three weeks of practice trying to avoid injury while without the financial protection of a pro contract. Buehler came to terms with his new team in the days leading up to the first official preseason game in Birmingham, Alabama against the Kansas City Chiefs. Only Art Thoms remained out of the Oakland loop and while his rookie deal was being finalized, the number of available players had slimmed. Cornerback Harold Lewis broke his arm in two places defending a pass against Dallas, while an injured calf muscle postponed veteran Tom Keating's comeback. The coaches withheld Dan Birdwell and Kent McCloughan to further recuperate from their injuries while Chip Oliver was unavailable due to his obligations as an Army reservist. Taking in the game from the stands was quarterback Ken Stabler. Having established himself as a front-runner to be Oakland's future starting quarterback with his 8 for 15, 138-yard, 2-touchdown outing in his rookies' game start, the Alabama snake confessed to tiring of playing football and returned to his Tuscaloosa home where he said he planned to finish 10 hours of work needed for a degree in physical education and possibly venture into coaching. Seventh round draft selection, Finnis Taylor, a safety from Prairie View A&M, left camp of his own accord.

There were still plenty of available bodies to fill out the Oakland roster. Ike Lassiter, having slimmed to 265 lbs. in the off-season, was quicker than ever according to coach Madden and had made a disruptive impact during drills. Sixth round selection Ken Newfield, continued to impress with his pass-catching abilities out of the backfield. Having also trimmed down, John Eason moved from tight end to receiver while 20lbs. of bulk were added to the frame of second-year man George Atkinson after four months of training with the National Guard.

Inserting Bill Laskey into the starting lineup in place of Chip Oliver and Al Dotson for Dan Birdwell were the only changes from the team, which came within a game of a second consecutive AFL championship. At the end of a scoreless opening quarter, Oakland lost the services of Daryle Lamonica, who injured his hand on the helmet of defensive end Aaron Brown and finished the contest on the sidelines holding an ice pack. Down 6-0 Oakland's lone backup Eldridge Dickey (as George Blanda and Cotton Davidson weren't yet slated to see exhibition action) erased the deficit with a 20-yard scramble for a touchdown. Ineffective through the air (completing just 5 of 16 for 54 yards with 3 interceptions) his footwork earned him the praise of the "best scrambling quarterback ever" from coach Hank Stram citing Oakland's lone offensive highlight. Following a field goal, Bill Budness intercepted a Jacky Lee pass on the 48 and returned it for a score and the lead at 17-13. Oakland, however, wouldn't threaten again. A Lee touchdown pass to Robert Holmes and a 23-yard field goal by Jan Stenerud in the fourth quarter dealt Oakland a 23-17 loss as they opened their tenth preseason.

With no imminent roster cuts in the coming week and the signing of first round draft choice Art Thoms, who agreed to a two-year, no cut arrangement, left Oakland stronger in the lineup than it was against the Chiefs in Birmingham. Awaiting them after a week of two-a-day drills in Santa Rosa was the same Baltimore Colts team that opened Oakland's exhibition slate in 1968. Now featuring the previous two National Football League MVPs, coach Don Shula chose to start the most current, Earl Morrall, at The Coliseum, and with the aid of a Lou Michaels' field goal, he led Baltimore to a 10-0 edge.

For George Atkinson, persistence would be rewarded. Dominating All-Pro receiver Willie Richardson, Atkinson's interception ended Morrall's afternoon and gave Oakland a prime scoring opportunity. Cashing in with a 10-yard toss from Lamonica to Warren Wells, the Raiders were ten down once again as Johnny Unitas completed a 10-yard scoring pass to John Mackey. A 49-yard blast by Roger Hagberg led to another Raiders' score as Rod Sherman hauled in a 14-yard touchdown pass. Oakland was trailing by 4 as a personal foul penalty set George Blanda 15 yards further back, aiding in a missed extra point. Touchdowns were traded and another Michaels' field goal concluded a wild, 47-point opening half. Scoreless through the third quarter, Oakland's attempt at a tie backfired as Lenny Lyles stepped in front of a Blanda pass and raced 51 yards to the end zone. A 7-yard pass to Buie midway through the final period provided a glimmer of hope for a comeback that failed to materialize as the home team fell 34-30.

Dealt away for a draft pick, fourth round draft choice, Ruby Jackson, was sent east to Cincinnati while Tom Keating, out of action since the 1967 All-Star game, returned to action and made an immediate impact against San Diego. With a first and goal from the 8-yard line following a Lamonica interception, John Hadl handed off to Dickey Post, who was met hard by Keating. Remaining on his feet and fighting for yardage, Post was unable to break free though the ball broke free from him and rolled into the end zone where Ike Lassiter recovered for an Oakland touchback. Responding with a 14-play drive, the offense took a 7-0 lead early in the second quarter when Lamonica fired to Wells for 32 yards. Out-gaining their opponents by 187 yards the week before, the Oakland offense seemed to be out of gas after their scoring march. Pitching a combined 5 completions in 23 attempts, they never threatened again. A Dennis Partee field goal got the Chargers on the board while linebacker Rick Redman stole an Eldridge Dickey pass on the 27-yard line in the third quarter and returned the error for a score for a 10-7 San Diego win.

The blame of three consecutive losses could be distributed across the Oakland roster but George Blanda would have none of it. "I'm rushing the kicks," said the 20-year veteran of his six misses over the past two weeks, owning up to his own responsibility. Coach Madden was more analytical, blaming his preseason evaluation for his kicker's erratic performance because the regular wings Billy Cannon and Hewritt Dixon hadn't performed in their kicking team roles. The upcoming Coliseum match-up against the Jets would be a last hurrah for many Raiders as the team was required to cut eight from their current 57-man roster to reach the league mandated limit of 49. Forty-eight of those would be filled by players currently seeking to make the squad while the final spot was reserved for the wayward Kenny Stabler, who, despite the lack of communication between him and coach Madden, a great deal of optimism was held for the young quarterback to be a part of Oakland's future.

Even in Stabler's absence there would be an Alabama quarterback at work in the sold out Oakland Alameda County Coliseum, in the form of Joe Namath. Speaking midweek on his intentions to pick apart the Oakland defense by concentrating on throwing to his outside receivers, Namath's plan was to neutralize safety Dave Grayson and pick on George Atkinson where Namath and Don Maynard had found success in the past. Their plan backfired.

Beginning a month-long home stand that would extend through the second week of the regular season, the Oakland defense allowed the Jets' offense 216 total yards and a pair of Jim Turner field goals in the opening half that accounted for their entire scoring output. Ahead at the break 7-6 as Lamonica capped the Raiders' opening drive with a 13-yard touchdown pass to Warren Wells. George Blanda's 6 of 7 fourth quarter outing netted a 23-yard scoring strike to Larry Todd. A field goal was added and the final bit of insurance in the form of a 6-yard completion to Drew Buie from Lamonica with just 14 seconds remaining sent the world-champion Jets home a 24-6 loser.

Knee injuries suffered by Art Thoms, Ken Newfield and Hewritt Dixon against New York aided Madden in his first player cut down. Rodger Bird was also waived injured as his shoulder was slow in healing and Cotton Davidson joined those on the wire as he was expected to be used in a coaching capacity, taking in games from the press box. Kent McCloughan jogged lightly in practice while still a couple weeks away from being eligible for action while Dan Birdwell, despite his claims of readiness, was given more time for his knee to heal. Becoming ever secretive, no other Raider releases were revealed to the media prior to Oakland's final Coliseum tune-up, though Bird and Thoms were recalled after being claimed by John Rauch in Buffalo.

The importance of this final exhibition game was driven home to John Madden by general partner Ed McGah, who informed his rookie head coach midweek that he was unconcerned about the teams win-loss record during the regular season just so long as he beat the San Francisco 49ers. Down by seven after a quick 4-play, 47-yard drive that resulted in a 14-yard John Brodie scoring pass to tight end Bob Windsor, Oakland answered with a 20-yard field goal from Blanda and the claimed the lead at 10-7 when Lamonica and Warren Wells connected for a 29-yard score to open the second quarter. When Oakland regained possession, the pace again was being set by the visiting 49ers. A 22-yard touchdown pass from Brodie to Gene Washington finished a 7-play, 70-yard drive giving San Francisco a 14-10 lead. Seesawing, the lead exchanged hands twice more in the opening half as a 1-yard touchdown run by Lamonica (on which he pulled a hamstring) was answered by a screen pass to 49ers running back Doug Cunningham, who raced 69 yards to lead 21-17.

Missing a 51-yard field goal attempt as the first half ended, Blanda made his second field goal of the day early in the third quarter before Brodie connected with Clif McNeil (who coach Dick Nolan said midweek wouldn't play because his contract holdout kept him out of practice) with a 68-yard bomb for an 8-point lead. Remaining in the game despite troubles from his hamstring, Lamonica finally gave way to Blanda, who immediately went on a tear. Slicing up the San Francisco defense, professional football's most tenured veteran needed seven plays to cover 58 yards, concluding the drive with a 10-yard touchdown to Billy Cannon. A pivotal end-zone reception by Marv Hubbard gave Oakland a 28-point tie that the defense would not relinquish. A battle between Nemiah Wilson and McNeil resulted in both players sprawled out on The Coliseum turf while Brodie's pass sailed straight to Dave Grayson on the Oakland 45. Following a 47-yard return, Blanda found Wells on second and goal from the 8 for Oakland's second score in 1:46. The valiant play that allowed San Francisco to control most of the contest turned to desperation in the end and Grayson victimized the 49ers for the second time as he stole a pass intended for Windsor on the San Francisco 43 and brought it back 29 yards to the 14. Using five plays to run time off the clock, Blanda hit Wells with a 12-yard pass for his third touchdown climaxing a 22-point fourth quarter that crushed the 49ers 42-28.

With 48 men remaining on the Oakland roster the unusual circumstance of two mandatory roster cuts the week before league play required coach Madden and his staff to cut four players twice to bring the roster to the 40-man maximum. Coupled with the task of preparing for an opening-day visit from the Houston Oilers, Madden and his staff requested waivers on veteran safety Howie Williams, second year man John Eason, sophomore linebacker Dave Ogas and rookie center Tom Freeman, who had little hope of supplanting the American Football League's iron man Jim Otto.

After less than stellar outings in the pre season and being surpassed by George Blanda as the main understudy to starting quarterback Daryle Lamonica, Eldridge Dickey was waived with hopes of obtaining him on the taxi squad. Veteran offensive lineman Ernie Park was dealt to Cincinnati, initially completing the first round of roster adjustments that allowed the coaching staff to recall some players who were claimed on the waiver wire by other franchises, as was the case with Dickey, whose mobility impressed Hank Stram enough for the Chiefs' coach to claim him and Dave Ogas, who was targeted by his former mentor John Rauch in Buffalo.

In the end only five could be retained for the taxi squad and as the final cuts were announced three players, Ogas, defensive tackle Ray Jacobs and Roger Bird were let loose while Heidi game hero Preston Ridlehuber decided to leave on his own and would find employment in Buffalo. His defection allowed Bird to latch on to the taxi squad.

With roster spots being held for the injured Dan Birdwell, Kent McCloughan and Ken Stabler the tenth edition of the Oakland Raiders moved forward into 1969. Telling boosters midweek that this was the toughest opener since his arrival in Oakland, Madden's players, early on, looked to make 1969's opening more reminiscent of the previous two, where they outscored their opponents by a combined 99-6. Reportedly better than ever according to Oilers' coach Wally Lemm, a pair of Pete Beathard passes found their way to Dave Grayson, whose returns to the Houston 24 and 16 yard lines left a short field for the Oakland offense and enabled two five-yard Charlie Smith touchdown runs for a 14-0 first quarter lead. Enduring one of his worst days as a pro, the boos from The Coliseum crowd rained down on Lamonica as his 10-for-31 performance and 3 interceptions bogged the offense down and allowed the Oilers to climb back into the contest. Lagging 14-10 heading into the fourth quarter, Beathard engineered an 11-play, 80-yard march and passed Houston into the lead with a 15-yard toss to rookie receiver Jerry Levias.

The ensuing kickoff, returned to the 35, provided Oakland with excellent field position. A second and nine play from the Raiders' 36 recaptured the lead as 1/10 of Lamonica's completions found its way to Warren Wells for a 64-yard touchdown. Attempting to both answer and beat Oakland at their own game, a deep Beathard pass to a wide-open Levias went through the receiver's hands and fell to the turf. Houston's chances ended in the dirt infield used by the Oakland Athletics as a sack by Tom Keating halted the final Oilers' drive and Oakland captured their first official win of the John Madden era, 21-17.

A 16-point underdog Miami Dolphins team was next to visit Oakland. Featuring one of the bright young quarterbacks in professional football in Bob Griese, the third-year man from Purdue had three dangerous and healthy targets in Howard Twilley, Karl Noonan, who tied Warren Wells for the league lead with 11 touchdown catches in 1968, and ranked third in the league with 58 receptions and Jack Clancy, who accounted for 67 catches in 1967 before missing action the year before due to a knee injury. Together they accounted for 327 yards through the air in week one against Cincinnati, who managed to survive the aerial bombardment for a 27-21 victory. These recent credentials, coupled with the acquisition of Nick Buoniconti from Boston to quarterback the defense from his middle linebacker spot, gave the Dolphins an air of confidence as they faced the AFL powerhouse in Oakland. Post-game, coach George Miller reflected on his squads' performance calling it "the best in our four-year history."

Struggling against Oakland's stingy defense (managing just 9 completions in 34 attempts with a trio of interceptions) Miami's passing game provided Oakland its first touchdown as a harmless screen pass to Stan Mitchell bounced out of the fullback's hands to Dave Grayson and the master thief returned the interception 76 yards for a 7-0 lead. An interference call against Nemiah Wilson aided Miami in tying the game at 7 but a 37-yard Blanda field goal and a 13-yard scoring reception by Biletnikoff gave the Raiders a 17-7 advantage as the first quarter concluded. Instead of falling apart, the upstart Dolphins made things interesting. A Lloyd Mumphord interception led to a field goal and a questionable pass interference call against Howie Williams, who was recalled from waivers and regained a spot opposite Grayson in the starting lineup, enabled a Miami touchdown that deadlocked the score at halftime. Scoreless through the third quarter and the first 12:47 of the fourth, Miami took over first and 10 on their own 20. Picking up 6 with a Larry Seiple run the Dolphins came out of the two-minute warning with a 2-yard gain by Jim

Kiick running over right guard. Going to Kiick again on the ground for a first down and the opportunity to run out the clock and preserve a tie met with an unexpected turn as the Miami runner lost a yard in the grasp of Al Dotson. With the Dolphins forced to punt, Oakland took possession on their 34. With two time outs remaining the Raiders' offense was able to move to the Miami 39. A screen pass on third down to Charlie Smith fell incomplete with 15 seconds left and George Blanda was sent on to attempt the winning field goal. Otto's snap to Lamonica was down and the 46-yard attempt sailed through as the Raiders snatched their second win of the season, 20-17.

For the first time in a month the Oakland Raiders would depart their home for a road swing to last nearly as long. Visiting Fenway Park in September, before the air froze and snow fell, they would face a Patriots team that had managed an 0-2 record while being outscored by a combined 66-7 over the season's first two weeks. These were welcome breaks for the Oakland club. As an underdog to a team that for the second consecutive week was a 16-point favorite, most football observers felt that, given their recent struggles, that Boston had little chance against their visitors, but their gracious guests gave them life. A failed fake punt deep in Oakland territory gave the Patriots a short field on the 20 that led to a quick touchdown and an 8-play, 65-yard drive on their next possession extended their first lead of the season to 13-0.

Methodically, Oakland directed its assault at Boston's defensive weakness, the middle. Picking up 165 yards on the ground opened the airwaves for the Raiders, who cut their deficit to three at halftime following a 27-yard Wells touchdown pass from Lamonica and a Blanda field goal. Wasting no time in the second half, Duane Benson's violent hit on return man Sid Blanks forced a fumble that Grayson secured on the Patriots' 20 for his fourth takeaway in three weeks that he returned 9 yards to the 11-yard line. A trio of touchdown passes followed, including a 55-yard bomb to Wells and a 1-yard Hewritt Dixon run, overwhelming Boston 38-13. With victory secure the defense allowed a late Carl Garrett touchdown and a Gino Cappaletti field goal that brought the hapless Patriots to within 15 in a 38-23 loss.

Unbeaten in September, Oakland looked to extend their win streak well into October by basing themselves in Boston to alleviate some of the strain of a long road trip, taking in practices at nearby Tufts University to prepare for a still winless Miami team in Orange Bowl Stadium that had played them tough in Oakland two weeks prior. Taking a tie well into the fifty-ninth minute against Oakland was a milestone of sorts for the Dolphins, who in four previous meetings had never been truly competitive with the squad in silver and black after being forced by their tormentors to make an early comeback. Week four would be a near reversal. After exchanging field goals Miami earned excellent field position as Frank Emmanuel hammered rookie defensive back Jackie Allen who was returning a kickoff and forced a fumble that Dolphins rookie Barry Pryor recovered on the 21-yard line. A 9-yard Griese to Karl Noonan pass put Miami ahead 10-3 in the waning moments of the opening quarter.

Scoreless through the second, Lamonica struggled through a 19-of-43 performance but his first touchdown, a 15-yard pass to Wells following a Bill Laskey interception, tied the game at 10. Connecting 13 times in 27 tries, Griese didn't fare much better in the humidity but managed a moment of brilliance, engineering an 80-yard drive in 9 plays that pulled his club ahead 17-10 just before time ran out in the third quarter. Chipping away with Blanda's second field goal in four attempts on the afternoon, George Atkinson redeemed himself for being beaten on Noonan's first quarter score by picking off a Griese pass on the Dolphins' 21. In three plays Oakland had the lead. Lamonica's second scoring pass, a 9-yard completion to Biletnikoff put Oakland up 20-17 with 9:19 to go. Blanda was not the only kicker to struggle; Karl Kremser managed just his fourth field goal of the season in eight attempts, knotting the game at 20. Unyielding, the Dolphins defense wouldn't allow Oakland to threaten the rest of the afternoon and with a 20-20 tie the Miami Dolphins finally managed to not fail against Oakland's Raiders.

The tie wouldn't hurt Oakland in the standings. While a loss would have dropped them into a three-way tie for first place in the West with Kansas City and the surprising Bengals, the deadlock wasn't enough for them to lose possession of first place. The entire division had experienced early success. So much so that no team owned a losing record entering the fifth week. Pulling up the rear and tied with San Diego at 2-2 was the Broncos, undefeated over the first two weeks. Denver was in the midst of a two-game slide and would host the Raiders on the final stop of their three-week, cross-country expedition.

Injuries and improvements dictated changes on the defensive side of the ball. Carleton Oats joined Tom Keating on the sidelines while Dan Birdwell was activated for the first time and would plug the middle with rookie Art Thoms making his first start. Improved play from Nemiah Wilson earned him the starting role opposite Willie Brown at cornerback while George Atkinson still performing well in the role had learned the strong safety position and would assume the starting role ahead of established starter Howie Williams.

Cleared weather made conditions slightly easier for the visitors but subfreezing temperatures and 15 inches of snow fortunately plowed from the field were foes as formidable as any pro team and played a major role in slowing the Oakland running game which accounted for 79 yards on the afternoon including a 9-yard Lamonica scramble. With the running attack hampered, a bit of special teams innovation from the rookie head coach gave his squad an excellent opportunity to break a scoreless tie early in the second quarter. "We didn't think there was any way they would block someone up the middle," explained Madden post-game. Replacing Wayne Hawkins, who normally lined up over center on punt teams with Art Thoms, the Raiders headman was proved prophetic as his rookie defensive tackle barreled unmolested toward Broncos punter Billy Van Heusen. Coming up-field like a shot, the rookie Thoms thought for a brief flash that he'd jumped off sides but was brought back to reality as the ball ricochet off his body backward where it was recovered for an Oakland first and goal at the Denver 6.

"That in essence was the game," according to coach Saban, despite his Broncos' matching Pete Banaszak's 4-yard touchdown reception with a 4-yard Al Denson catch. Ahead 10-7 at the half, Oakland built upon their lead. Executing a 50-yard drive in six plays the advantage grew to 10 points before the third period elapsed. Denver would not surrender. Grinding out a 71-yard drive in 9 plays, the Broncos pulled to within a field goal on a 4-yard run by Floyd Little. Given the opportunity to win the battle for field position as the foul weather wasn't conducive to offensive production, the Broncos watched as their hopes for their first win over Oakland since 1962 and their first division triumph since defeating the expansion Bengals in 1968's fourth week slipped away as Daryle Lamonica began to pick their defense apart. Converting a pair of crucial third down plays with passes to Banaszak and Billy Cannon, nine other plays were utilized to put the game out of reach. A 2-yard scoring toss to Cannon secured Oakland's fourth win, a 24-14 triumph they would relish on the warm flight back to Oakland.

Sold out for weeks in advance, the lone contest scheduled for the month of October in the Oakland Alameda County Coliseum had special significance. Not only would it feature the return of Bay Area native Orenthal James (O.J.) Simpson, the current Heisman trophy winner and most pro-ready rookie to emerge from the college ranks since Billy Cannon, but also that of former Raiders' coach John Rauch. Having either traded or cut seven starters from the season prior, John Rauch's Buffalo Bills were a different bunch from the year before and, at 2-3, had already doubled their win total from 1968. Even as "Heidi" was set to repeat on NBC Television and the network executives now possessed the foresight to allow the game to finish before entertaining the nation's children, the people of Buffalo were forced endure the final eight minutes of a contest that was never in doubt. Setting an American Football League record by throwing six touchdown passes in a half, the oft-struggling Daryle Lamonica directed an offense reminiscent of an unstoppable force building a 42-0 lead 25 minutes into the contest. After tossing a pair of interceptions Jack Kemp was benched in favor of James Harris, the Grambling rookie who was the first African-American quarterback to start a season for a pro team. In turn, Harris launched a 39-yard strike to Haven Moses to avoid a shutout late in the second quarter, but rough treatment from Ben Davidson and Ike Lassiter rudely forced him onto the injured reserve list. Kemp retook the field trailing 48-7 with a quarter to play. Deep passes to Bill Enyart and converted quarterback Marlin Briscoe went for scores but the relentless Oakland defense had the last word in the contest as Kemp was planted by Al Dotson in the end zone for a safety, dispatching the resurgent Buffalo Bills from The Coliseum, who were abused throughout a 50-21 ordeal.

The Raiders' season reached its halfway point in San Diego against a Chargers club on a roll. Winning four straight after dropping their first two decisions against Kansas City and Cincinnati, surged the Chargers into third place in the West behind the Chiefs and Raiders, who were separated by a mere half game. As it was the year before, San Diego stood to stop Oakland from breaking their mark of 14 consecutive league games without a defeat that began in 1960's eleventh week at the Los Angeles Memorial Coliseum against an Oakland Raiders team in black and gold and ran through 1961's eleventh week before falling on the road in Houston 33-13. Ending Oakland's bid for AFL immortality the year before aided in dropping the then undefeated Raiders into third place and ultimately forced a Western Division playoff game at the seasons end. In the seventh week of 1969, history belonged to the Oakland Raiders.

Running a fever of 103 and hospitalized the night before this most crucial contest, Daryle Lamonica erased a 3-0 deficit by launching a 48-yard bomb to Larry Todd. A trio of interceptions by Dave Grayson did more than half the Chargers offense, it gave him 45 for his career and a tie with retired Houston Oiler Jim Norton for most all time by an AFL defender and fourth overall in pro football history behind Bobby Boyd, Dick "Night Train" Lane and Emlen Tunnel. Oakland never looked back. Padding their lead with touchdown passes of 15 yards to Wells and 16 yards to Roger Hagberg, Lamonica was again named the American Football League's Player of the Week (after his decimation of the Bills) and the offense set a 21-6 pace as the third quarter came to an end. Fending off the Chiefs who hammered Cincinnati 42-22 for the division lead, Oakland added insurance in the form of a 28-yard field goal and left San Diego with a 6-0-1 record and a 24-13 victory.

Enjoying what was far and away the best start in franchise history, the Raiders stopped off in Oakland before departing for Cincinnati where they were the obvious favorites to extend their unbeaten string into the second half of the season. Dan Birdwell was added to the injured reserve list ending a season that began for him just three weeks prior, as his knee injury hadn't healed as sufficiently as once thought. A bruised hip caused a crisis situation at tight end as Billy Cannon was held out while fullback Roger Hagberg assumed his role in the starting lineup.

Since taking over the role of starting quarterback for the Bengals, Sam Wyche had passed himself into the top ranking as an AFL quarterback while his team slid to the bottom of the division on a four-game losing streak. Prepared for Wyche and a high-powered offense that saw four receivers average more than 20 yards per catch, Oakland instead found Greg Cook under center. With an incredible 17.5 yards per completion average on the season, Cook riddled the Oakland secondary and provided Cincinnati its last taste of football glory in 1969. Completing 11 of 19 for 189 yards, Cook's two touchdown passes accelerated the Bengals into a 24-0 halftime lead. Getting help on the ground from Jess Phillips, who scampered 15 times for 120 yards including an 83-yard jaunt to set up the Bengals third touchdown. Phillips finally found the end zone on a 2-yard run following one of Lamonica's five interceptions giving Cincinnati a 31-3 edge as the fourth quarter began. With an insurmountable advantage, the Bengals relaxed against a flat Raiders club, which added a pair of late touchdowns. Losers for the first time 31-17, Oakland fell from its perch atop the AFL's Western Division and returned home trailing the Kansas City Chiefs by one-half game.

After eight weeks the top two spots in the Western Division were nearly assured for Oakland and Kansas City. The only issue to be resolved was that of post season seeding. The top Western Division club would enjoy home field advantage throughout the postseason while the runner-up would be forced to travel to New York to face a Jets team in the dead of winter as they were a cinch to wrap up the Eastern Division as its only winning team. Downing the San Diego Chargers at home 27-3, the Chiefs gave Oakland no room for error in the ninth week against the Broncos, forcing the Raiders to respond with one of their most dominating performances of the year. A pulled muscle sidelined Bill Laskey, who had recently regained his starting role, and an errant Steve Tensi pass falling to his understudy Chip Oliver gave Oakland a 7-0 lead after a 29-yard return. Grinding away 88 yards with a 16-play drive, Denver tied the contest with 1:40 to go in the half on a 1-yard run by Fran Lynch.

The time remaining following the Broncos' scoring drive left ample opportunity for an alert Oakland team. Sensing a trick play, Duane Benson jumped on an onside kick at the Raider 47 and the offense displayed some trickery of its own. A fake handoff and a pump fake to Fred Biletnikoff in the flat aided in helping the league's leading receiver out-distance the defense and broke the dead-lock in just one play with a 53-yard reception. Abused by Ike Lassiter, who forced losses of 5 and 12 yards, Tensi and the Broncos were forced to punt. Starting from their side of the field on the 44 with no time outs, Oakland was given a free pass into Bronco territory with a pass interference penalty on Grady Caveness, who was unwilling to be burned for another Biletnikoff touchdown and a roughing the passer penalty on Richard Jackson, who was unable to reach Lamonica cleanly. Shaken up by the rough treatment from Jackson, Lamonica was on the sidelines as Blanda connected with Charlie Smith for an 11-yard touchdown pass for a 21-7 lead at halftime. Returning for the third quarter, the Raiders' "Mad Bomber" connected with Biletnikoff for his second scoring grab. An exchange of field goals closed out the third quarter and Oakland added 10 insurance points with Biletnikoff's third score and a Blanda field goal as Oakland rebounded at home with a 41-10 triumph.

The remainder of the home-stand was rounded out by a meeting with a team on the decline. The San Diego Chargers, who had been unable to reach the end zone since a meaningless 3-yard pass from John Hadl to Lance Alworth when Oakland visited Balboa Stadium three weeks prior. Marty Domres was named the starting quarterback by coach Sid Gillman following a dismal 10 for 31 performance with five interceptions in the loss in Kansas City. Yet the quarterback found himself on the bench once again as a hernia and a stomach ulcer ended Gillman's 9-½ year tenure as the Chargers' head coach. Staying on as general manager, Gillman named Charlie Waller as his successor. For his troubles in replacing Domres with Hadl, coach Waller saw two more passes completed than the week before and the interceptions completely eliminated; however for the third week in a row the Chargers offense' failed to find the end zone. Their defense would compensate. Stepping in front of a Lamonica pass on the 28, Speedy Duncan silenced the 54,372 on hand at the Oakland Alameda County Coliseum by racing 72-yards for a San Diego touchdown. Retaliating with a 19-yard scoring pitch to Biletnikoff, Oakland took the lead when Dan Conners stole the ball from tight end Willie Frazier's grasp and cashed in with a touchdown 25 yards up-field. As Dennis Partee kicked true on 3 of 4 field goal attempts, the first-time head coach Charlie Waller watched his squad surge ahead 16-14 1:47 into the final quarter. From their 21, the Raiders offense found themselves a yard poorer on second down after losing a yard. When Lamonica broke the huddle, he instructed Warren Wells to not quit on the ball no matter the circumstance and promised its delivery. Immediately, Wells was given ample reason to disregard his orders. Dropping back to pass, Lamonica stumbled and fell. This episode of bad luck proved advantageous as the Chargers' pass rush ran past the fallen quarterback who picked himself up and launched a pass that sailed 58 yards through the air to Wells, who had pulled free from safety Jim Hill, who hesitated when Lamonica dropped to the ground. Without opposition, Wells wandered into the end zone and Oakland captured its eighth win of the year 21-16.

The final regular-season road trip proved to be the most crucial time of the season. Still lagging a half game behind Kansas City, the Raiders needed only a tie to secure a spot in the AFL's post-season. Forced to play away from The Coliseum against two of the AFL's best in late November, Oakland needed to win first in Kansas City to reclaim first place in the West, then against the world-champion Jets in Shea Stadium to avoid the brutal post-season handicap. Aid came their way like a flood. While being out-gained 436 yards to 262 on the afternoon, Oakland benefited from seven Chiefs turnovers. Howie Williams' rough treatment of rookie Ed Podolak freed him from the football and led to a 10-yard field goal less than two minutes into the game. Even with the Chiefs' generosity a clash of this magnitude would not come without adversity. A pair of

Kansas City touchdown drives gave an early indication of a home team runaway but a pass intended for Fred Arbanas was intercepted by George Atkinson and the miscue was returned 22 yards to pull within four points at 14-10. Churning out 60 yards of offense in 10 plays after a Chiefs' field goal, Oakland managed a 17-point tie at halftime when Lamonica found Wells open for a 22-yard score. Dave Grayson, obtained in 1965 for Fred Williamson secured his place in American Football League history by nabbing his forty-sixth career interception from the team that dealt him away with a troublemaker tag, preserving a tie at the break.

Down three as Oakland took the lead on a 14-yard field goal, Len Dawson directed the Chiefs' offense into Raiders' territory. Firing to running back Wendell Hayes on the Oakland 25, Dawson's pass was met instead by Dan Conners, who headed up-field with the errant throw and outlasted both the quarterback and his intended receiver for a touchdown. Kansas City retaliated with a 42-yard bomb to Frank Pitts for a score, Grayson's forty-seventh interception and the second fumble forced by Howie Williams rendered Kansas City's further efforts useless as the Raiders left for New York with a 27-24 victory, a 9-1-1 record and sole possession of first place in the Western Division.

Even with history working against them (manufacturing just two wins in ten years in New York and none since 1966's seventh week) the Oakland Raiders were favored coming into Shea Stadium to close out their road slate on a winning note. They were given a break seven days prior to kick off. A broken bone in Don Maynard's foot kept him out of action and elevated veteran Bake Turner into the starting role. It was there that Oakland coaches executed their defensive plan of attack. Implementing a disguised coverage with a fifth defensive back that called for Turner or tight end Pete Lammons to be double covered at any given time caused Joe Namath a great deal of difficulty in deciphering the Oakland zone. Choosing to concentrate on George Sauer, 11 of Namath's 12 passes in his direction fell to the ground as Willie Brown rendered him a non-factor despite his quarterback's otherwise insistence. Completing just 10 of 30 on the day, Namath's lone highlight came in the form of a 54-yard bomb to Turner, which tied the contest at seven toward the end of the opening quarter. The next time New York found the end zone, with a 1-yard Bill Mathis run they had been buried by a 1-yard Lamonica blast that capped a 12-play, 80-yard drive and Wells' second touchdown of the afternoon to pull ahead 21-7. A pair of field goals added an unnecessary cushion as the Jets' offense proved lifeless in the second half as Oakland breezed to a 27-14 victory.

While Namath struggled against Oakland's defensive ingenuity, his counterpart enjoyed a stellar afternoon. Apart from his two touchdown passes to Wells and a scramble for another, Lamonica completed 19 of 28 for 333 yards of offense while earning American Football League Offensive Player of the Week honors for the third time in 1969. Personal accomplishments aside, Lamonica's club gained no ground in their bid for a third consecutive division championship as Kansas City hammered the Denver Broncos in week 12, 31-17. Kansas City remained a half game off the pace and pulled out a last minute 22-19 decision at home against Buffalo in week 13.

Even with home field advantage against an opponent sporting a record of 4-7-1, The Cincinnati Bengals owned the distinction of being the only American Football League team to defeat the Oakland Raiders in 1969, and the home squad would have to overcome a great deal of pre-game adversity. For the second time in six weeks Daryle Lamonica was hospitalized the night before a game. He was held for observation overnight as a stiffness in his back from a shot delivered by the New York defense turned into an agonizing knot that threatened to keep him out of the crucial Coliseum rematch. Unable to sleep the night before the game despite being administered sedatives and muscle relaxers, Lamonica was unsure he would be able to dress for action. After a lengthy rub down, the application of heat pads, a half-hour workout and the assurance from doctors that he couldn't injure himself any worse, the former Notre Dame passer joined his squad as four of his teammates were being honored. Original Raiders Wayne Hawkins and Jim Otto along with Billy Cannon and George Blanda who had joined them later from Houston, were each given a gold wristwatch by *Oakland Tribune* sports editor George Ross, serving as a representative of the American Football League, for their 10 years of on-field service. Praised in a telegram sent by President Richard Nixon as "The very best in professional football," these four and their well-treated quarterback went to work and immediately began to exact revenge for their sole loss of the season. With Bob Svihus missing due to a leg injury sustained in New York, second year man Art Shell stepped in and Oakland's ground attack amassed a record 309 yards on 44 carries for an astounding 7 yards per carry average. The Raiders' offense then sank Cincinnati through the air as Lamonica launched a 51-yard bomb to Wells midway through the first quarter and a pair of 16-yard strikes to Wells and Biletnikoff to take a 21-7 lead at halftime. With the running game in high gear Lamonica rested while Blanda needed to pass just four times in the second half. Adding a trio of field goals the second and final Blanda completion found Wells for his second 16-yard scoring grab and third of the afternoon as professional football's grand old man reached the milestone of 20,000 passing yards as the Raiders steamrolled the Bengals who managed 10 second-half points in a 37-17 loss.

In all, 12 Oakland Raiders were named to the Associated Press' All-American Football League team. Center Jim Otto for the tenth consecutive season, Fred Biletnikoff, Gene Upshaw, Harry Schuh, Dave Grayson, Willie Brown and 1969's Most Valuable Player award recipient, Daryle Lamonica, rounded out the first team. While expressing his pride in those who were selected, coach Madden spoke of pressure on the 30 sportswriters (three from the ten AFL cities) against voting for teammates at the same position. Thus explaining why Warren Wells, professional football's leader in touchdown receptions, total yards and yards per catch (with an astronomical 26.8 yards per average) was excluded. Madden was also displeased with the snub of guard Jim Harvey. Tom Keating had fully recovered from his ailments that haunted him for a year and a half and was named to the second team despite being double teamed throughout the year was joined by line-mate Ike Lassiter and linebackers Gus Otto and Dan Conners.

These 12 and their teammates had one final battle before them to wrap up their third division crown in as many years and the team who looked to steal this laurel from them were dealt a definite advantage. Rains poured upon the Oakland Coliseum midweek and the tarp laid across the field eventually served little use as the water it was meant to keep out eventually found its way underneath and stood. The footing was treacherous, especially for a pass-happy team like the Raiders and the defense charged with stopping the Kansas City Chiefs running attack, the American Football League's most prolific. The Chiefs played to their strength. Len Dawson attempted only 6 passes (completing 2) on the afternoon as a barbaric defensive battle ensued. Taking a 3-0 lead captured in the second quarter into the final period, Lamonica lobbed an 8-yard touchdown pass to Charlie Smith over a fallen Johnny Robinson. Answering with a scoring drive that consumed more than eight minutes, Kansas City found the end zone on third and goal from the 1 as Wendell Hayes beat George Atkinson to the outside to bring the Chiefs within four at 10-6. Playing to win instead of a tie that would guarantee Oakland the division crown, Coach Stram called for a 2-point conversion. Mike Garrett's run through the middle of the

Oakland defense was abruptly halted by Tom Keating and Chip Oliver and with 5:25 remaining, the Chiefs, needing a touchdown to win, would never see the ball.

The remaining time was consumed by a half-dozen carries from Marv Hubbard, who gained 39 yards and the crucial first downs to retain possession. A helpless Kansas City club watched the clock tick down to zero as the Oakland Raiders gained their third consecutive division championship with a 10-6 victory.

(4)

The 72-yard bomb hauled in by Warren Wells in the second quarter that set up George Blanda's 30-yard field goal was feared to be his last reception of the season. His midair collision with Emmitt Thomas while reaching for Lamonica's pass left a marble-sized knot in his shoulder that caused numbness and forced his doctors to schedule surgery that would sideline him for six weeks while he recuperated in a cast. John Madden, the second Raiders coach to earn a Coach of the Year honor in his rookie season was left with an interesting dilemma. Behind Wells at the split end position were Rod Sherman, the third-year pro and expected starter who was yet to catch a pass upon his return from Cincinnati where he led the Bengals in receiving in their inaugural season and Drew Buie, who managed 34 yards of offense on his lone reception in 1969.

If there was a silver lining to be found it was in the form of the Houston Oilers. Coming off a meaningless 27-23 win over the Boston Patriots, who were three games behind the 6-6-2 Oilers for second place and a trip to Oakland for a chance at Super Bowl infamy. Despite posting six more victories in the regular season no one in the Raiders' organization forgot the near miss that nearly dealt them their first opening week loss since 1964. Ignoring the crucial divisional round match-up in New York as the runner-up Chiefs won a tough defensive battle, earning a return trip to Oakland, the Raiders concentrated on the task at hand and annihilated their guests.

With one hand held behind his back by defensive back Miller Farr, Fred Biletnikoff secured the game's opening touchdown with the other, taking in a 13-yard pass for a 7-0 lead and beginning what Raiders beat writer Blaine Newnham mused in print was the most beautiful 1:59 of football ever played. Pete Beathard's third down pass to All Star tight end

Alvin Reed inconceivably found its way into the hands of George Atkinson. After the pass was stolen from Reed's fingertips, middle linebacker Dan Conners added intimidation to insult by decking the intended target, giving his opportunistic teammate room to roam. Sprung again by a Nemiah Wilson block on the 20-yard line, Atkinson completed his 57-yard return by crossing the goal line putting his squad ahead 14-0. The shell-shocked Oilers then fell apart as Hoyle Granger's fumble on first down was smothered by Gus Otto on the Houston 24-yard line. Running a post pattern, Rod Sherman caught his first pass of the year on the 8 and dragged both Farr and Zeke Moore goal-ward before breaking free to bury Houston 21-0.

The magical 119 seconds had elapsed and with more than 51 minutes of game time remaining a team could settle down and work to erase such a deficit. Instead the Oilers proved to be their own worst enemy. Managing to hold onto the ball for two plays successfully, the third was disastrous as Beathard fumbled the snap and Oakland took control on the 34. With Biletnikoff having beaten Zeke Moore on the first play from scrimmage, Lamonica fired his third consecutive pass to go for a score as the former Seminole ran the score to 28-0 with 4:05 to go in the opening quarter. Leading by 35 at halftime as Lamonica found Charlie Smith mismatched on the Raiders' 40 with weak side linebacker and East Bay native Ron Pritchard, who was helpless in stopping Smith's 60-yard touchdown jaunt. After finding Sherman for his second score of the afternoon with a 23-yard strike, Lamonica matched his career best six-touchdown performance against Buffalo with a 3-yard pass to Billy Cannon in the waning seconds of the third period. A comfortable lead allowed Oakland's reserves a chance to obtain some valuable post-season experience and against a relaxed squad with its understudies on the field Houston finally found the end zone, finishing a 95-yard march with an 8-yard Beathard pass to Reed. Oakland's ground attack chimed in with a 4-yard Marv Hubbard run behind Roger Hagberg to re-establish the teams' scoring mark and finishing Houston's season with a 56-7 massacre.

There was a two-week break between the only divisional round the American Football League's postseason would ever know and its final championship. A two-week period where both the host Oakland Raiders, owners of professional football's best record over the past three seasons with 37 regular season wins compared to 4 losses and a tie, and the Kansas City Chiefs who had the best winning percentage in the league's 10-year history would completely heal their wounded and be ready for the league's final showdown. Based in Long Beach (Southern California) leading up to the championship game, the Chiefs would not reveal their strategy against Oakland but Oakland's quarterback was more candid. "We need to score the first touchdown," revealed Daryle Lamonica prior to kickoff, underscoring the need to make the opponent play from behind and allowing Oakland to dictate to them. In front of the 54,544 in attendance at the Oakland Alameda County Coliseum (the eight consecutive sellout) and the 50 million more watching on television, he would do precisely that. Against a Kansas City defense that gave up yardage begrudgingly all afternoon, Oakland took 10 plays to march 66 yards for the opening score. Following a 24-yard reception by Warren Wells (his only catch of the day upon returning to the starting lineup) Charlie Smith powered in from 3 yards out for a 7-0 lead. The Chiefs dug in and for the remainder of the afternoon, held Oakland out of the end zone. Halting the momentum Lamonica had hoped to build, Kansas City erased the early deficit, stringing together a 7-play, 75–yard drive and matching their hosts with a 41-yard deep ball from Dawson to Frank Pitts over a fallen Nemiah Wilson. This gave the Chiefs a first and goal from the 1, then Wendell Hayes slammed it home to knot the game with 1:50 remaining in the half.

An encore of preseason misfortune occurred in the third quarter. Aaron Brown, already having dropped Lamonica twice for losses, inadvertently dealt the Oakland passer the worst blow of all. Following through on a pass Lamonica's hand was bruised on Brown's helmet sending the passer to the sidelines in pain. Unable to capitalize twice in the third quarter as a pair of Blanda field goal attempts missed, the 42-year-old quarterback's struggles continued under center. Completing just 2 of 6 for 24 yards, a slip by Wells caused Blanda's sure touchdown strike to be intercepted by Emmitt Thomas in the end zone. Choosing to return the interception instead of downing the ball for possession on the 20, Thomas was tackled by Billy Cannon on his 6. Oakland's advantage of field position was fleeting. Dropping back into his end zone, Dawson fired to Otis Taylor, who made a circus catch for 35 yards along the sidelines. Though landing out of bounds, Taylor and the Chiefs were given a break when the officials ruled Taylor had been forced out. Staying on the ground initially, Dawson quickly went long to Taylor again. Drawing a pass interference call against Nemiah Wilson, the Chiefs had a first and goal on the Oakland 7. Blasting in on second and goal from the 3 Robert Holmes put the Chiefs ahead for good.

With assurances that his passing hand was only bruised and not broken and a reasonable amount of success connecting 12 times in 22 tries prior to his injury, John Madden had no quarrel with sending his MVP quarterback into action to steal a championship from the jaws of defeat. No stranger to adversity after being hospitalized twice the night before victories in 1969, Lamonica took the stage for an Oakland miracle that would never come. Completing 3 passes in 17 attempts in the fourth quarter, three Raider drives ended in interceptions as the Chiefs' defensive backfield rendered Oakland's receivers useless as Wells, Biletnikoff and Rod Sherman combined for 4 catches for 69 total yards (3 by Sherman for 45 yards). The final interception was returned 62 yards by Thomas to the Oakland 18. With a 22-yard Jan Stenerud field goal the game was now out of reach though a fumbled handoff allowed the Raiders a final gasp. Three Lamonica passes fell incomplete before Brown buried him for the third time on fourth and 10 for a 7-yard loss. Victory was at hand for the Chiefs and league-founder Lamar Hunt's club earned their third AFL Championship with a 17-7 defensive triumph.

(5)

Once the new league's weakest link, the Oakland Raiders, even in defeat were still considered by many to be its finest team. Jim Otto, Mr. Raider, who never missed a regular or postseason game he was eligible for in the 10 seasons of the American Football League, spoke of his distaste for the Kansas City Chiefs, a team his Raiders' club had handled in five of the last six meetings leading up to the fateful championship game. Standing in contrast to his coach and teammates who sang the Chiefs' praises and expressed confidence of an AFL victory a week later in New Orleans against the Minnesota Vikings, Otto's negative sentiments were echoed in the press box at halftime as the Chiefs, outperforming Minnesota in every aspect of the game opened up a 16-0 lead. "It's a good thing the Oakland Raiders aren't in this game or you wouldn't be able to find the Vikings, they'd be buried so deep," expressed a Buffalo sportswriter even with the knowledge that Lamonica would have been lost for the Super Bowl as he was for the All Star game. The double-digit underdog Kansas City squad added another touchdown before allowing a meaningless third quarter score. With this 23-7 conquest, the upstart American Football League would forever be regarded as the equal of its former antagonist and saboteur, while proving to be their better.

CREDITS AND THANK YOUS!

If you've made it this far you've earned my eternal gratitude. The previous pages are the result of three years worth of work, compiled from a few sources mostly from the microfilm copies of *The Oakland Tribune* contained at the Oakland Public Library so first I need to give thanks to their entire wonderful staff, for the attention, patience and encouragement you've all given me over that time. That and the approximately 5,500 pages of paper that they'd supplied me with.

Next, I need to give credit to the folks at the history department of the Oakland Museum of California, namely Stacy Zwald. Thanks to Miss Zwald I was able to find pictures of the early Raiders in their black and gold uniforms. One would think that these shots were plentiful, for me however, they were not. I found a few great shots through a phone call made to Miss Zwald and a couple of those are contained within. So to fulfill a legal obligation I must type the following. With the exception of the cover image and the photo of Alan Miller the pictures in this book are courtesy of the Oakland Museum of California. Thanks also to Dianne Curry. The cover image is courtesy of Ron Riesterer, *Oakland Tribune* photo editor who took that shot one gray afternoon at Frank Youell Field. With that shot and the brilliant photo of Gus Otto, Mr. Riesterer can now identify his biggest fan, ME! Thanks go out to Randy Reed, son of Russ Reed who took most of the pictures found within for his gracious permission to use his fathers' work. The Alan Miller shot is courtesy of Alan Miller himself at the behest of Frank Denevi of Denevi Camera, who was kind enough to speak with me even though I walked into his corporate offices unannounced asking to speak with him. So if you need a camera see Frank, if you need an attorney contact Mr. Miller through his website www.alanrmillerpc.com. I'm sure they'd be glad to help you.

While writing is a solitary exercise I was encouraged and supported by a great many people. First I must give thanks to Phyllis Wright, the first to give me a nudge into actually writing and for listening to me complain about it over the next couple of years. Same for Chuck Foltz as well as my mother and Mr. Steve, I hope you guys are as proud of this as I am. To my son Craig, who has a date with his old man at the ballpark real soon, love you buddy. To Wayne Crow and Scotty Sterling for taking the time to talk to me, and to Mr. Bill Lincoln at Fremont, California's Robertson High School for putting me in touch with Mr. Crow. Finally gratitude must be bestowed upon the entire crew at Raider Fan Radio, Rob, Stef, Mort, Stoner, Mike D and the Mutt. The Our Raider Nation group on MSN and the Oakland Raiders Group on Yahoo who I thank for their constant interest and enthusiasm and of course to the Raider Nation itself, as well as Morris Bradshaw and Al LoCasale of the Oakland Raiders for their time. Last but not least I must mention Charles Oakey who contributed many pictures for this book however none made it to the final cut and to Ange Coniglio who preserves the history of the American Football League at his American Football League website, you can find it at http://www.RemembertheAFL.com/. Thanks also to my sisters and brothers in I.A.T.S.E Local 134 for their trust and to Justin Axlroth at Authorhouse for his patience.

Jim McCullough
4/18/2005

LaVergne, TN USA
21 February 2010

173810LV00004B/79/A